# CLOSE-UPS

# CLOSE-UPS

From the Golden Age of the
Silent Cinema

FOR JORIFIN:
John Richard Finch
*Planning, Design, and Direction*
Paul Elby
*Historical Research and Liaison*
Roland Liot
*Photographic Consultant*

South Brunswick and New York: A. S. Barnes and Company
London: The Tantivy Press

A. S. Barnes and Co., Inc.
Cranbury, New Jersey 08512

The Tantivy Press
Magdalen House
136–148 Tooley Street
London SE1 2TT, England

Library of Congress Cataloging in Publication Data

Finch, John R.
Close-ups (from the Jorifin collection).

Includes indexes.
1. Moving-picture actors and actresses—Portraits, caricatures, etc. 2. Moving-picture actors and actresses —Biography. I. Elby, Paul A., joint author. II. Title.
PN1998.A2F535 791.43'092'2 [B] 74-30974
ISBN 0-498-01723-0

SBN: 0-904208-41-9 (U.K.)

PRINTED IN THE UNITED STATES OF AMERICA

# CONTENTS

*Close-Ups* is dedicated to the men and women of the motion picture industry, in all its facets of operation, who helped to build "movies" from the nickelodeon stage to the greatest single medium of entertainment in our time, and to the memory of my good friend WALLACE REID, a great star who died on January 18th, 1923, and whom I remember so vividly and with so much affection.

"You and the song are gone,
but the melody lingers on—"

from *The Song Is Ended*

"One picture is worth a thousand words——"

*Confucius*

# FOREWORD AND COMMENT

*Close-Ups* is the product of a collection of photographs of motion picture stars that began more than fifty years ago and which now comes to you as a pictorial history book in close-up of the actors and actresses who created the great golden era of the silent screen.

This book is for collectors—those who already have collections and those who wish to start collections. It is also a book for those who will derive pleasure from reminiscing, and for those of the younger generation whose interest in the cinema prompts them to delve into its early history.

*Close-Ups,* too, is a book for the motion picture industry itself, for it contains those faces that made the industry possible. *Close-Ups* presents many rare photos, many difficult to secure, and some now quite impossible to obtain. *Close-Ups* is also a Who's Who of the stars of the silent era of the screen.

*Close-Ups* is, then, a picture book of the cinema for *everyone*—unique in its design—comprehensive and intimate in its content.

Many books have been written on the film industry. A great many words have been used, but few books have ever given the viewer a close-up of faces—sans words, props, production stills, and film clips. Those who wish written history have almost an unlimited source from which to choose. But for those who want to look into the faces of the stars—big and clear and intimate—this is what you will get in *Close-Ups.*

In planning the "personal appearances" of the stars in *Close-Ups* it was decided that the format should be entirely different from the usual book design. Only the portrait and the name of the star appears on each page. The arrangement is "loosely" chronological according to the stars' period in screen history. An alphabetical list appears in the back of the book giving the plate number of each star's portrait, together with a succinct profile. Each part contains 242 portraits plus an 8-page colour section.

I began my collection in 1921, at which time I was working for the Famous Players Lasky company then housed in an old green wooden building on the corner of Sunset and Vine in Hollywood. Down Sunset a block or so was the Christie Comedies studio, and only a few blocks farther down Sunset, at the corner of Western, was the old William Fox studio. Warner Brothers at that time was also on Sunset, and Robertson-Cole was not far away on Melrose Avenue. Most of us had friends and acquaintances at all the studios and we used to fraternise and talk shop. Many of us youngsters had started a collection of star photos and proudly displayed those personally autographed by the celebrities.

It was the day of "the beautiful people." Stars dressed in the height of fashion, immaculate and regal. Their cars were often Rolls-Royces or Cadillacs, mostly with special bodies designed to their individual specifications. The great *premières* were fantastically outstanding events with every star in Hollywood appearing in full dress—the men in faultless white tie and tails and the women in evening gowns fashioned by the world's most famous couturiers. Throngs of fans crowded the streets for blocks around to get a glimpse of this fabulous galaxy. The crowds were orderly, smiling and happy. The movies and the stars were their escapism—not something they wanted to associate with their own lives, as many mistaken people think, but rather to associate with their dreams.

In Part One, the historical chronology is fairly strict,

although it is sometimes put together a little loosely for the sake of groupings—the comics, the character people, and personal associations which brought certain stars together through marriage, relationship, or career parallels.

In many cases *Close-Ups* has more than one portrait of a star. Sometimes the rareness of the photos determined this. In other cases, it is to show the star in some outstanding role. In the case of Wallace Reid, who shares the dedication of this book, his photo appears five times, twice in Part One and three times in Part Two. For eight straight years Wallace Reid topped all popularity polls as a motion picture star. Yet, strangely enough, good portraits of him are difficult to obtain. *Close-Ups* gives you five.

In Part Two of the book the historical chronology is less strict. In this period actors and actresses appeared on the scene who made no great impression in silent films but blossomed into "greats" with the coming of sound. Clark Gable may be mentioned as a case in point. The comics are grouped together regardless of historical period. So are the Western stars.

As to acknowledgements, many of the photos appearing in *Close-Ups* were given to me directly by the stars, their secretaries or some member of their family whom I knew. In those days the studio photographers took mostly action stills from the working productions. The stars themselves usually had their portraits made independently and the two most popular photographers I recall at that time were the Hartsook Studio and the Witzel Studio, both in downtown Los Angeles.

In any acknowledgement made for the earlier photos, I would undoubtedly have to name all the old companies which passed out of existence almost half a century ago. John Bunny, Flora Finch, Florence Turner, Maurice Costello, Norma Talmadge, and Anita Stewart were all famous names with Vitagraph. The Kalem Company had Alice Joyce, Tom Moore, Pat O'Malley, and the famous "Kalem Girl," Gene Gauntier, among many others.

Broncho Billy Anderson made 376 Westerns for Essanay, of which he was part owner. The beautiful Marguerite Clayton was his leading lady in most of those films. Broncho Billy's Essanay company boasted among its stars such celebrities as Francis X. Bushman, Charlie Chaplin, Henry B. Walthall, Bryant Washburn, and Wallace Beery. Some of the stars in *Close-Ups* worked for Biograph, including Florence Lawrence, screen history's first movie star. Others were with Triangle, Pathe, Keystone, Mack Sennett, Selig, Lubin, Christie Comedies, Hal Roach, and Robertson-Cole. Many of the stars whose portraits appear herein were with the great David Wark Griffith.

Some of the photos in *Close-Ups* were undoubtedly taken by studio photographers, but there is no possible way now of knowing by whom. Remember, the silent screen era ended before 1930, and most of the photos appearing in *Close-Ups* were all taken prior to that time—most of them many years earlier.

Some of the stars in *Close-Ups* continued very successfully into the sound era which began in 1927. You will note that the photographs of these stars were taken when they were very young and before they became associated with the major studios. Virtually all the big studios were represented later by these stars so we must include Columbia, Universal, Fox, Paramount, RKO, First National, Goldwyn, United Artists, Republic, Warner Brothers, and Metro-Goldwyn-Mayer.

All of the above studios where any of the photos appearing in *Close-Ups* might have originated, are hereby acknowledged.

When I made up my mind to release the JORIFIN COLLECTION in book form or, more accurately that part of it covering the silent era, it had to be decided how the photos in the collection were to be reproduced. Because of the very considerable value and also because of the age and condition of some of the photos, I could not permit the originals to be handled directly. At this point, Roland Liot, one of the most talented photographers in Paris, was contacted and he accepted with enthusiasm the immense job of photographing originals, cutting for most attractive and uniform viewing, and making the finished prints which required the most expert knowledge of the use of many different types of paper according to the quality of the image on the negative. Roland Liot's work is hereby acknowledged with appreciation.

There are a few portraits in *Close-Ups* that may appear to be and *are* reproductions taken from an old "paste-up" album in my collection which is more than fifty years old. I included these because I felt that you, the viewers, would appreciate seeing these old and rare photos.

My greatest regret is for the many stars who were very famous in films but who do not appear in either section of the book. It was not a matter of choice whether or not to include them. It was just that I didn't have their photos in my collection, very much to my regret. But I must, however, mention some of them by name. Collectors especially should be interested in the following named stars, portraits of whom would materially enhance their collections if it is possible to obtain them.

Among the early husband and wife teams was Carter and Flora de Haven, the parents of Gloria de Haven who became a star in the sound era, the Sidney Drews, and, later, Jimmy and Lucille Gleason. For the very early days I must mention Miriam Cooper, Carol Dempster, Rosemary Theby, and Seena Owen—all Griffith stars. Then there was Gibson Gowland, Charles Ogle, William Faversham, Thomas Santschi, Phillips Smalley, Lars Hanson, Nigel de Brulier, Holbrook Blinn, Leon Errol, and Joseph Swickard—all greats.

So-jin, the Japanese film star, gained fame with Douglas Fairbanks, Sr. in *The Thief of Bagdad,* and continued his success in American films for many years. Among the comedians were Kalla Pasha, Andy Clyde, Billy Bevan, Hank Mann, Billy West, Johnny Hines, Billie Ritchie, Arthur Kennedy, and lovable Arthur Houseman. Mention, too, must be given to Harry Myers, Tom Wilson, Henry Armetta, Karl Dane, Lucien Littlefield, and Leo White. One of the great Western stars was Art Acord, an authentic cowboy.

Glamour stars who belong in every collection include Vivian Martin, Marie Doro, Pauline Garon, Jetta Goudal, Eileen Percy, Olga Petrova, Dorothy Phillips, Arleen Pringle, Jobyna Ralston, wife of Richard Arlen and leading lady for Harold Lloyd, Vivienne Segal, Lillian Rich, and Barbara Bedford. Some of the great character people include Russell Simpson, Nigel Barrie, William V. Mong, Claire McDowell, Ethel Wales, Huntley Gordon, Louise Dresser, Allison Skipworth, Vera Gordon, George Marion, Conrad Veidt, Emily Fitzroy, Mary Boland, Harry Morey, and Holmes Herbert. Vernon Steele and Robert Cain should also be mentioned as should Gertrude Astor, Mary Nolan, Virginia Pearson, Mary MacLaren, and Alice White.

David Powell was a threat to Ronald Colman in his time. To be remembered for leading and young character parts are Philo McCullough, Francis MacDonald, and Gayne Whitman. Important supporting actors, more often than not co-stars, were Earle Foxe, Cullen Landis, Niles Welch, George Hackathorne, Lawrence Gray, Theodore von Eltz, and James Murray.

Richard Talmadge, who bore the same name as the famous Talmadge sisters, but was not related, became an "athlete" star almost rivalling the great Douglas Fairbanks, Sr.

I also wish to gratefully acknowledge the kind cooperation of Mary Corliss with the Film Division of The Museum of Modern Art in New York; Clyde Jeavons of the British Film Institute in London; and John H. Dorr and Sam Gill of the Special Projects Division of The Academy of Motion Picture Arts and Sciences in Hollywood.

I sincerely hope that every single viewer of *Close-Ups* will experience a deep nostalgic pleasure in looking into the faces of the great stars of the golden era of the silent screen. These are the faces that emerged in the beginning of an industry that progressed to sound and eventually to modern television. These are the people who were "first" in the greatest single medium of entertainment of the Twentieth Century for all the people of the world.

It was a great industry and a golden era.

I trust *Close-Ups* will bring some of the faces close to you.

JORIFIN

# PART ONE

**1 Broncho Billy Anderson**

2 **Broncho Billy Anderson**

**3 Marguerite Clayton**

**4 Florence Lawrence**

**5 Florence Lawrence**

6 John Bunny

7 Flora Finch

8 King Baggott

**9 Kathlyn Williams**

**10 Pearl White**

**11 Crane Wilbur**

**12 Gene Gauntier**

**13 Maurice Costello**

**14 Blanche Sweet**

**15 Blanche Sweet**

16 Francis X. Bushman

**17 Beverly Bayne**

**18 Frank Keenan**

**19 Florence Turner**

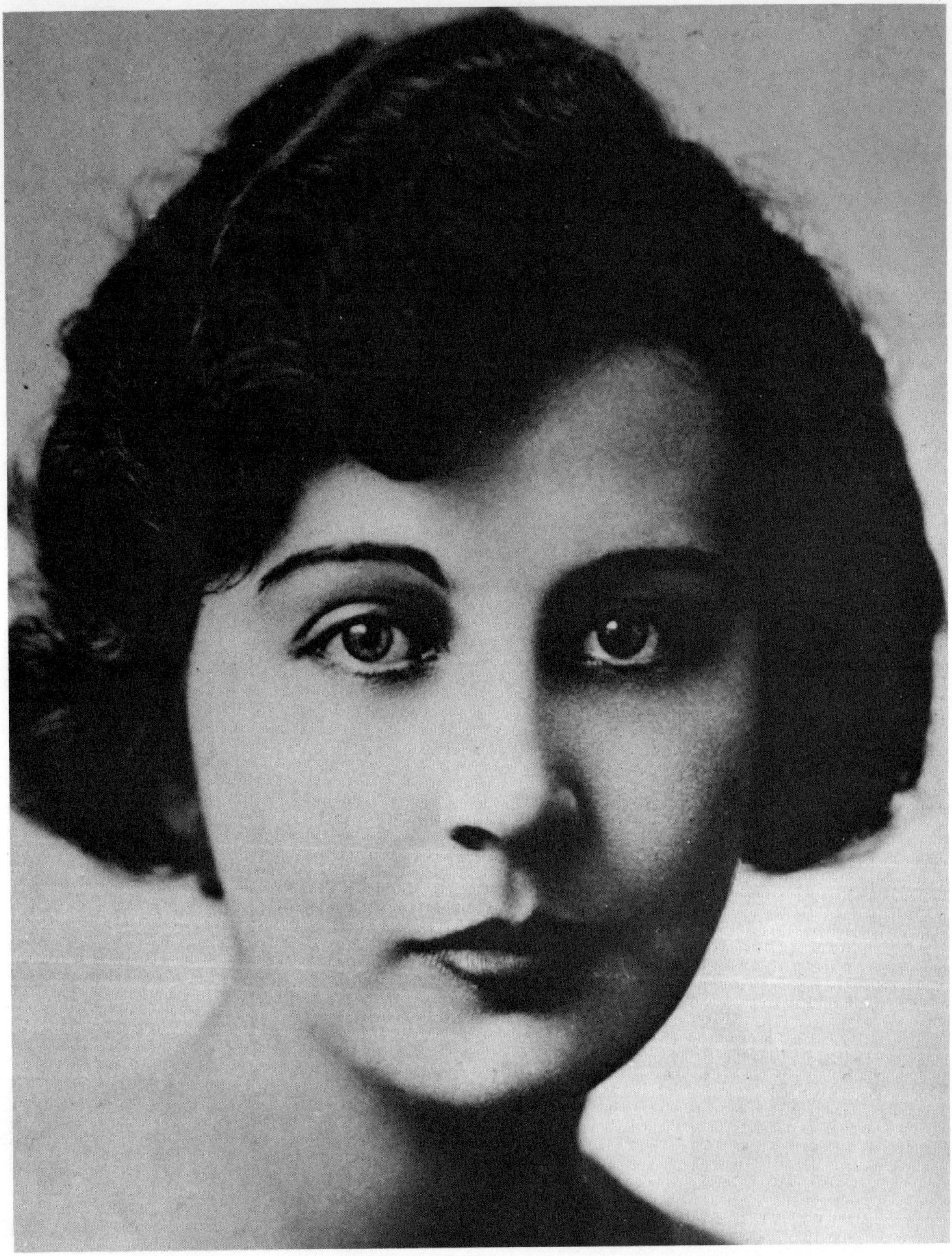

**20 Dorothy Dalton**

**21 Paul Panzer**

**22 Alice Joyce**

23 William Farnham

24 Arthur Johnson

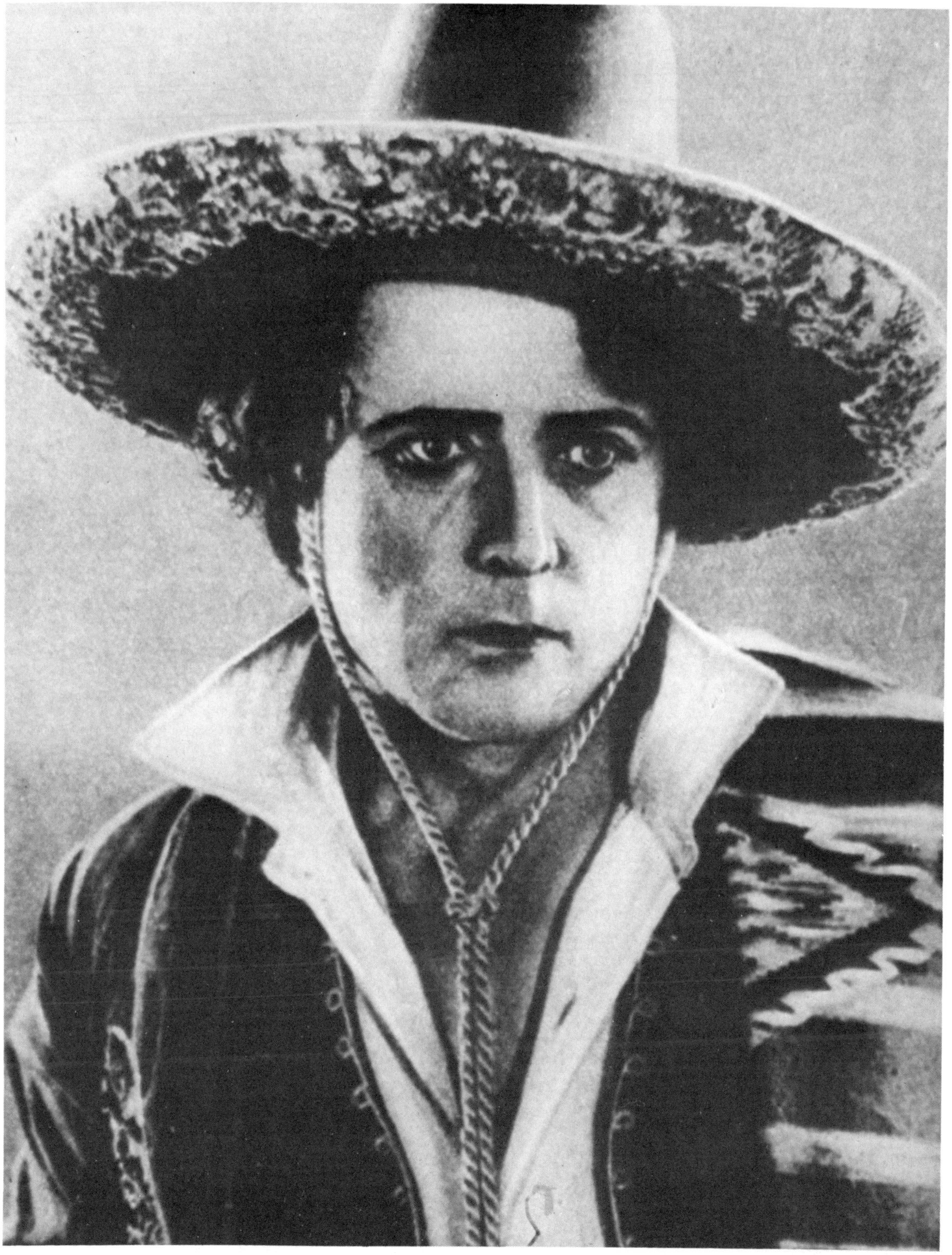

25 J. Warren Kerrigan

26 Marc MacDermott

**27 Helen Holmes**

28 Earle Williams

**29 Lillian Walker**

30 **Owen Moore**

**31 Dorothy and Lillian Gish**

32 Lillian Gish

33 Dorothy Gish

34 Francis Ford

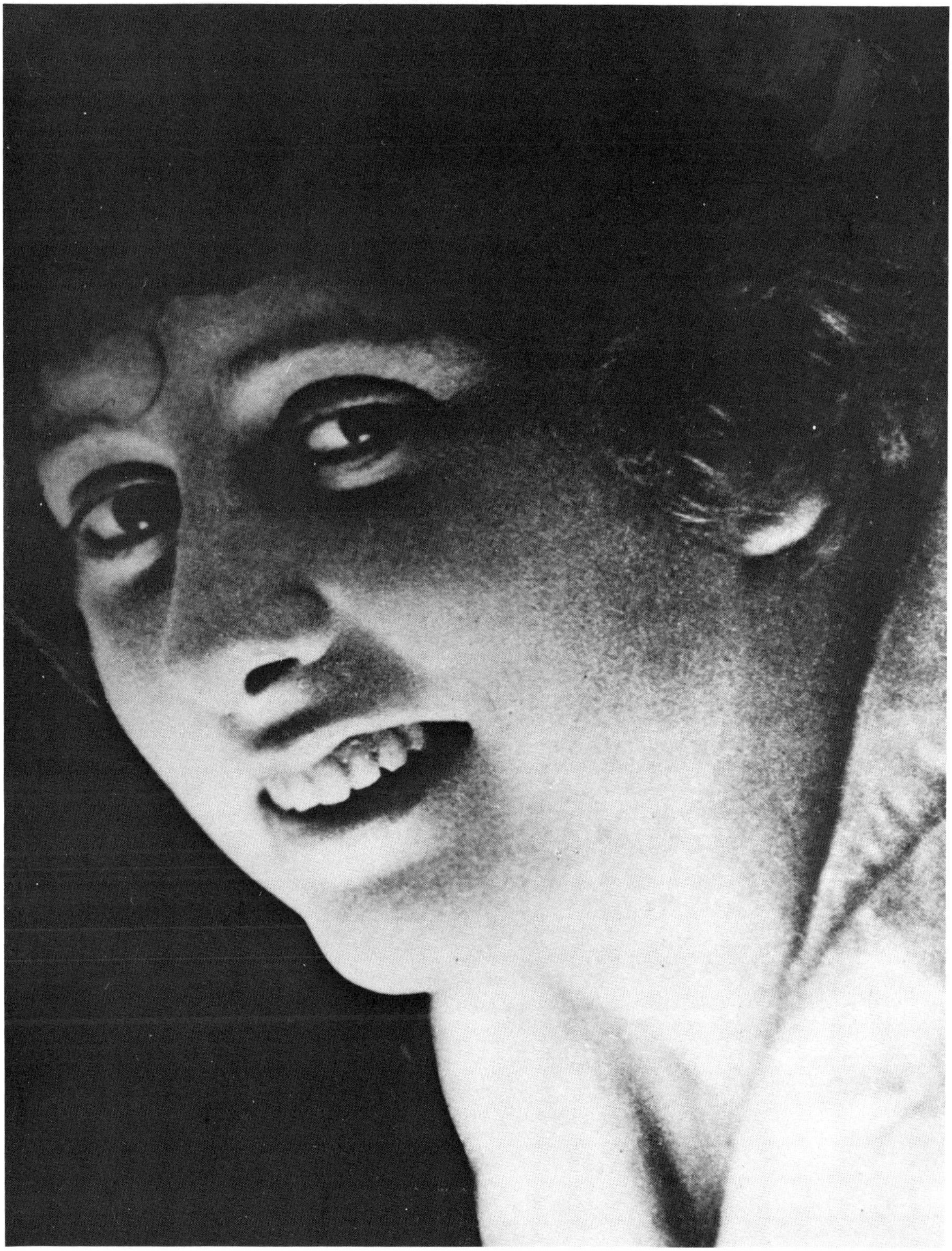

35 Grace Cunard

**36 Theda Bara**

**37 H. B. Warner**

38 Edith Storey

39 **Richard Bennett**

40 Mitchell Lewis

**41 Pauline Frederick**

**42 Lionel Belmore**

**43 Pauline Frederick**

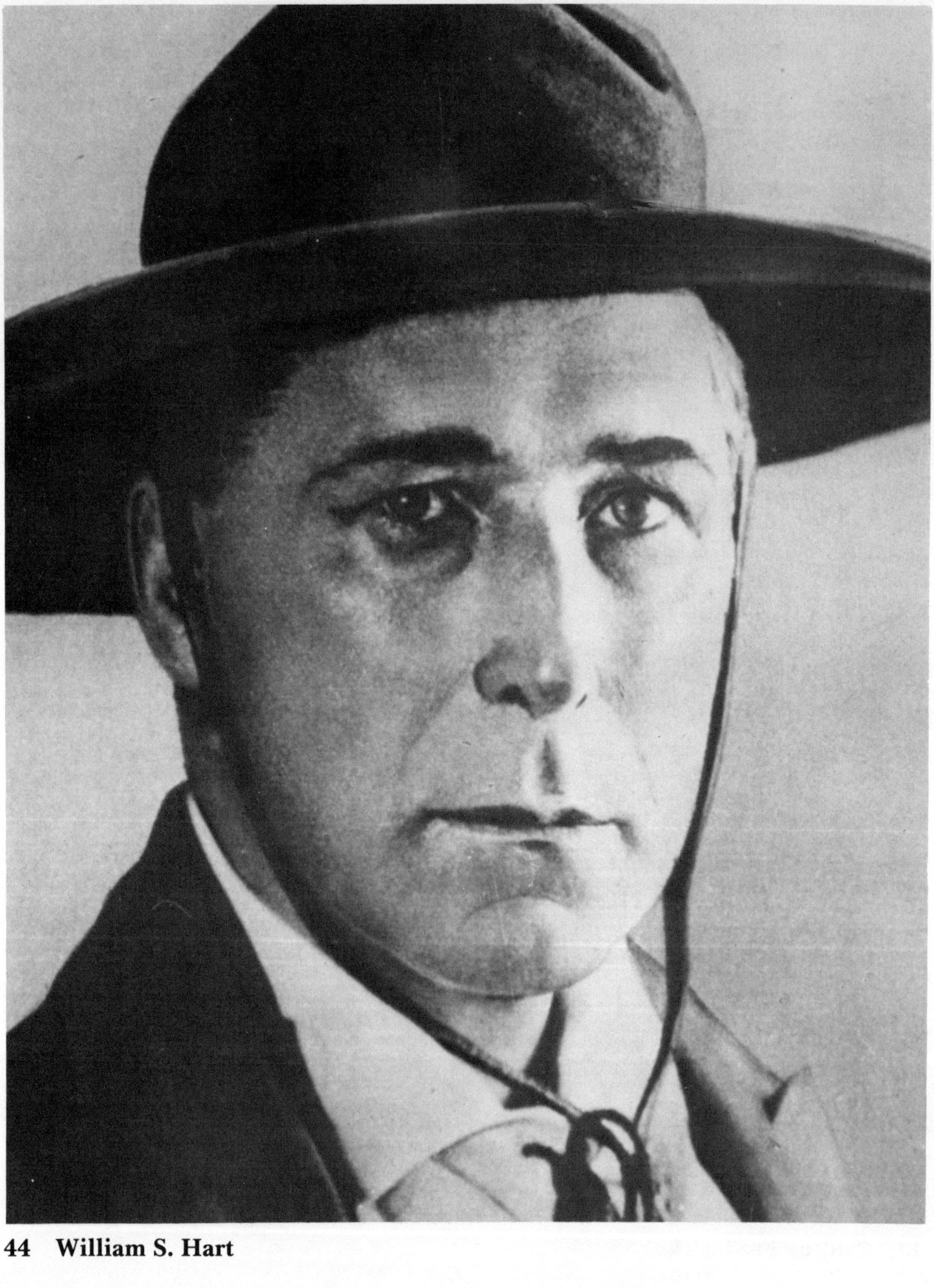

**44 William S. Hart**

**45 Louise Glaum**

46 Charles Chaplin

**47 Charles Chaplin**

**48 Edna Purviance**

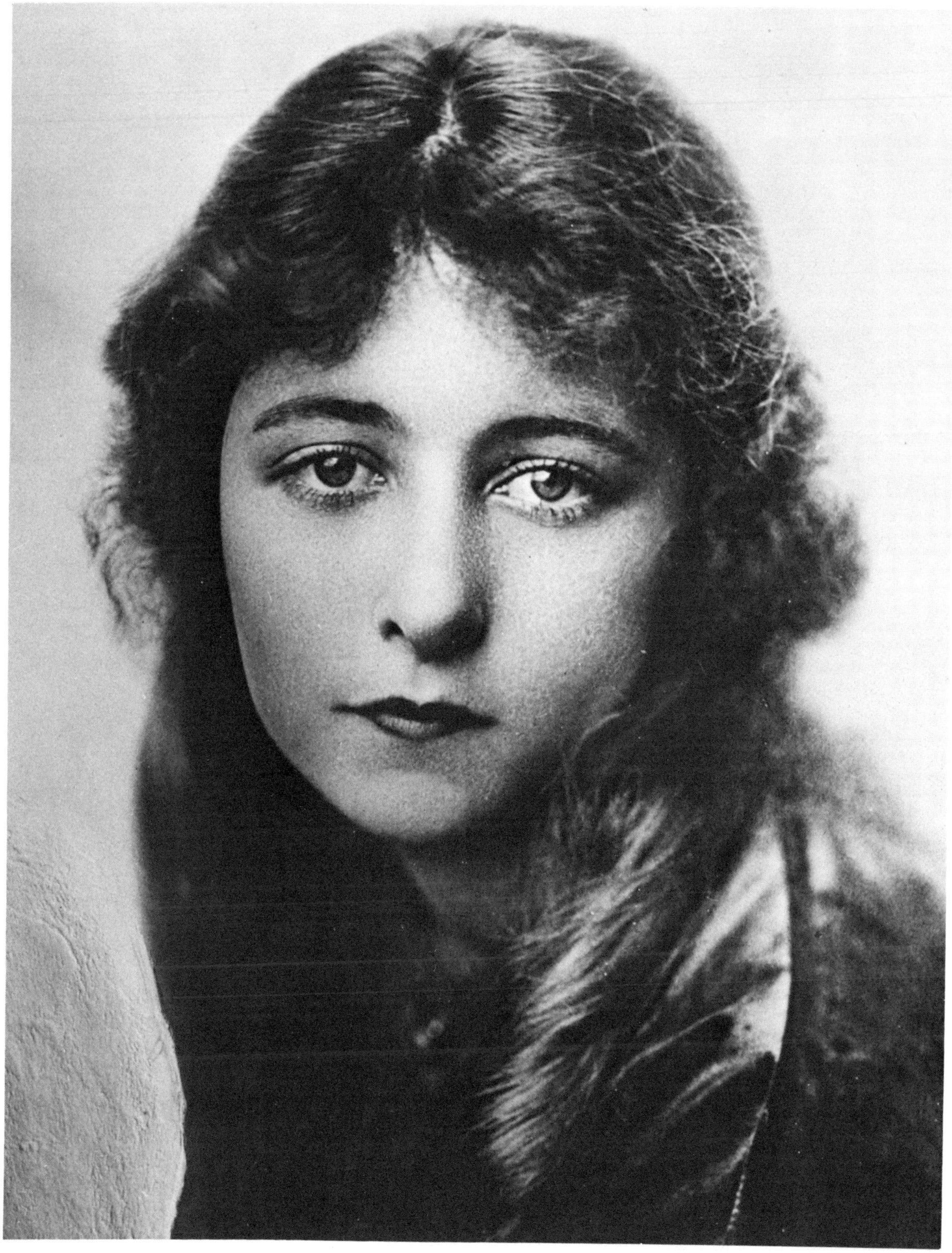

**49 Mildred Harris**

**50 Alla Nazimova**

**51 Pat O'Malley**

**52 Constance Talmadge**

**53 Lowell Sherman**

54 Mary Pickford

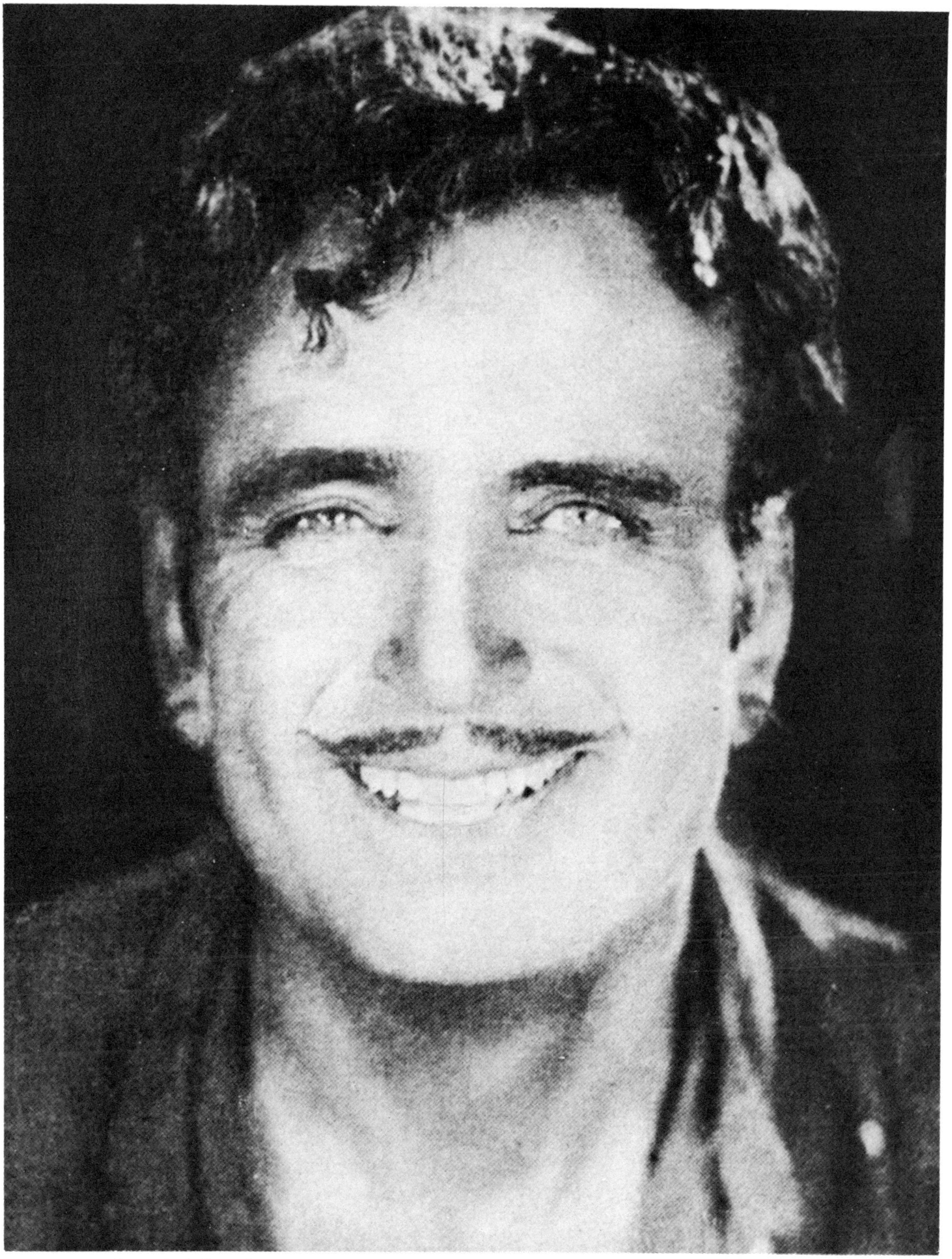

**55 Douglas Fairbanks, Sr.**

56 Mary Pickford

**57 Douglas Fairbanks, Sr.**

**58 Sarah Bernhardt**

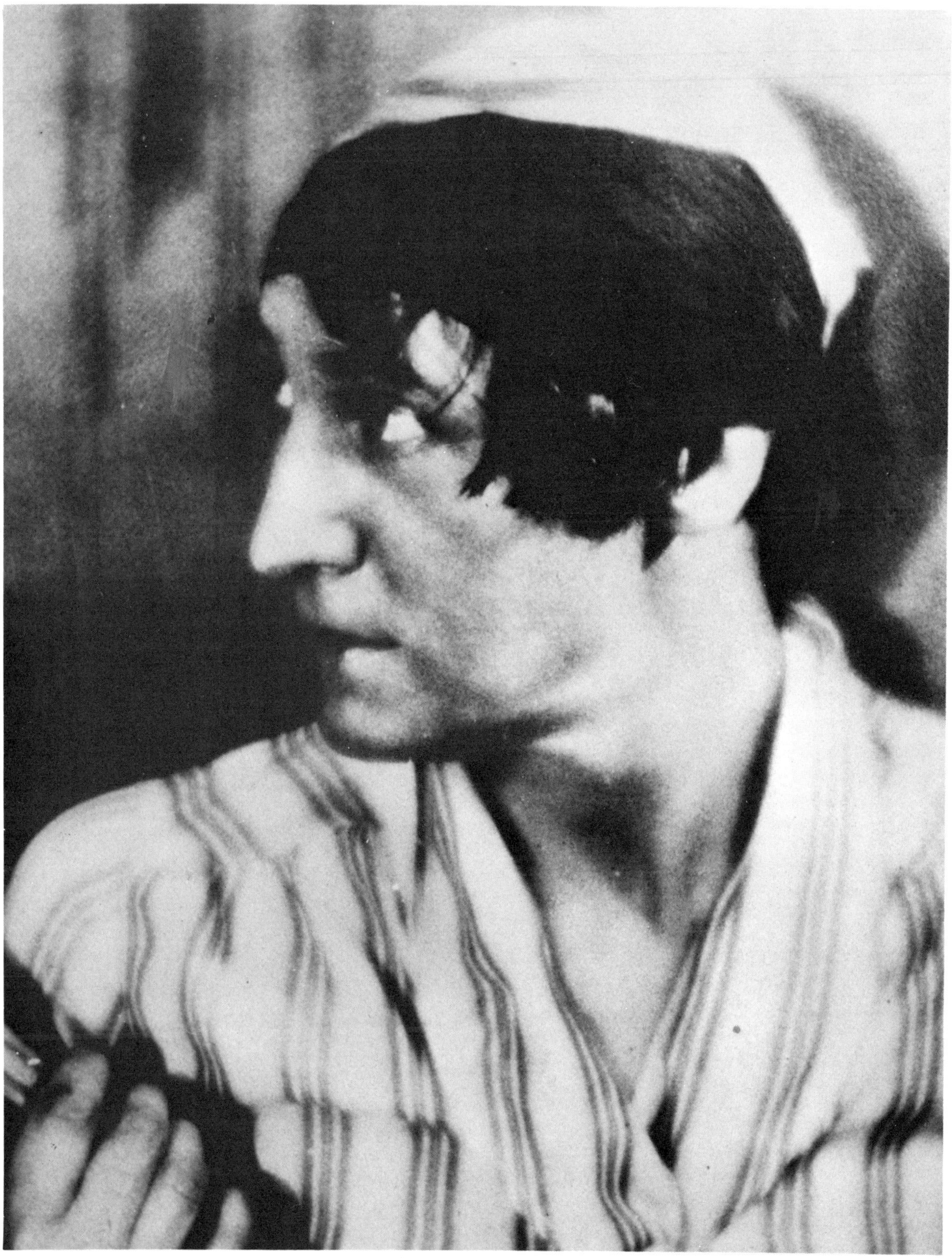

59 Lou Tellegan

60 Geraldine Farrar

**61 Wyndham Standing**

62 Irving Cummings

**63 Mary Miles Minter**

64 **Wallace MacDonald**

**65 Marie Prevost**

66 Mae Marsh

**67 Robert Harron**

**68 Vivian Oakland**

**69 Robert McKim**

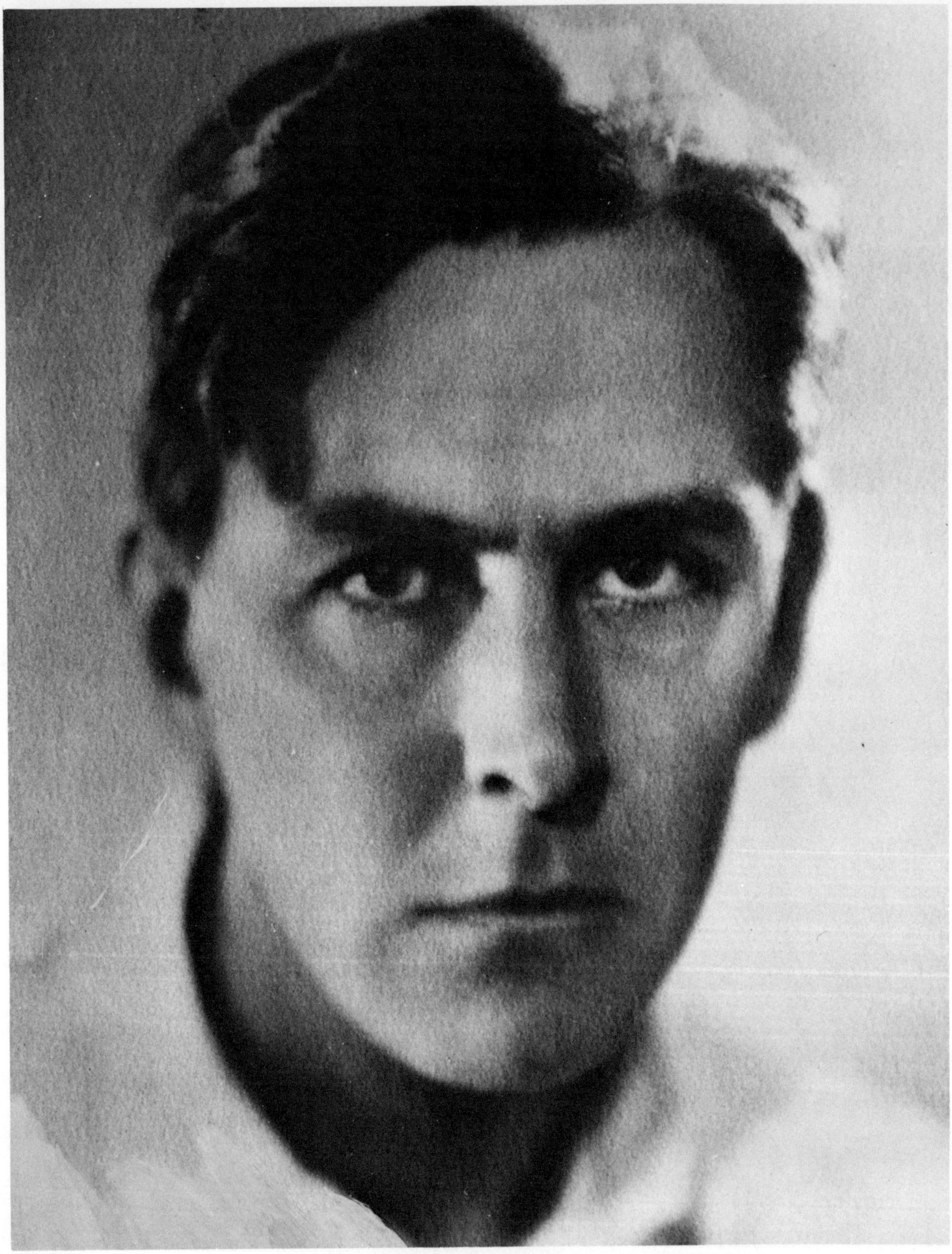

70 Percy Marmont

**71 Ruth Roland**

**72 Gladys Brockwell**

**73 Donald Crisp**

74 Ruth Stonehouse

**75 William Russell**

**76 Fannie Ward**

**77 Sessue Hayakawa**

**78 Ethel Clayton**

**79 Henry B. Walthall**

80 Jean Hersholt

**81 Clara Kimball Young**

82 Katherine MacDonald

**83 Lewis S. Stone**

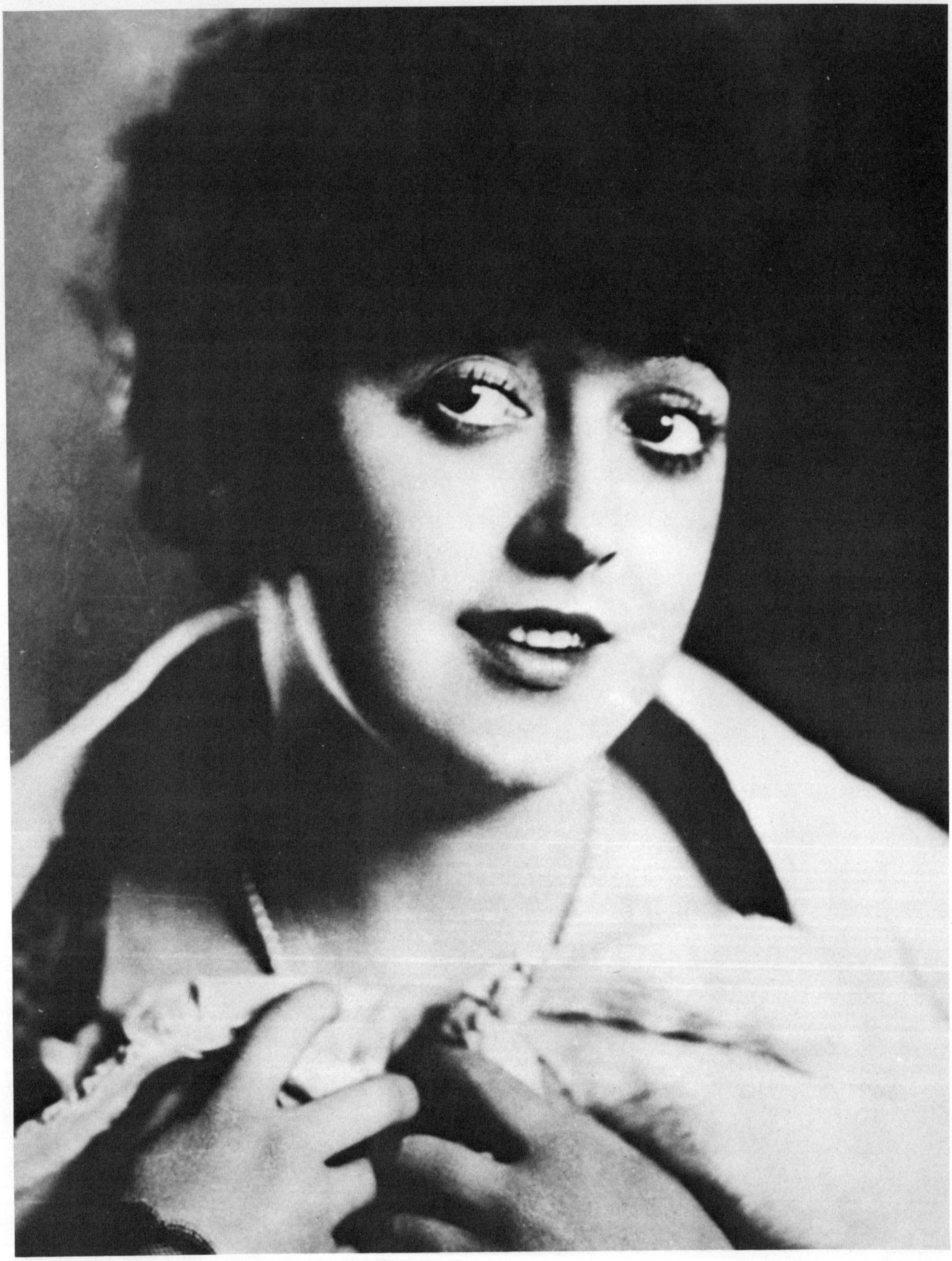

84 Mable Normand

**85 Frank Mayo**

86 Belle Bennett

**87 Carlyle Blackwell**

88 **Montague Love**

**89 Betty Blythe**

**90 Antonio Moreno**

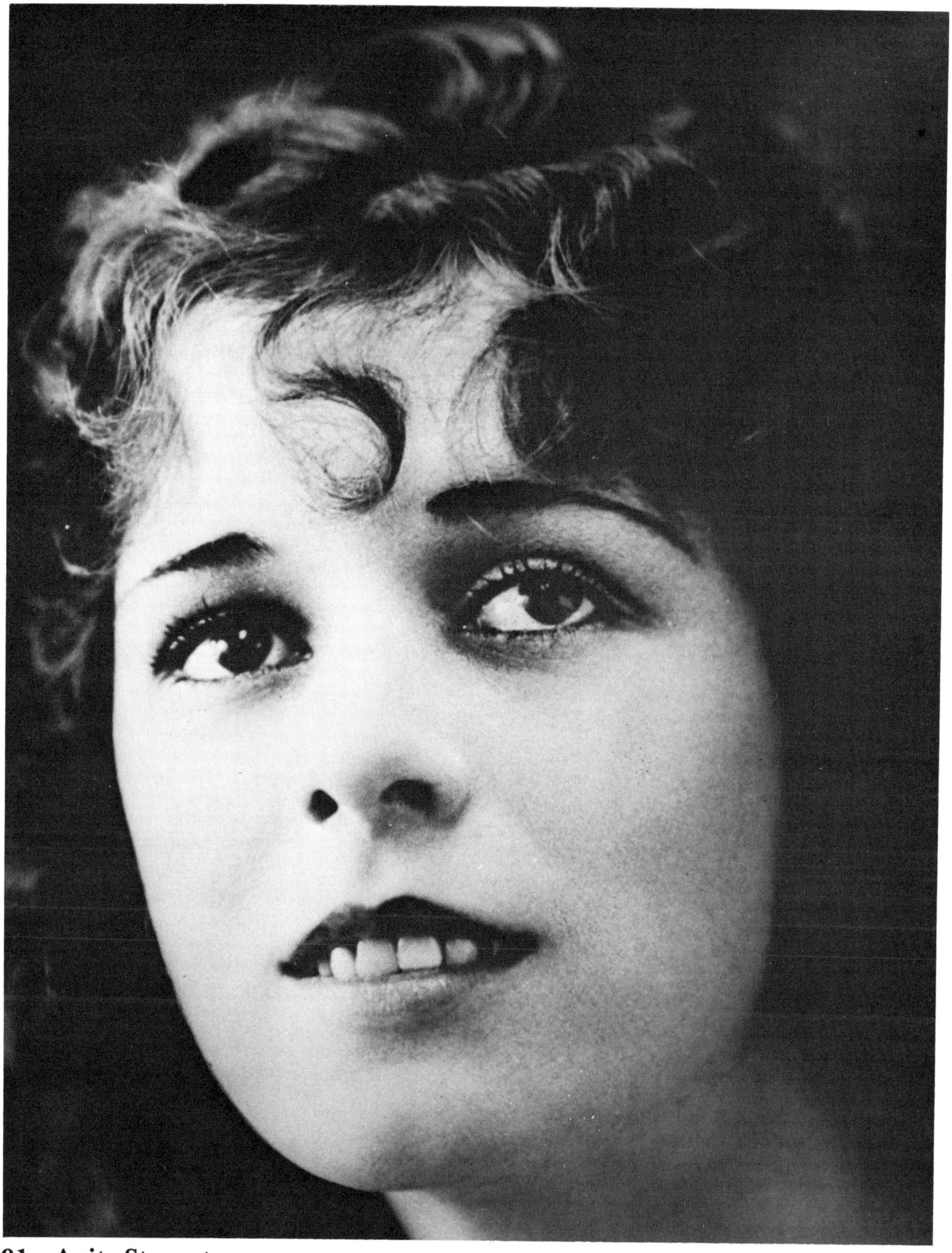

**91 Anita Stewart**

92 George Beban

**93 Billie Rhodes**

**94 Marguerite Clark**

**95 Dustin Farnham**

96 Corrine Griffith

**97 Tyrone Power, Sr.**

**98 Lya de Putti**

**99 Hobart Bosworth**

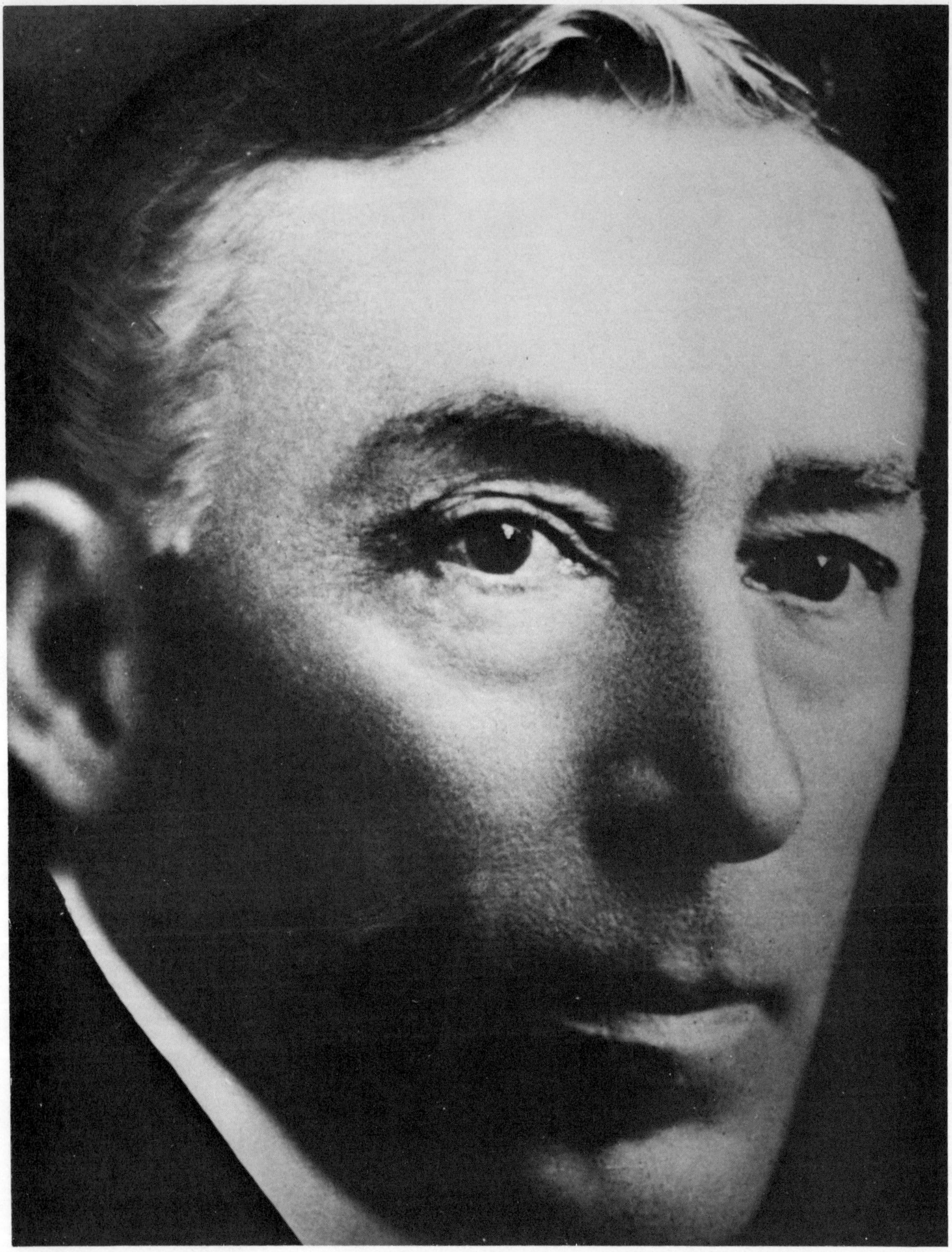

**100 Tully Marshall**

**101 Mary Carr**

**102 Jack Pickford**

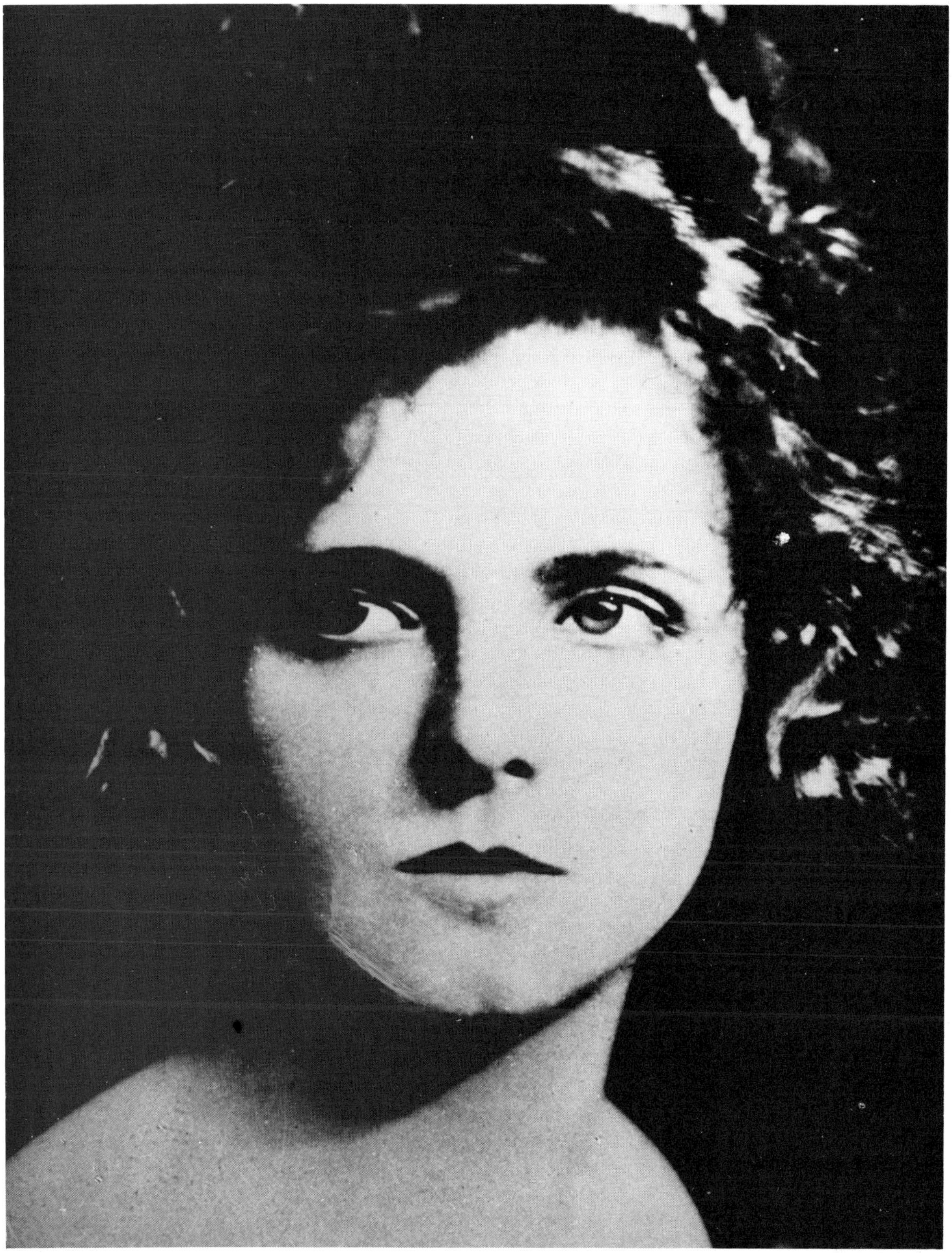

**103 Olive Thomas**

**104 Marilyn Miller**

**105 Richard Barthlemess**

**106 Joseph Schildkraut**

**107 Fay Tincher**

**108 Billie Burke**

**109 J. Farrell MacDonald**

**110 George Seigmann**

**111 Barbara Castleton**

**112 Gaston Glass**

**113 Alma Rubens**

**114 Charles Ray**

**115 Charles Ray**

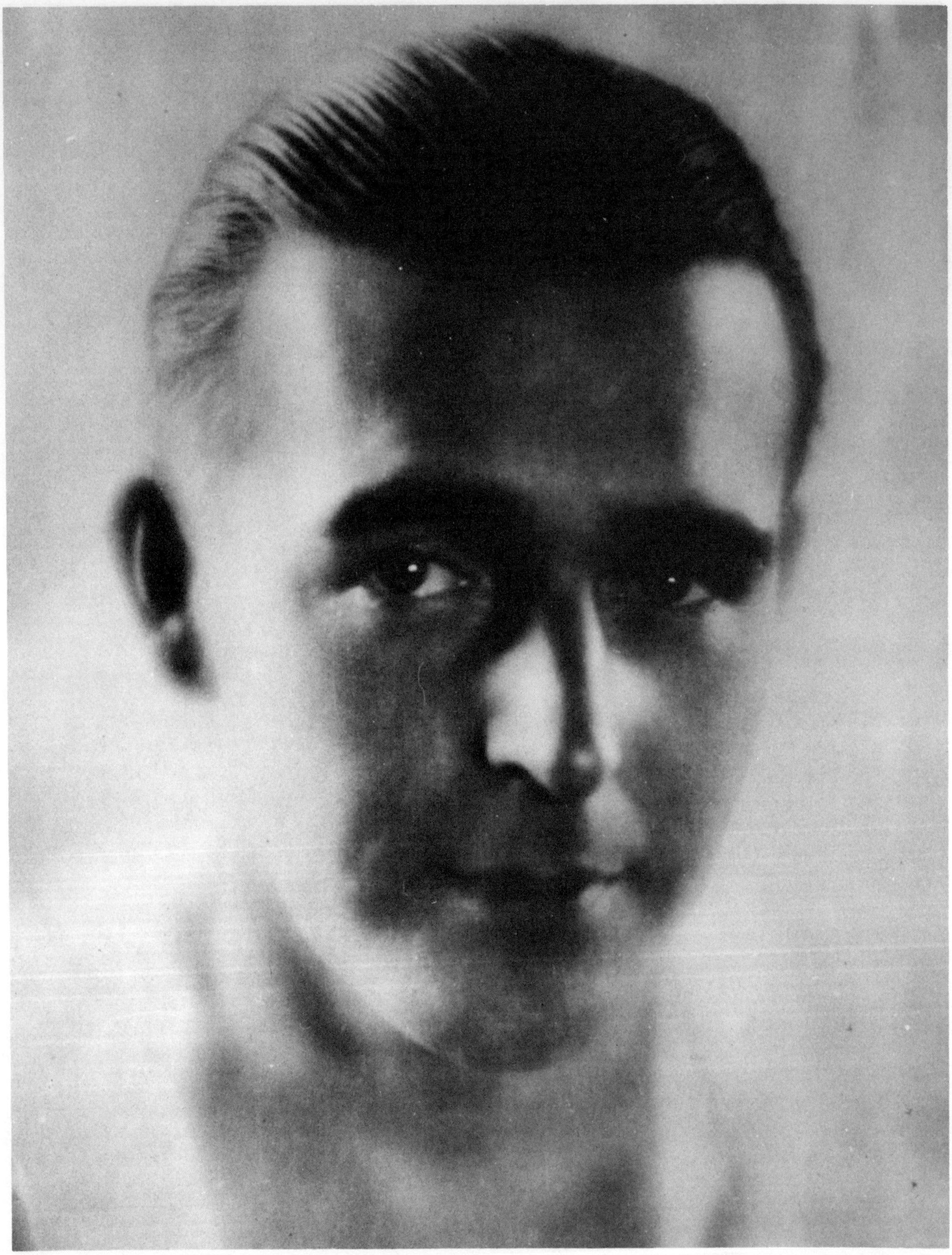

**116 Wallace Reid**

**117 Wallace Reid**

**118 Douglas MacLean**

**119 Anna Q. Nilsson**

**120 Gladys Walton**

**121 Roy D'Arcy**

**122 Pauline Starke**

**123 Tom Moore**

**124 Roscoe "Fatty" Arbuckle**

**125 Roscoe "Fatty" Arbuckle**

**126 Roscoe "Fatty" Arbuckle**

**127 Helene Chadwick**

**128 Eva Novak**

**129 Jane Novak**

**130 Norma Talmadge**

**131 Gilbert Roland**

**132 Monroe Salisbury**

**133 Leatrice Joy**

**134 May Allison**

**135 Harold Lockwood**

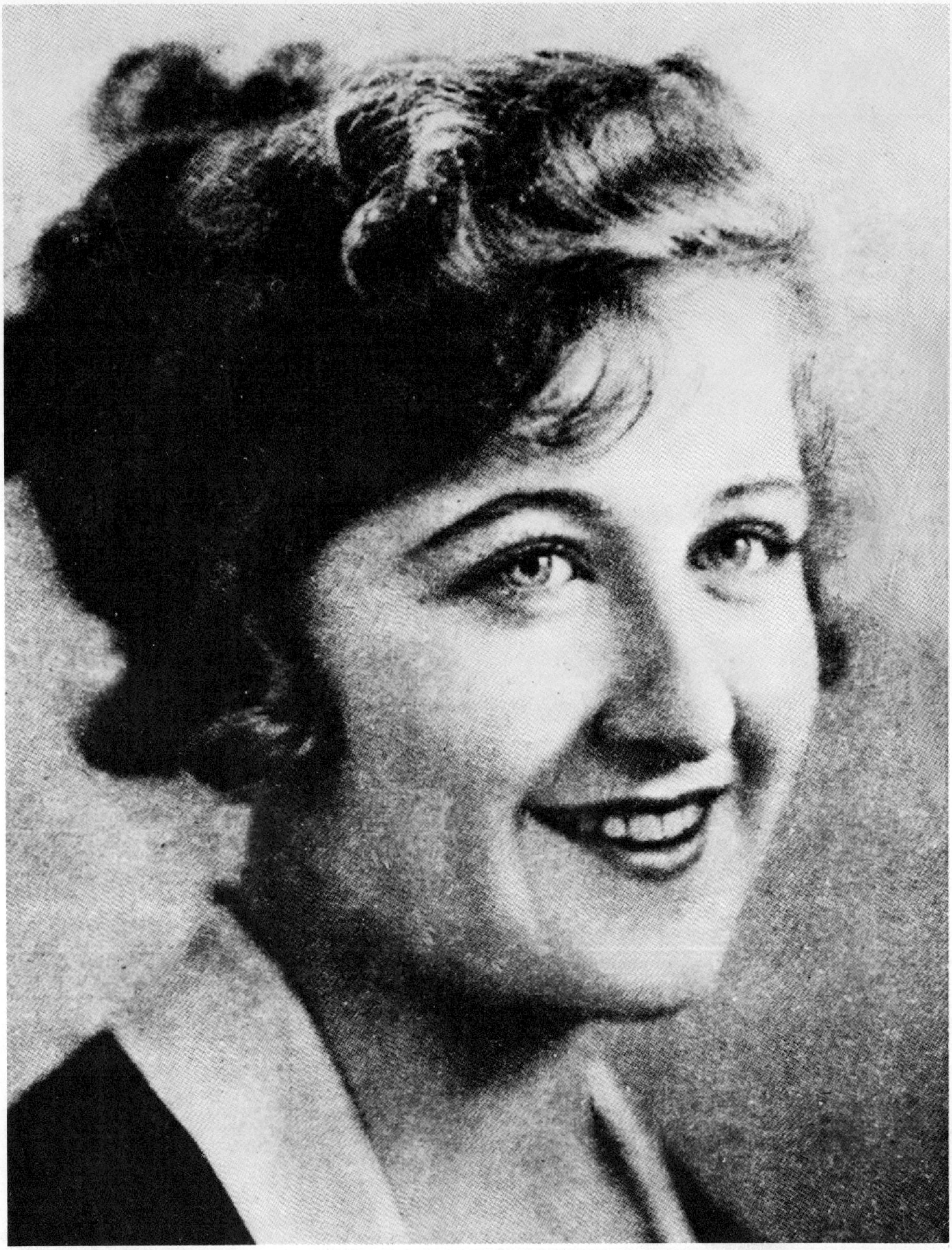

**136 Ruth Clifford**

**137 Bryant Washburn**

138 Vilma Banky

**139 Bert Lytell**

**140 Matt Moore**

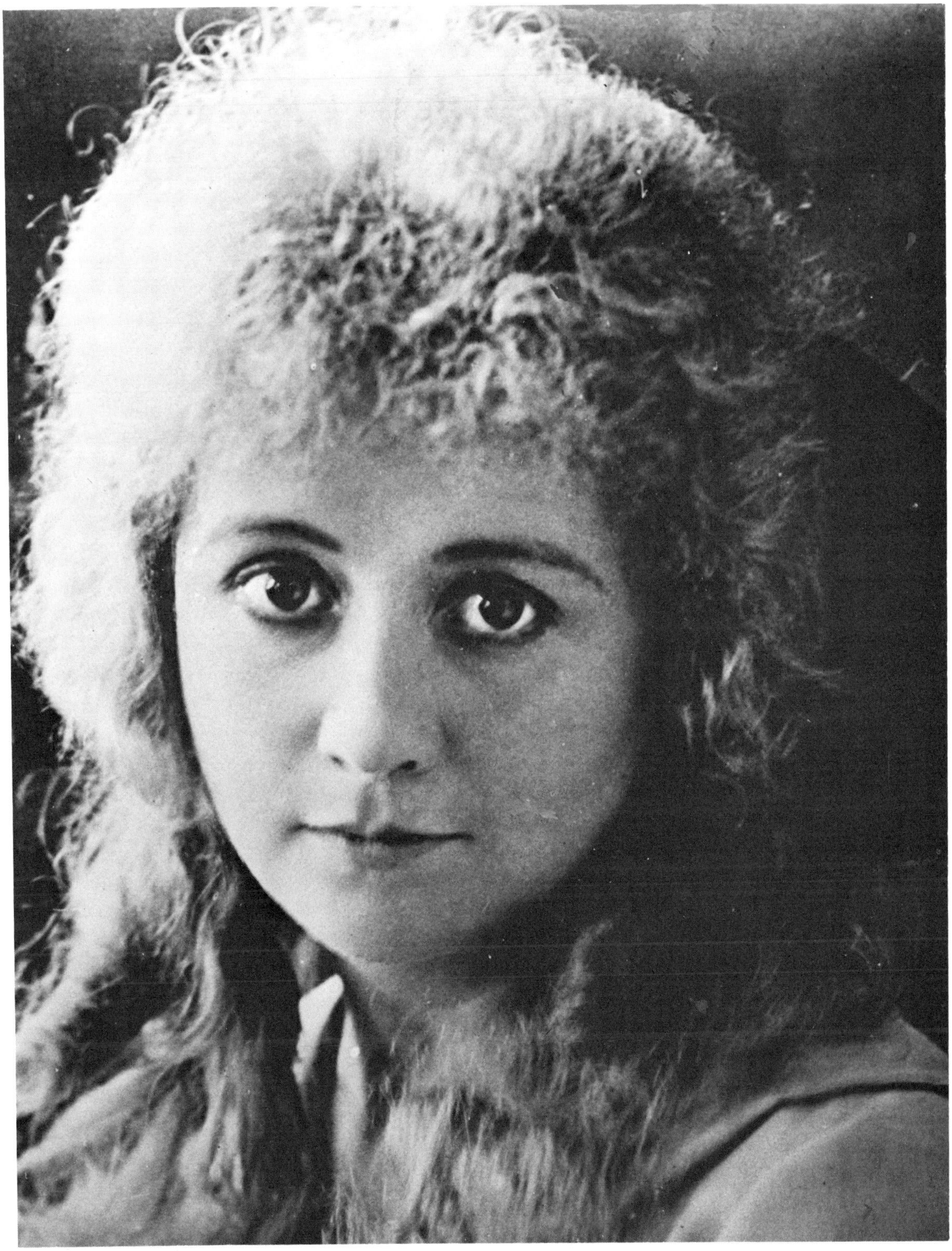

**141 Bessie Barriscale**

**142 Laura LaPlante**

**143 Charles de Roche**

**144 Margarita Fischer**

**145 Thomas Meighan**

**146 House Peters**

**147 Alice Brady**

**148 Norman Kerry**

**149 Mary Philbin**

**150 Stuart Holmes**

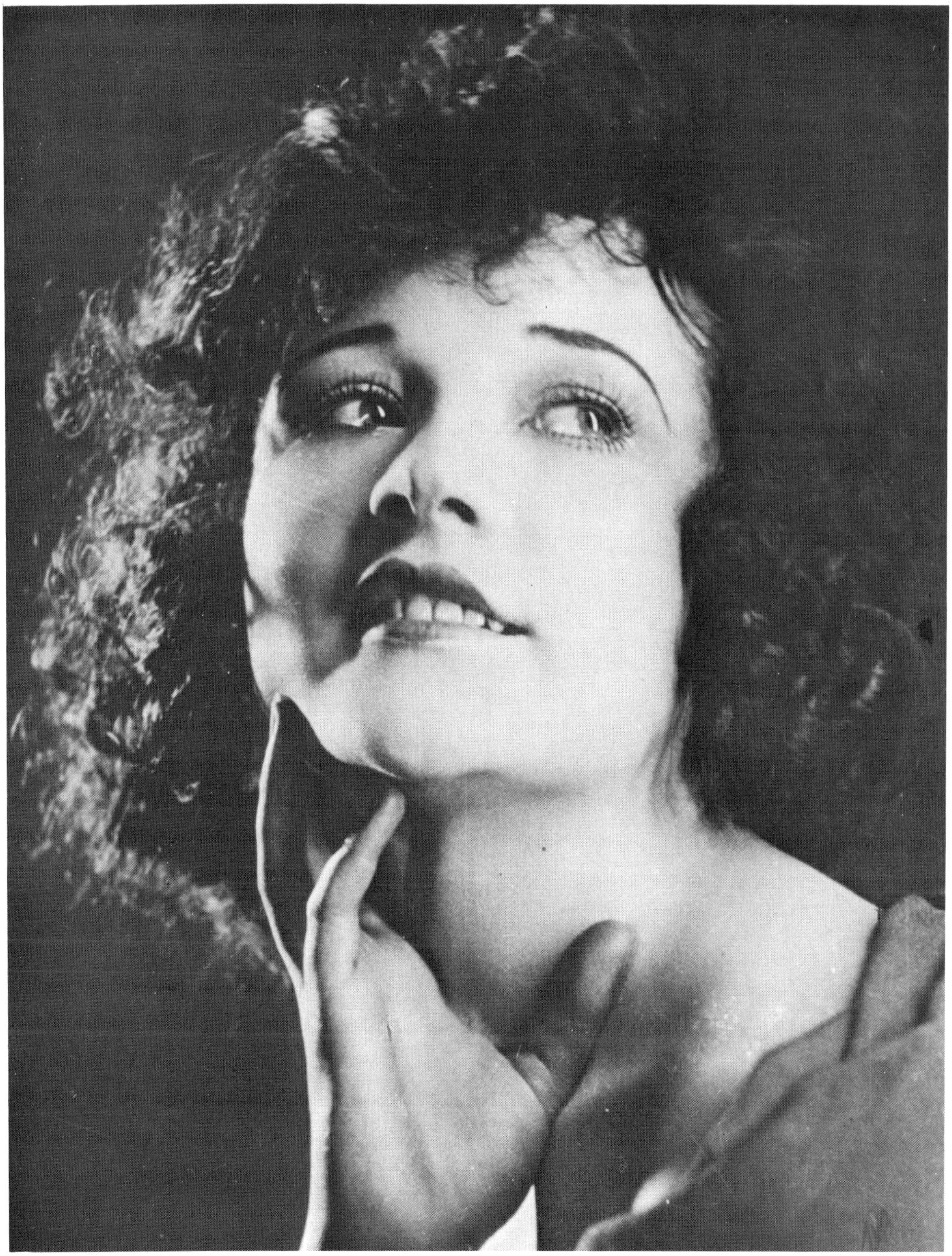

**151 Betty Compson**

**152 George Walsh**

**153 Madge Bellamy**

**154 James Kirkwood**

**155 Bessie Love**

156 Phyllis Haver

**157 Ralph Graves**

**158 Eugene O'Brien**

**159 Barbara Lamarr**

**160 Norma Talmadge**

**161 Rudolph Valentino**

**162 Rudolph Valentino**

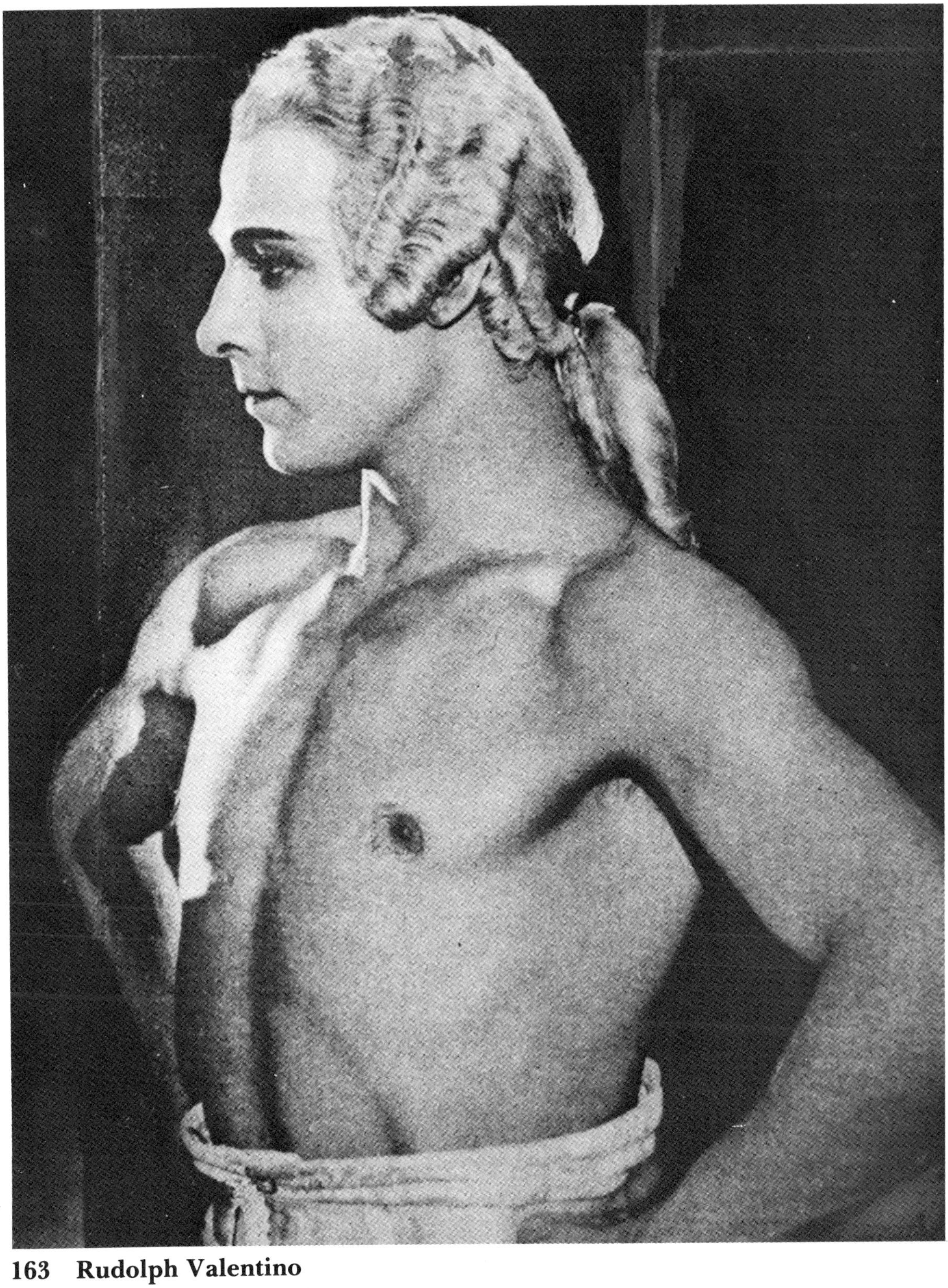

163 Rudolph Valentino

**164 Delores Costello**

**165 Harrison Ford**

**166 Creighton Hale**

**167 Bebe Daniels**

**168 Emil Jannings**

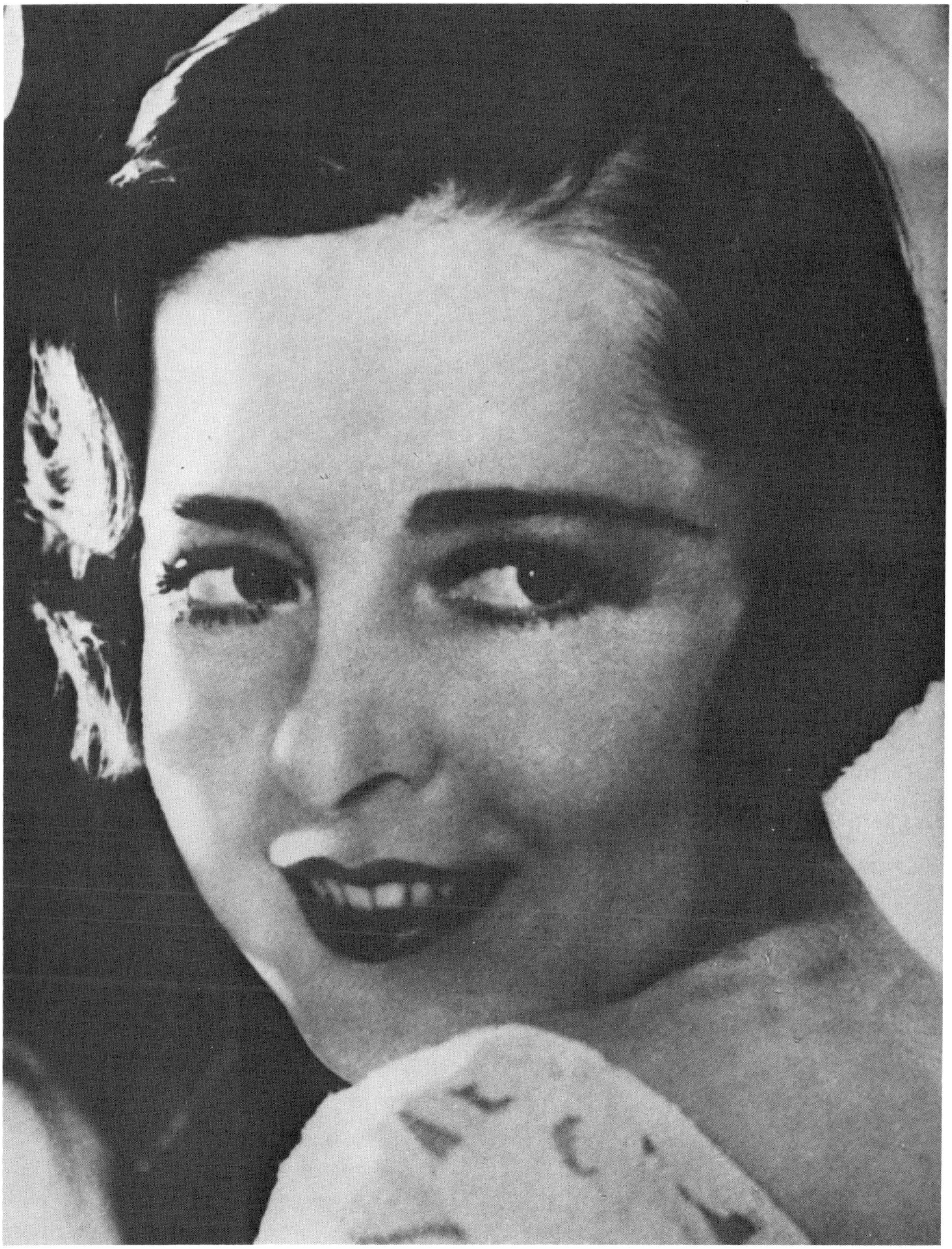

**169 Colleen Moore**

**170 Walter Long**

**171 Alice Terry**

**172 Mae Murray**

**173 Frank Mayo**

**174 Robert Frazer**

**175 Mae Busch**

**176 Lon Chaney**

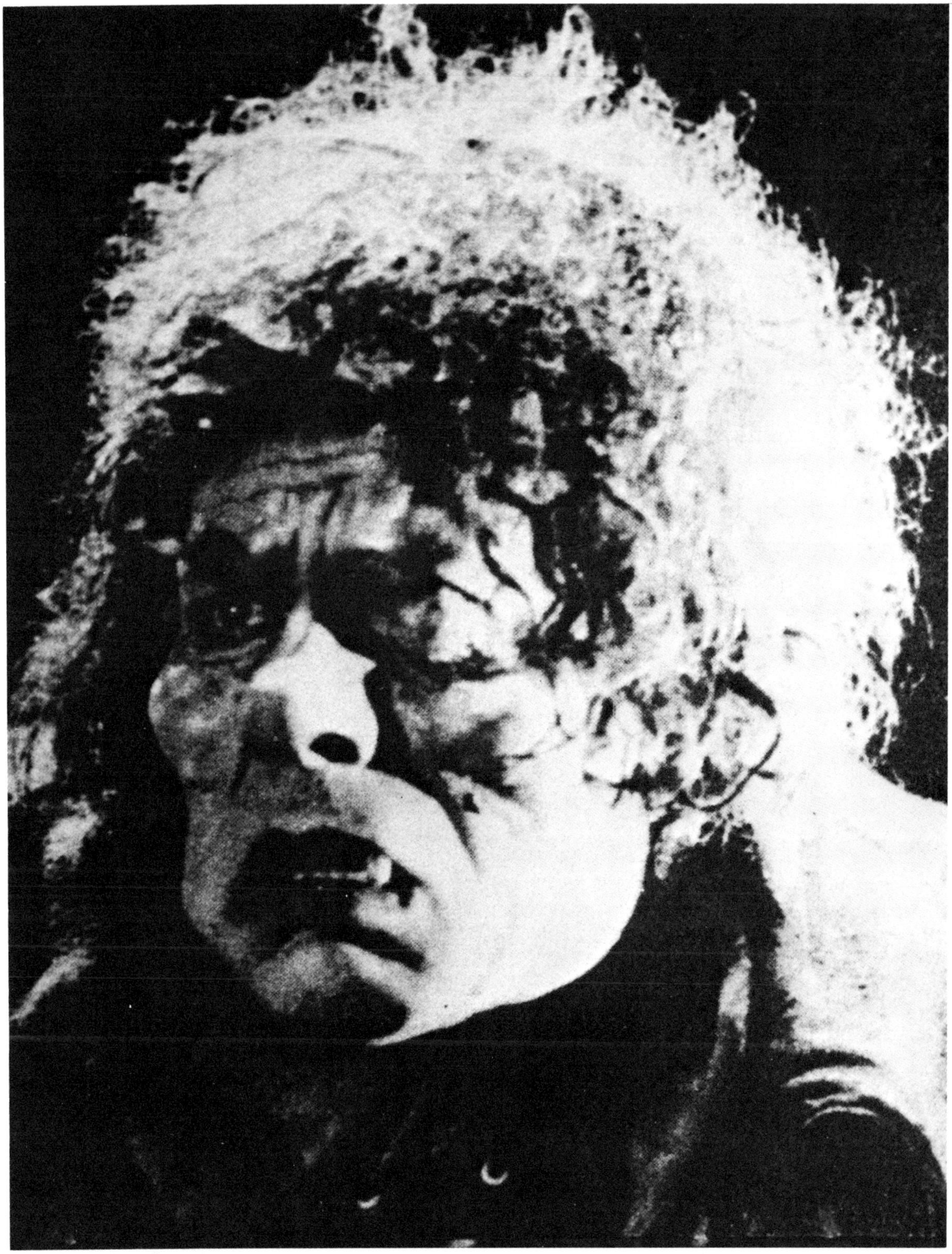

**177 Lon Chaney**

**178 Louis Wolheim**

**179 Marion Davies**

**180 Rod LaRocque**

**181 Rod LaRocque**

182 George Fawcett

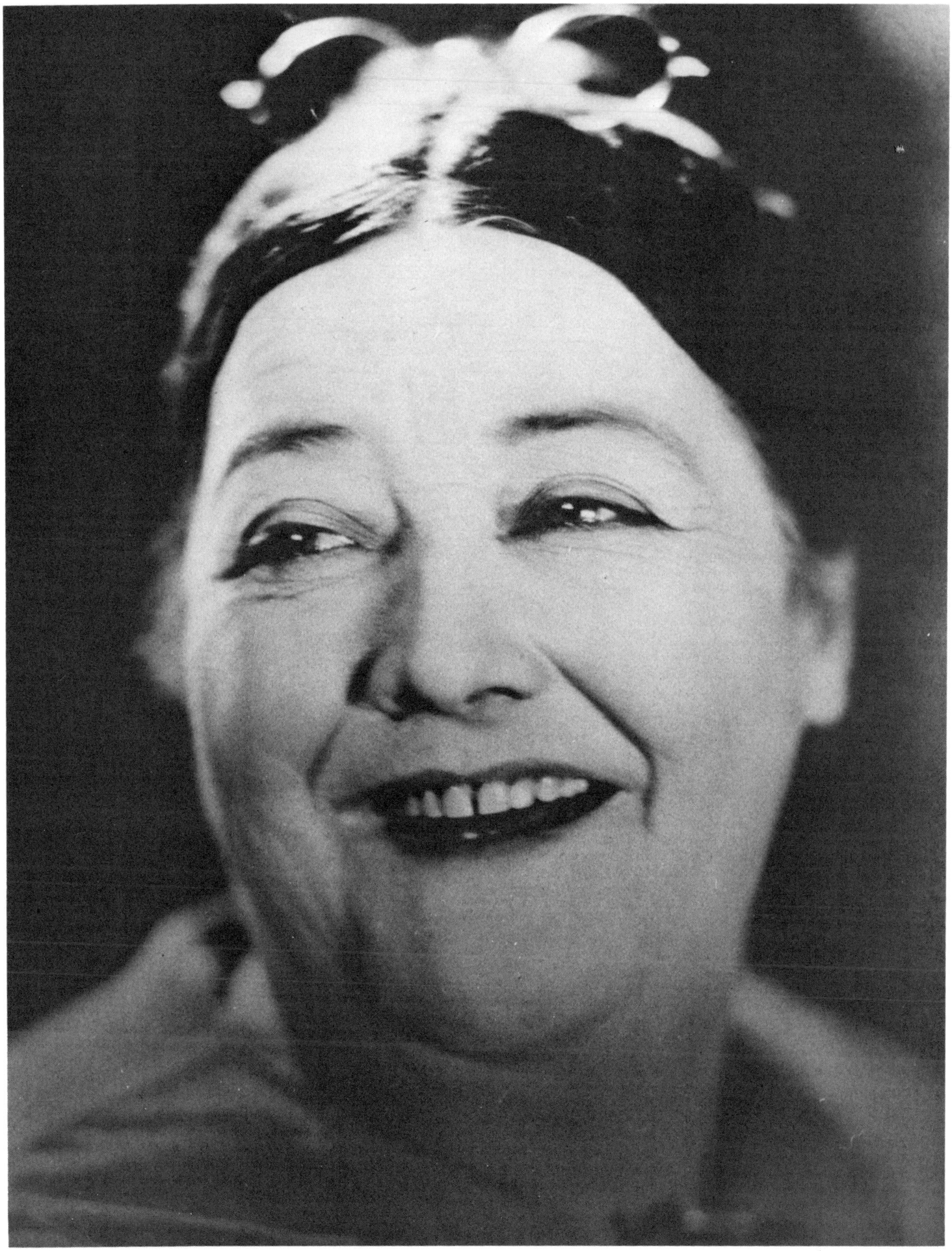

**183 Kate Price**

**184 Julia Faye**

**185 William Boyd**

**186 Adolph Menjou**

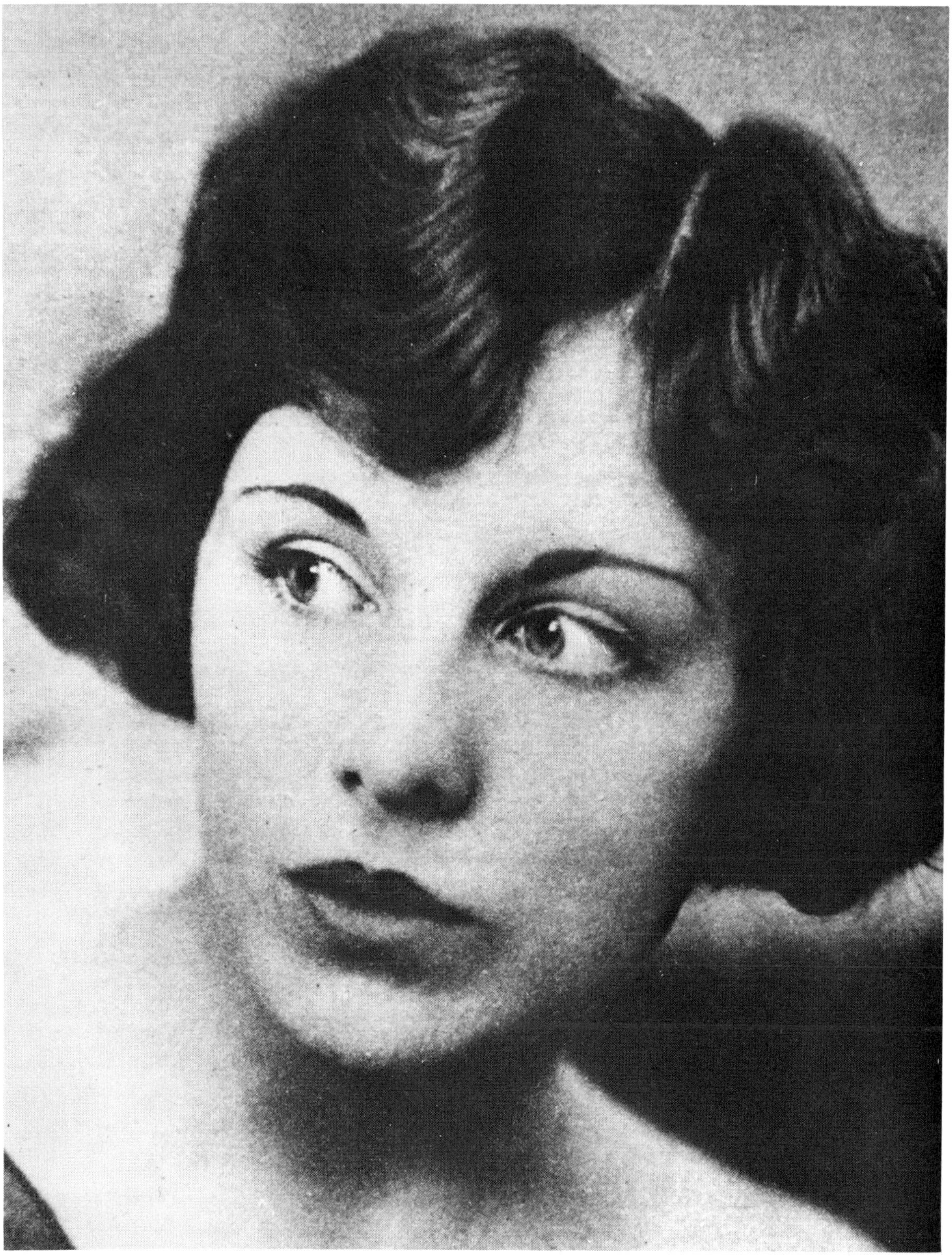

**187 Shirley Mason**

**188 Enid Bennett**

**189 Roy Steward**

**190 Viola Dana**

**191 William Desmond**

**192 Monte Blue**

**193 Mae Marsh**

**194 Irene Castle**

**195 Walter MacGrail**

**196 Gloria Swanson**

**197 Neil Hamilton**

**198 Tim McCoy**

**199 Natalie Talmadge**

**200 Estelle Taylor**

**201 Jack Mulhall**

**202 George O'Brien**

**203 Constance Binney**

**204 Sidney Chaplin**

**205 Priscilla Dean**

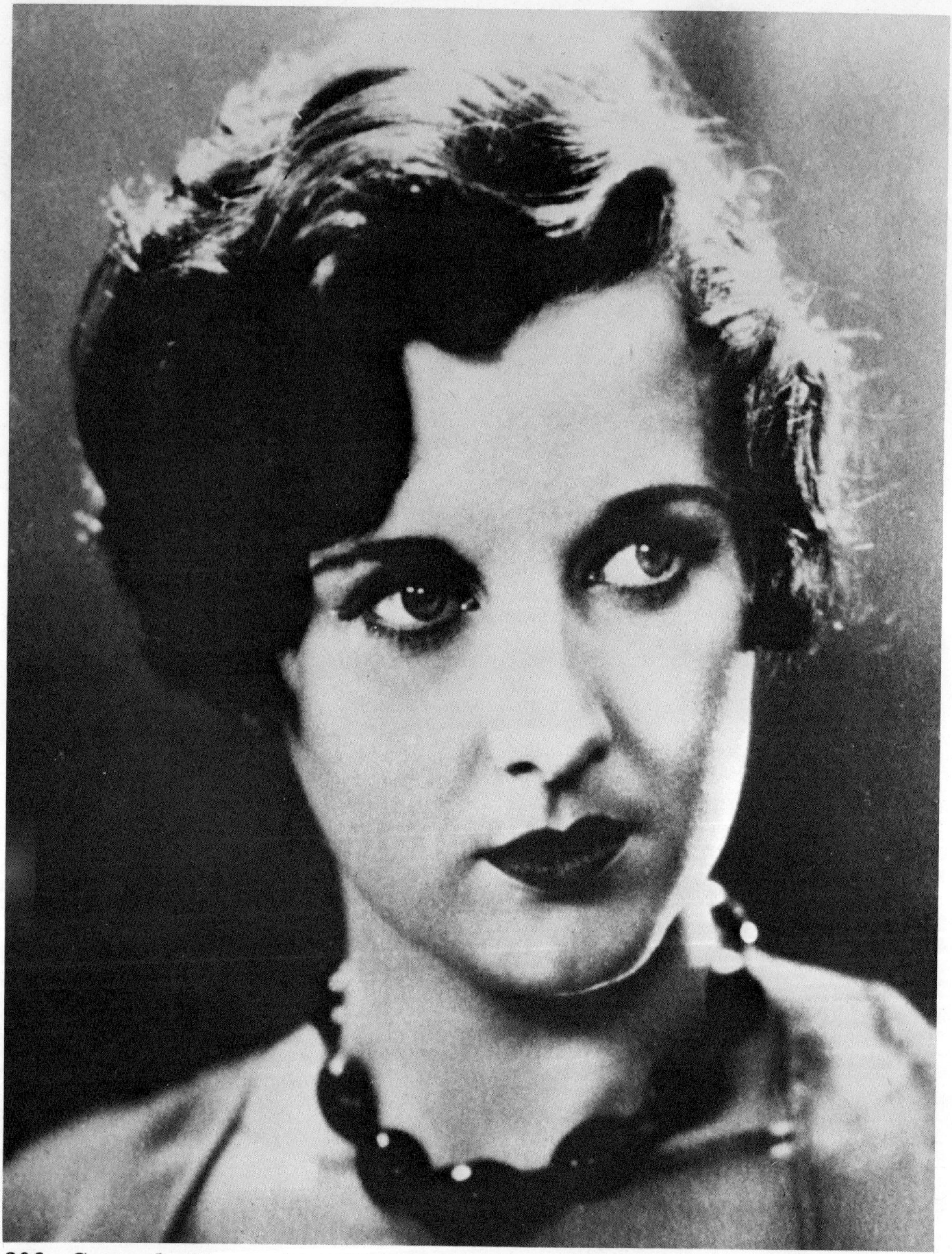

**206 Gertrude Olmstead**

**207 Lew Cody**

**208 Nita Naldi**

**209 Nils Asther**

**210 George Bancroft**

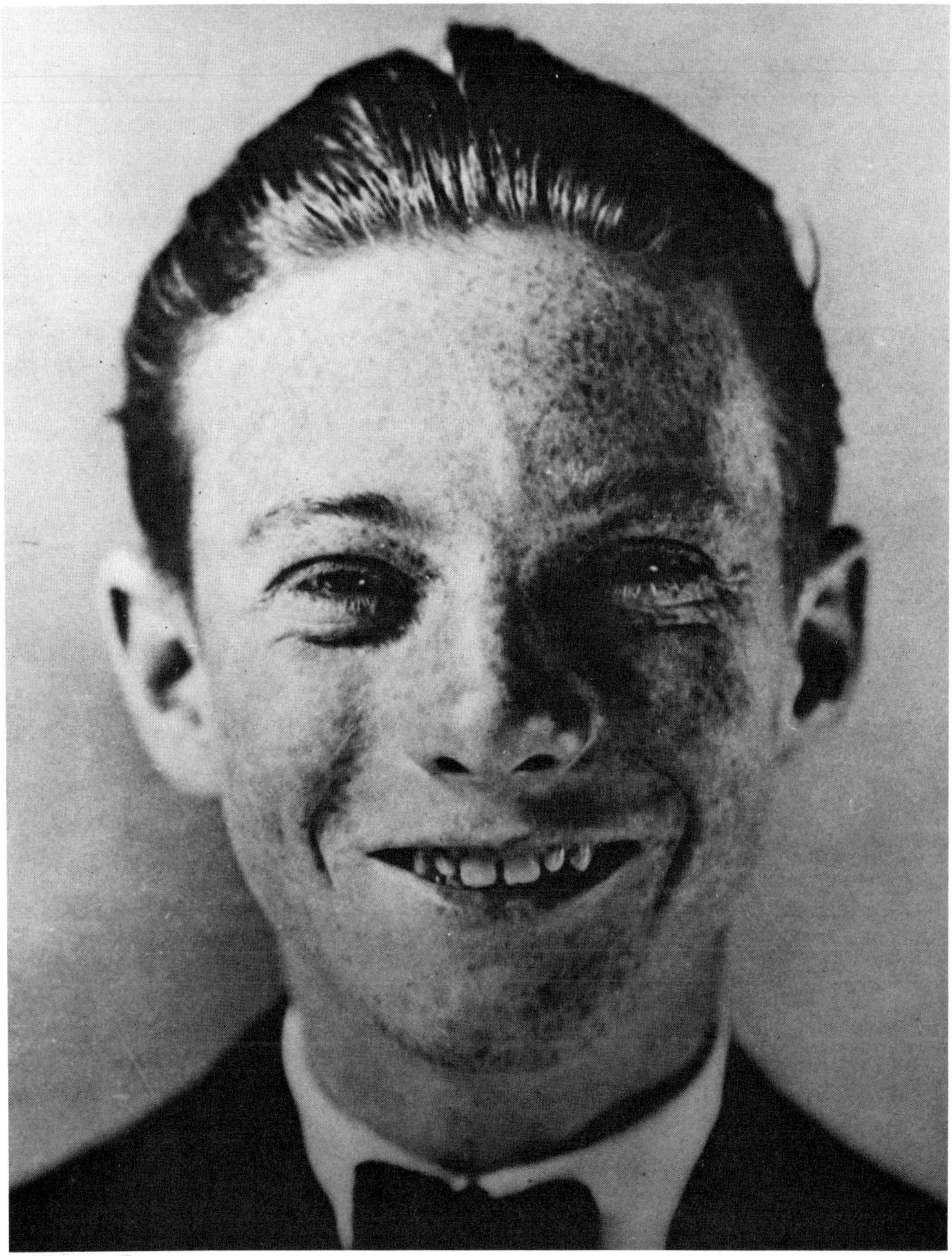

**211 Wesley Barry**

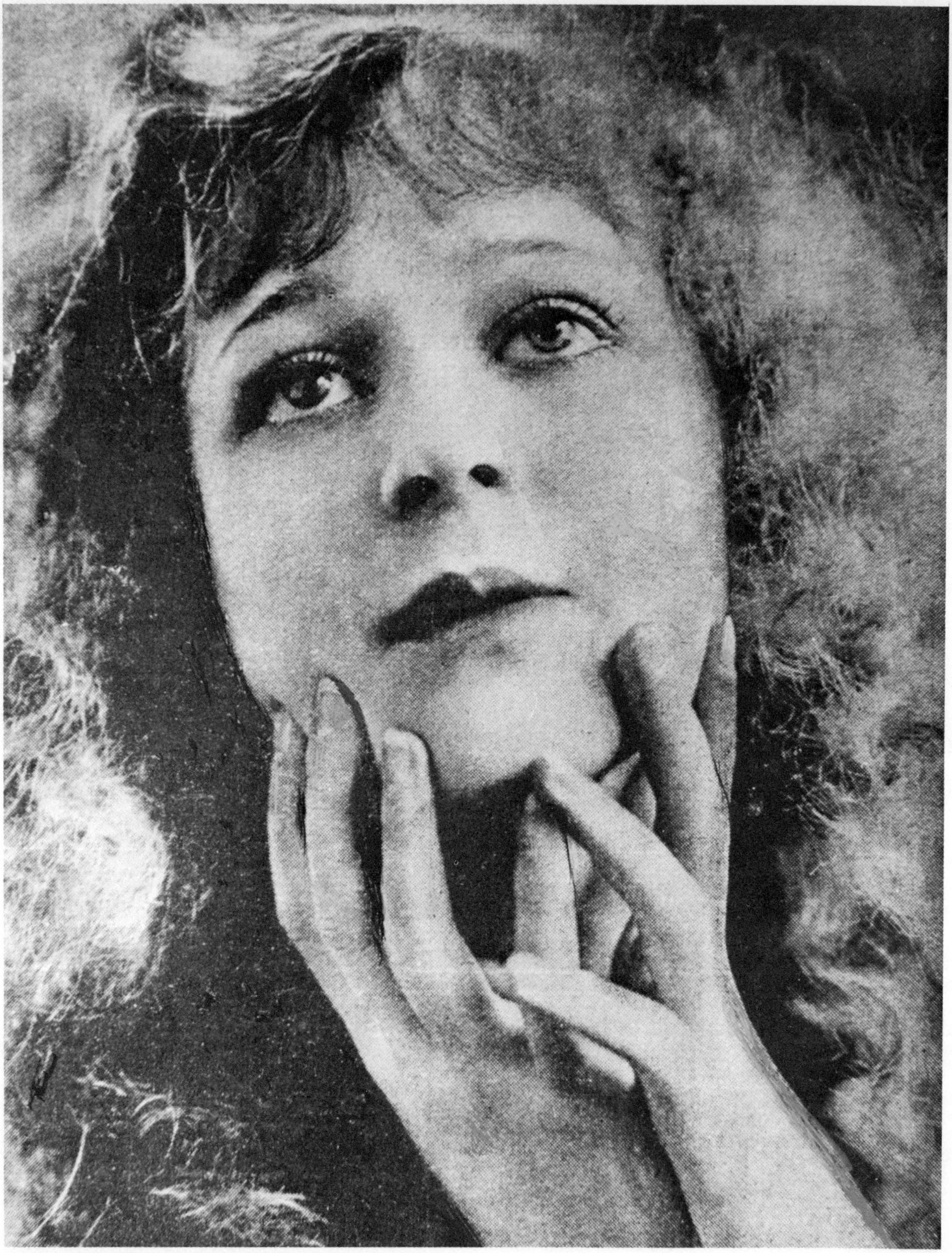

**212 Marguerite de la Motte**

**213 Max Linder**

**214 Charles "Buddy" Rogers**

**215 Fifi Dorsay**

**216 Theodore Roberts**

**217 Theodore Roberts**

**218 Ramon Novarro**

**219 Ramon Novarro**

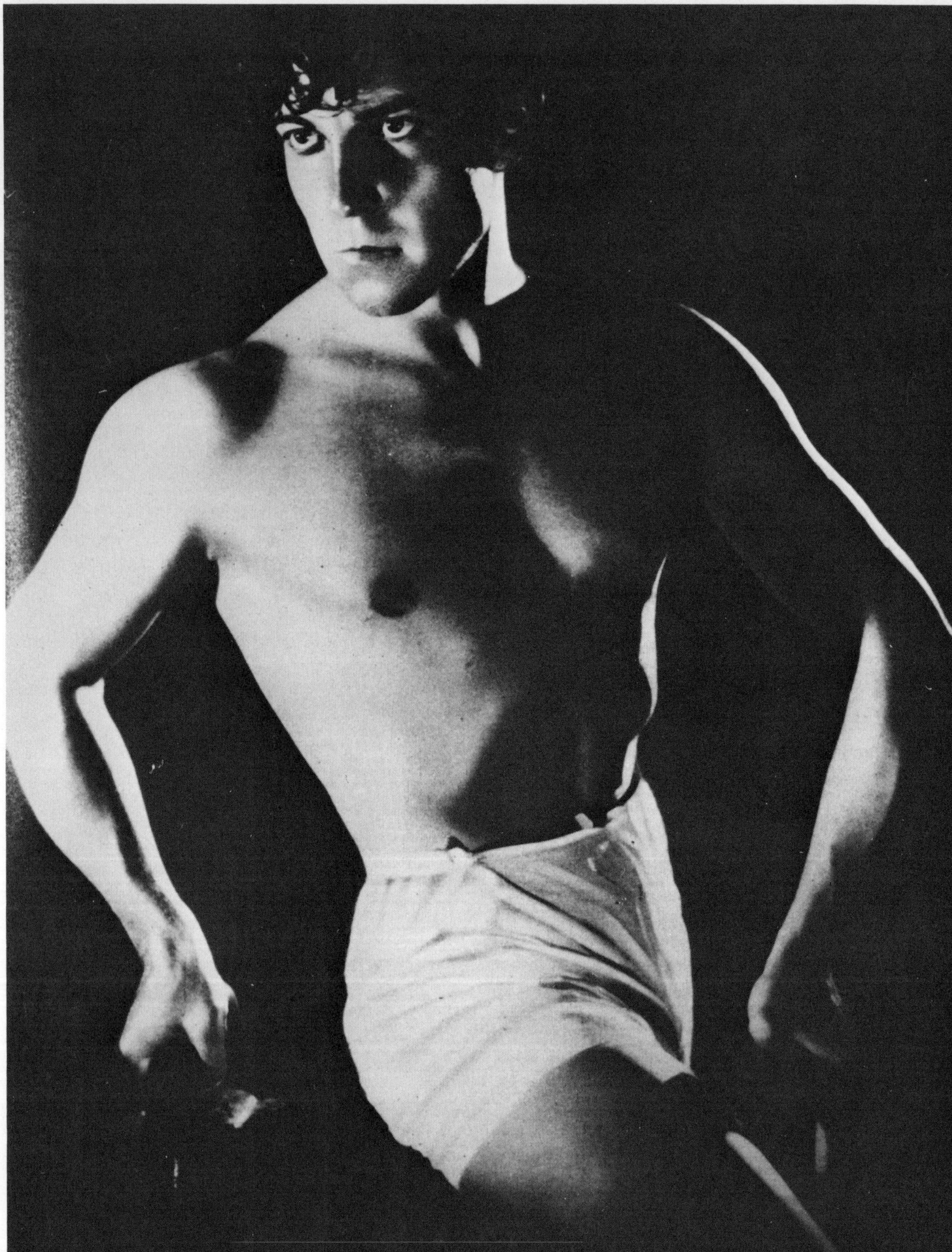

**220 Ramon Novarro**

**221 Victor Moore**

**222 Pola Negri**

**223 Pola Negri**

**224 Alan Hale**

**225 Eugene Pallette**

**226 George Barbier**

**227 Ned Sparks**

228 Bull Montana

**229 Polly Moran**

**230 Edward Everett Horton**

**231 Franklin Pangborn**

**232 W. C. Fields**

**233 Al St. John**

234 Walter Hiers

**235 Joe E. Brown**

**236 Larry Semon**

**237 Charlie Chase**

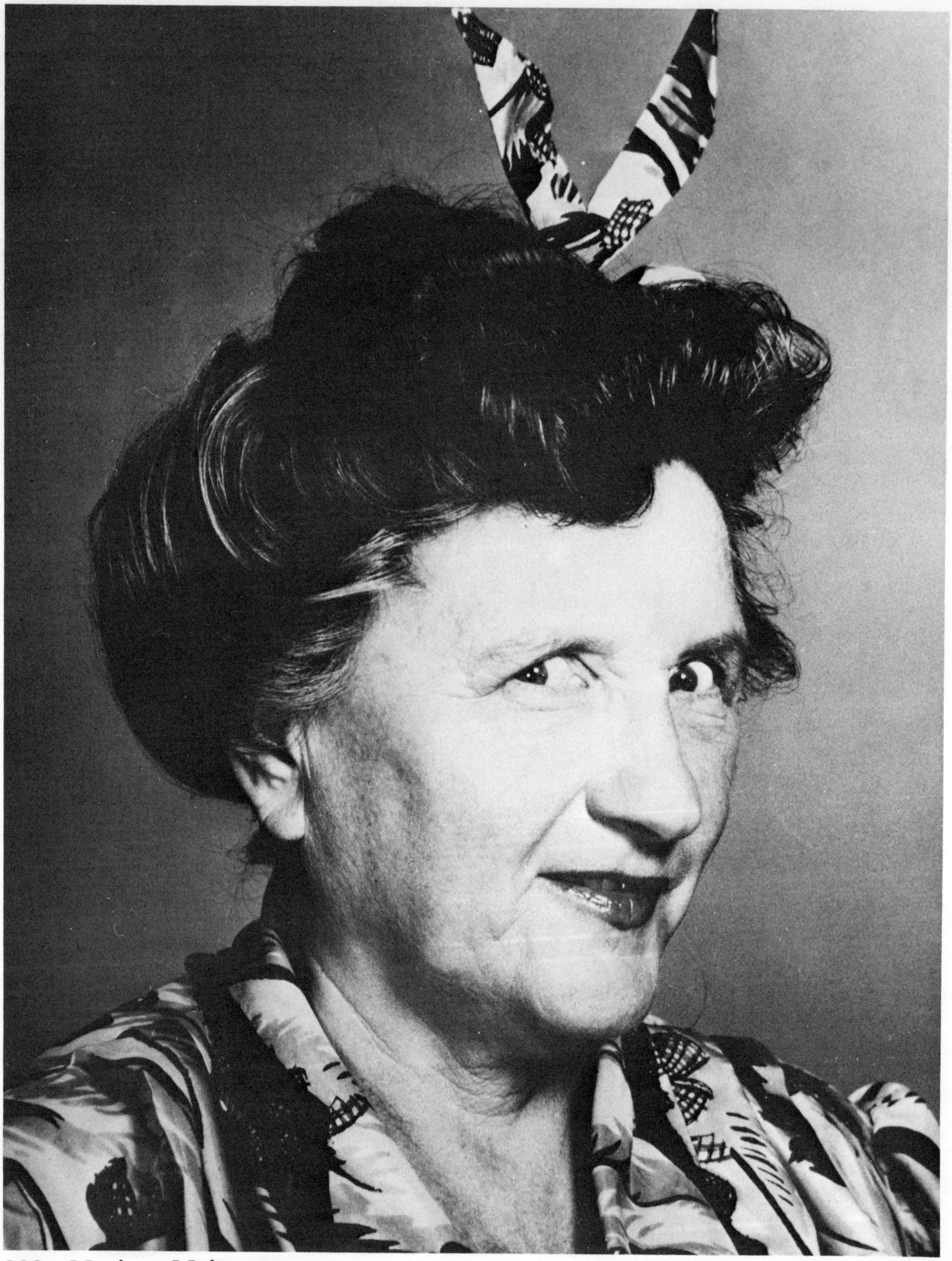

**238 Marjory Main**

**239 Harold Lloyd**

**240 Marie Dressler**

**241 Slim Summerville**

**242 El Brendel**

# INDEX AND PROFILES TO PART ONE

A

**ALLISON, May**—plate 134. Born on a farm in Georgia, in 1898, and was educated in Birmingham, Alabama. Had a very successful stage career before entering films. Starred in EVERYMAN and THE QUAKER GIRL on Broadway and was persuaded by Will Rogers to play the leading role with him in a film called DAVID HAREM in 1917. Many films followed including ONE INCREASING PURPOSE, THE WOMAN WHO FOOLED HERSELF, MEN OF STEEL, THE CITY, and MISMATES. Height 5 ft. 6 in. with golden hair and blue eyes. Flew her own private plane.

**ANDERSON, Broncho Billy**—plates 1, 2. Born in Pine Bluff, Arkansas, April 30, 1883, he started his film career under the name of G. M. Anderson. Because he was the first great Western star, he became known affectionately as Broncho Billy. His real name was Max Aronson. He was the earliest pioneer of Western drama. Historically, he was the first male "movie star," having worked in THE GREAT TRAIN ROBBERY with the old Edison Company in 1903. Moved from Edison to Vitagraph to Selig and finally formed his own company with George Spoor under the name of Essanay (S and A, Spoor and Anderson). BRONCHO BILLY AND THE BABY was the first of 367 of his Westerns. Many of the great stars of the era worked for him, including Chaplin, Francis X. Bushman, Wallace Beery, Bryant Washburn, and Ethel Clayton. Height 5 ft. 11 in. Brown hair and blue eyes. He died in 1971.

**ARBUCKLE, Roscoe "Fatty"**—plates 124, 125, 126. Born in Smith Center, Kansas, March 24, 1887. Educated in Santa Clara, California, and entered the theatre in 1900. Worked in vaudeville, carnival, and burlesque. He joined the Selig Company in 1907, and began his movie career. He was with Mack Sennett from 1913 to 1917. After producing pictures independently in partnership with Joseph Schenck for a time, he signed with Famous Players Lasky, where he made a long series of films the most famous of which were BREWSTER'S MILLIONS and THE ROUNDUP. He was one of the great comics of his day. A very stout man, he was known internationally as "Fatty." He died in New York in 1933.

**ASTHER, Nils**—plate 209. Born on January 17, 1900, in Malmö, Sweden. Made his stage *début* in Stockholm at the age of thirteen. Entered films with the UFA Company in Berlin, where he made many films and was already a star when he was brought to Hollywood to play the leading male role in TOPSY AND EVA with the famous Duncan sisters. He was the star of Herbert Brenon's film SORREL AND SON, which was filmed in England. Other films include THE SINGLE STANDARD with Greta Garbo, HER CARDBOARD LOVER with Marion Davies, LAUGH CLOWN LAUGH, WILD ORCHIDS also with Garbo, and THE COSSACKS. He married Vivian Duncan. Height 6 ft. 1 in. Black hair and grey eyes.

B

**BAGGOTT, King**—plate 8. Born in St. Louis, Missouri, on October 21, 1868. Began a stage career at an early age and with quite some success, but left it for the screen. He pioneered through the early days of film-making and, with Francis X. Bushman and Maurice Costello, was one of the three great "matinee idols" of his day. He later changed from actor to director and became one of the leading film directors in America. His film credits include RAFFLES, LADY AUDLEY'S SECRET, IVANHOE, THE CORSICAN BROTHERS, and DR. JEKYLL AND MR. HYDE. Dark brown hair with a white streak through the centre. Blue eyes. A big man—about 6 ft. tall. Died in 1948.

**BANCROFT, George**—plate 210. Born in Philadelphia, Pennsylvania, on January 13, 1882. Educated at the Tomes Institute and the United States Naval Academy. Renounced his naval career for the theatre. Became a Broadway star and was highly acclaimed in PAID IN FULL and in THE TRAIL OF THE LONESOME PINE. PONY EXPRESS, his first picture for Paramount, brought him to the attention of director James Cruze, who cast him for a leading part in other films. Among his films are included OLD IRONSIDES, DERELICT, LADIES LOVE BRUTES, DRAGNET, and THE WORLD AND THE FLESH. Height 6 ft. 2 in. Brown hair and eyes. One of the screen's great character actors. He died in 1956.

**BANKY, Vilma**—plate 138. Born in Budapest, Hungary, on January 9, 1903, the daughter of a prominent politician. Real name Vilma Concit. Made her stage *début* in Vienna and later made films in Austria and Hungary. Samuel Goldwyn, travelling in Austria, was impressed by her picture in a shop window. He contacted her and brought her to Hollywood to star. She played the female lead with Rudolph Valentino in THE EAGLE and in the SON OF THE SHEIK, and was in THE DARK ANGEL with Ronald Coleman. Other screen credits include THE WINNING OF BARBARA WORTH, THE AWAKENING, NIGHT OF LOVE, and INNOCENT. Height 5 ft. 6 in. Blonde and blue eyes. Married to film star Rod LaRocque.

**BARA, Theda**—plate 36. Born in Cincinnati, Ohio, in 1890. Her real name was Theodosia Goodman. She had a brief stage career and then joined the Pathe Company for whom she played minor roles under the name of De Coppet. She was "discovered" by William Fox and given the role of the vampire in A FOOL THERE WAS, made by the Fox Company in 1915. Fox immediately signed her as a star and there followed a long line of spectaculars which carried her fame around the world. Among her great successes was CLEOPATRA and DU BARRY. Theda Bara was the first "vamp" of the screen. She died in 1955.

**BARBIER, George**—plate 226. Born in Philadelphia, Pennsylvania, on November 19, 1879. Entered Crozier Seminary to study for the ministry, but gave it up to go on the stage. He began in light opera and then spent several years in repertory and stock and the Broadway stage. His first important film was THE BIG POND. He played countless roles in films including ON THE AVENUE, IT'S LOVE I'M AFTER, MIGHTIER THAN THE SWORD, and WAIKIKI WEDDING. A character actor of great ability. Height 5 ft. 9 in. Grey hair and blue eyes. Died in 1945.

**BARRISCALE, Bessie**—plate 141. Born on September 30, 1889, in Hoboken, New Jersey. Her real name was Elizabeth Barry Scale. She was a dramatic actress on the stage before entering films in the early days of the industry. Jesse Lasky brought her to his Famous Players company where she worked in DeMille films. She made THE ROSE OF THE RANCHO with Monroe Salisbury, NOT MY SISTER with William Desmond, HOME with Charles Ray, among many other films. In later years, she played an important supporting role in SECRETS with Mary Pickford and Leslie Howard. One of her most lovable roles was in DUTCH SHOES. Height 5 ft. 3 in. Honey blonde hair and blue eyes.

**BARRY, Wesley**—plate 211. Born in Los Angeles, California, on August 10, 1907. Entered films as a child actor and was cast with Mary Pickford in DADDY LONG-LEGS in which he made a tremendous hit and became famous overnight as the grinning, freckled-faced urchin of films. He appeared in a series of films for director Marshall Neilan and continued his successful career in PENROD, THE COUNTRY KID, SCHOOL DAYS, SON OF MINE, and GEORGE WASHINGTON, JR. He gave up his film career at twenty, and never returned to the screen, but the freckled, red-headed, grinning boy is part of film history.

**BARTHELMESS, Richard**—plate 105. Born on May 9, 1895, in New York City. Educated at Trinity College. Made his film debut in 1916 in WAR BRIDES with Alla Nazimova. He was "discovered" by D. W. Griffith and immediately signed by him. Barthelmess became internationally famous for his role as the Chinese youth in BROKEN BLOSSOMS with Lillian Gish and Donald Crisp. His masterpiece was a film titled TOL'ABLE DAVID. Other great starring roles were in WAY DOWN EAST, THE ENCHANTED COTTAGE, DAWN PATROL, and SON OF THE GODS. Height

5 ft. 7½ in. Black hair and brown eyes. Was married to actress Mary Hay Caldwell. He died in 1963.

**BAYNE, Beverly**—plate 17. Born on November 22, 1892, in Minneapolis, Minnesota. She began her screen career in 1914 with the old Essanay Company. She was the leading actress of that company for several years. Starred in a great many two-reel films for Essanay with Francis X. Bushman as her leading man. She later married Bushman. In 1915 Bushman and Bayne made an eight-reel film version of ROMEO AND JULIET which, for its time, was not only a great success but an outstanding accomplishment for the infant film industry. Height 5 ft. 5 in. Dark hair and eyes.

**BEBAN, George**—plate 92. The screen's first portrayer of Italian roles, he was born in Fresno, California, on November 5, 1873. He made his stage *début* as a boy baritone at the age of eight. Before entering motion pictures he was the most famous impersonator of Italian characters on the American stage. After a five-year stage run of THE SIGN OF THE ROSE, it was filmed with Beban playing the lead. Other of his films include THE ALIEN, THE GREATEST LOVE OF ALL, THE LOVES OF RICARDO, and THE HEARTS OF MEN. His small son co-starred with him in the latter. Height 5 ft. 6 in. Black hair and brown eyes. Died in October 1928.

**BELLAMY, Madge**—plate 153. Born in Hillsboro, Texas on June 30, 1904. Real name was Margaret Philipott. Her stage career began as a child dancer at the age of ten. She had considerable stage experience before entering films in 1925. She was selected by Penrhyn Stanlaws, the well-known American artist, as the most beautiful girl of her type in America. She rose quickly to stardom following her success in the film epic THE IRON HORSE. Other films made by Miss Bellamy include WINGS OF YOUTH, TONIGHT AT TWELVE, HAVOC, THE FUGITIVES, and SUMMER BACHELORS. Height 5 ft. 3 in. Red-gold hair and violet eyes.

**BELMORE Lionel**—plate 42. Born in London, England, on March 23, 1878. He was well-known on the English stage before entering films. He made his screen *début* in 1914, and played in many films both in England and America. His character roles were famous. Among them are included OLIVER TWIST with Jackie Coogan, BARDELYS THE MAGNIFICENT with John Gilbert, THE LOVE PARADE with Maurice Chevalier, LOVE COMES ALONG, and EVIDENCE. Height 5 ft. 10 in. Grey hair and brown eyes.

**BENNETT, Belle**—plate 86. Born on August 6, 1891, in St. Paul, Minnesota. Her theatrical career began in a tent show and progressed to stock and finally Broadway, but it was a struggle until she joined the old Triangle Company in 1914. A few years later in the super production of STELLA DALLAS in which she played the title role, she attained top stardom. Followed THE IRON MASK with Douglas Fairbanks Sr., THE LILLY, THE WAY OF ALL FLESH, THE WOMAN WHO WAS FORGOTTEN, and COURAGE. Height 5 ft. 3 in. with fair hair and grey eyes. She died in 1932.

**BENNETT, Enid**—plate 188. Born on July 15, 1895, in Australia. Appeared on the American stage and was discovered for the screen by Thomas Ince. She starred with Douglas Fairbanks Sr. in ROBIN HOOD and in THE SEAHAWK with Milton Sills. Among the many other films she made were THE FOOL'S AWAKENING, THE WRONG MR. WRIGHT, and A WOMAN'S HEART. Height 5 ft. 6 in. Fair hair and blue eyes. Married to director Fred Niblo.

**BENNETT, Richard**—plate 39. Born on May 21, 1973, in Deacon Mills, Indiana, Richard Bennett was a top Broadway star when he came to films. He was the father of Constance and Joan Bennett, both screen celebrities. Among his many screen successes were BOUGHT, a film made with his daughter Constance. DAMAGED GOODS, NO GREATER LOVE, and ARROWSMITH with Helen Hayes and Ronald Colman, gave him important roles. He will be remembered with black hair greying at the temples. He had blue eyes and was 5 ft. 10½ in. in height. Richard Bennett died in Los Angeles in 1944.

**BERNHARDT, Sarah**—plate 58. Born in Paris, France, on October 22, 1844. The great French actress who started in the first feature length film made in America. She went to Hollywood under the auspices of Jesse Lasky and Adolph Zukor to star in QUEEN ELIZABETH. The film was five reels in length. She made another film in Hollywood called JEANNE DORE. The first film was made in 1912 and the second in 1915 when

Madame Bernhardt was seventy-one years old and had suffered the amputation of one of her legs. She made seven other films, all in France. They were LA TOSCA, ADRIENNE LECOUVREUR, MERE FRANCAISE, THE DUKE'S MOTTO, LA DAME AUX CAMELIAS, HAMLET, and SARAH BERNHARDT AT HOME. Her fabulous career ended with her death on March 26, 1923.

**BINNEY, Constance**—plate 203. Born in New York City on July 27, 1899. She made her stage *début* in musical comedy and, at nineteen, played the leading role in 39 EAST on the New York stage. She made her screen *début* in 1918 as the heroine in SPORTING LIFE, and then played the leading role opposite John Barrymore in THE TEST OF HONOR. Realart Studio elevated her to stardom in 1919 and cast her in the leading role of ERSTWHILE SUSAN. They followed it by SUCH A LITTLE QUEEN, and THE CASE OF BECKY with Glen Hunter supporting. Other films included A BILL OF DIVORCEMENT, SOMETHING DIFFERENT, and THE PASSIONATE QUEST. Height 5 ft. 2 in. Dark brown hair and eyes.

**BLACKWELL, Carlyle**—plate 87. Born on May 12, 1888, in Syracuse, New York. Made his stage *début* in New York and was a successful stage star when in 1909 he joined the Vitagraph Company to play the lead in UNCLE TOM'S CABIN. He played the leading role opposite Mary Pickford in SUCH A LITTLE QUEEN in 1914, and co-starred with Marion Davies in THE RESTLESS SEX. He made THE VIRGIN QUEEN with Lady Diana Manners in England and starred in several other British films. Returning to America, he joined the Kalem Company and was put in charge of operations for them in Hollywood. He was most famous for his interpretation of BULLDOG DRUMMOND. Height 5 ft. 11 in. Black hair and brown eyes. He died in 1955.

**BLUE, Monte**—plate 192. Born on January 11, 1890, in Indianapolis, Indiana. His father was half French and half Cherokee Indian. Worked his way through Purdue University and, in 1914, entered films under the direction of D. W. Griffith. Although he had no previous theatrical experience, he rose rapidly to prominence, especially following his role as Danton in ORPHANS OF THE STORM. Among his film credits are SKIN DEEP, TIGER ROSE, A MILLION TO ONE, and LIVES OF A BENGAL LANCER. Height 6 ft. 3 in. Dark brown hair and eyes. Married Tova Janson and had a son and a daughter. Died in 1963.

**BLYTHE, Betty**—plate 89. Born in Los Angeles, California, on May 18, 1894. Real name Elizabeth Slaughter. She was educated in a convent and trained in Paris for grand opera, but never played on the operatic stage. Instead, she began a film career. By 1915 she was well on her way to stardom. She attained fame with her portrayal of THE QUEEN OF SHEBA. Her other film credits include SINNER OR SAINT, SHE, THE TRUTH ABOUT WIVES, RECOIL, and HOW WOMEN LOVE. Height 5 ft. 7 in. Brown hair and grey eyes.

**BOSWORTH, Hobart**—plate 99. Born on August 11, 1867, in Marietta, Ohio. He ran away from home when he was twelve and shipped out on a sailing ship. After three years at sea he obtained a job in a theatre and by 1885 was launched on a stage career which he continued until 1909, the year he made his film *début*. He starred in many films, the most famous of which was Jack London's THE SEA WOLF. He was famous for his strong character roles. For a time he headed his own film company in Hollywood. He worked with Mary Pickford in MY BEST GIRL, THE BIG PARADE, THE CHINESE PARROTT, THE BLOOD SHIP, HURRICANE, and STEAMBOAT ROUND THE BEND. Height 6 ft. 1 in. Grey hair and blue eyes. He died in 1943.

**BOYD, William**—plate 185. Born on June 5, 1899, in Cambridge, Ohio. He arrived in Hollywood in 1919 and obtained work as an extra in the various studios. He was finally given a small part in WHY CHANGE YOUR WIFE. His work in this picture was noted by his studio and a few months later he played the lead in THE ROAD TO YESTERDAY. His blond handsomeness caught on with the public and with the film THE VOLGA BOATMAN with Elinor Fair, he was secure in stardom. He made a long series of successful films, among them DRESS PARADE, THE LAST FRONTIER, TWO ARABIAN KNIGHTS, and HIS FIRST COMMAND. In later years he became the great screen idol Hopalong Cassidy in a long series of Westerns

Height 6 ft. Blonde hair and blue eyes. He was married to Elinor Fair, and died in 1972.

**BRADY, Alice**—plate 147. Born on November 2, 1892, in New York City. She made her stage *début* at fourteen and began her screen career in 1914, but returned to the New York stage in 1918 and became a Broadway star. Back to screen work in the early Thirties, she abandoned straight dramatic roles for light comedy and delighted her audiences in such films as THREE SMART GIRLS, MIND YOUR OWN BUSINESS, CALL IT A DAY, MR. DODD TAKES THE AIR, and 100 MEN AND A GIRL. Height 5 ft. 7 in. Dark brown hair and eyes. She was the daughter of William A. Brady, the theatrical producer. She died in 1939.

**BRENDEL, El**—plate 242. Born in Philadelphia, Pennsylvania, on March 25, 1891. Made his stage *début* at the age of thirteen in vaudeville. Became known on the American stage as a character comedian. Was one of the stars of THE PASSING SHOW on Broadway. He made his screen début in 1919, and played the comedy relief in many films with great success. Among his film credits are THE COCK-EYED WORLD, SUNNY SIDE UP, THE GOLDEN CALF, ROLLED STOCKINGS, and WINGS. Height 5 ft. 8 in. Brown hair and eyes. Spoke with a Scandinavian accent. Died in 1964.

**BROCKWELL, Gladys**—plate 72. Born on March 21, 1894, in Brooklyn, New York. Made her stage *début* at the age of three, and was a popular star for many years before making her *début* on the screen in a "vampire" role. She became recognised as a great dramatic screen star. She was in SEVENTH HEAVEN with Janet Gaynor and Charles Farrell. Other films included THE DRAKE CASE, SPANGLES, STELLA MARIS, THE LAST FRONTIER, THE ARGYLE CASE, and THE HOTTENTOT. Height 5 ft. 4 in. Medium brown hair and hazel eyes. She died July 4, 1929, in a road accident.

**BROWN, Joe E.**—plate 235. Born in Holgate, Ohio, on May 20, 1894. Joined a circus troupe at the age of nine and remained with the circus until 1906. He was in San Francisco at the time of the earthquake and fire in 1906 and remained in that city for more than a year as an entertainer. He did acrobatic dancing, juggling, and a comedy vaudeville turn. He later starred in two Broadway musical revues before entering screen work. His first film was CROOKS CAN'T WIN. He was one of the first stars to make a sound film. The film MOLLY AND ME was actually a silent film with sound sequences. Other films included THE COCK-EYED WORLD, SALLY, SONG OF THE WEST, and SOME LIKE IT HOT. Height 5 ft. 9 in. Dark brown hair and eyes. He died in 1973.

**BUNNY, John**—plate 6. Born in New York City on September 21, 1863. Between 1911 and 1915 he was the most famous man on the screen. He was actually the first international star, his films were being seen all over the world. His father was an English naval officer who emigrated to America from Penzance. John Bunny began his acting career at the age of twenty and was an actor for nearly thirty years before he made his film *début* with the Vitagraph Company in 1910. He was the first great American comedian of the screen. A jolly, smiling "fat man", he was immensely popular with film audiences. He died at the peak of his career in 1915. Height 5 ft. 8 in. Grey hair and blue eyes.

**BURKE, Billie**—plate 108. Born in Washington, D. C., on August 7, 1886. She made her *début* on the English stage in 1903. After success in British musical comedy she returned triumphantly to Broadway where she became the toast of New York. She was starred in the Ziegfeld Follies and married the great Flo Ziegfeld. Her film career began after her husband's death, and her most famous roles were achieved later in life in Gracie Allen type characterisations. Among her films were MY AMERICAN WIFE, PARNELL, CRAIG'S WIFE, TOPPER, and GOOD GRACIOUS, ANNABELLE. Height 5 ft. 5 in. Auburn hair and blue eyes. Her real name was Ethel Burke. She died in 1970.

**BUSCH, Mae**—plate 175. Born in Melbourne, Australia, on January 20, 1894. Her father was conductor of the Australian Symphony Orchestra and her mother a grand opera singer. She spent much of her early childhood in Tahiti, where the Busch family owned property. The family emigrated to America where Mae made her stage *début* at seventeen and subsequently became a vaudeville favourite. She made her film *début* with the old Keystone Company in Mack Sennett comedies. She attained stardom in Erich von Stroheim's FOOLISH WIVES. Other films in which she played include THE UNHOLY

THREE with Lon Chaney, NAME THE MAN, THE CHRISTIAN, THE MIRACLE OF LIFE, and ALIBI. Height 5 ft. 6 in. Auburn hair and grey eyes. She died in 1946.

**BUSHMAN, Francis X.**—plate 16. Born on January 10, 1885, in Norfolk, Virginia. Was on the New York stage before starting his screen career in 1911 at which time he joined the Essanay Company. He appeared in more than 200 of that company's films. He was the undisputed romantic screen idol of his day and the most popular leading man in America and England. He married Beverly Bayne and appeared with her in many films including ROMEO AND JULIET in 1915. In later years he played the role of Messala in BEN HUR with Ramon Novarro and May MacAvoy. He played in a total of 417 films. Height 6 ft. Medium brown hair and blue eyes. Died in 1966.

## C

**CARR, Mary**—plate 101. Born in Philadelphia, Pennsylvania on June 8, 1870. She was famous for her mother roles both on the stage and on the screen. She made OVER THE HILL for the screen and it became one of the most popular films of its day. Her other films include SPECIAL DELIVERY, FRENZIED FLAMES, SOMEBODY'S MOTHER, and SECOND WIFE. Height 5 ft. 3 in. Grey hair and blue eyes.

**CASTLE, Irene**—plate 194. Born in New Rochelle, New York, on April 17, 1894. Her maiden name was Foote, and she was the daughter of a prominent physician. After some experience on the vaudeville stage, she met and married Vernon Castle, an English dancer. They became a dance team of international repute. After the death of her husband, she entered films and soon attained great popularity. Among her best known pictures were THE GIRL FROM BOHEMIA, THE WHIRL OF LIFE, THE FIRING LINE, THE FIRST LAW, and PATRIA. Height 5 ft. 7 in. with dark brown hair and grey eyes. Her film *début* was made in 1918. She died in 1968.

**CASTLETON, Barbara**—plate 111. Born in Little Rock, Arkansas, on April 19, 1897. Educated at a convent which was also attended by Anita Stewart. It was through Miss Stewart that she entered motion pictures. Her first film was with Annette Kellerman in Herbert Brenon's great water spectacle A DAUGHTER OF THE GODS. She was then cast with Alla Nazimova in WAR BRIDES. Firmly established by her work in these films she played leading roles in many pictures including VENGEANCE, THE SILVER KING, and THE NET. Height 5 ft. 6 in. Dark brown hair and brown eyes.

**CHADWICK, Helene**—plate 127. Born in New York City on November 25, 1897. After leaving school she attracted the attention of the famous artist Harrison Fisher for whom she subsequently posed. Her face adorned a vast number of magazine covers and attracted a Hollywood studio where she was put under contract. After several important roles in films she was elevated to stardom. Among her film credits are STOLEN PLEASURES, THE MASKED DANCER, BROTHERS UNDER THE SKIN, THE STILL ALARM, and DANCING DAYS. Height 5 ft. 7 in. Light brown hair and hazel eyes.

**CHANEY, Lon**—plates 176, 177. Born on April 1, 1883, in Colorado Springs, Colorado. His parents were both deaf mutes and from them he claimed he inherited the sense of pantomime. In his film career he became famous as a master of make-up Chaney went on the stage as a boy and became a musical comedy comic. He made his screen *début* in 1912 at Universal Studios in two-reel films which he produced and wrote. He was acclaimed for his role as the bogus cripple in THE MIRACLE MAN. Among his most famous films were THE HUNCHBACK OF NOTRE DAME, HE WHO GETS SLAPPED, THE UNHOLY THREE, THE PHANTOM OF THE OPERA, MR. WU, THE ROAD TO MANDALAY, THE PENALTY, and LAUGH CLOWN LAUGH. Height 5 ft. 10 in. Dark brown hair and eyes. Died on August 26, 1930.

**CHAPLIN, Charles**—plate 46, 47. Born in London, England, on April 16, 1890. Both his parents were show people. His mother sang and danced under the name of Lil Harvery. At the age of eight, Chaplin was a member of a music hall troupe known as THE EIGHT LANCASHIRE LADS. He played bit parts on the stage and as a young man with his brother Sydney became a member of Fred Karno's comedy company which toured America. Chaplin remained in the U. S. and joined the

Keystone Company in 1913. In 1914, he made TILLIE'S PUNCTURED ROMANCE with Mabel Normand and Marie Dressler, and from that time on was universally famous. After contracts with Essanay and then the Mutual Film Corporation, he formed his own company. Among his many films those perhaps best remembered are SHOULDER ARMS, THE GOLD RUSH, THE CIRCUS, THE KID with Jackie Coogan, and MODERN TIMES. His marriages were with film stars Mildred Harris, Lita Grey, and Paulette Goddard. His present wife is Oona O'Neill, daughter of the famous playwright Eugene O'Neill. Height 5 ft. 4 in. Black hair and blue eyes.

**CHAPLIN, Sydney**—plate 204. Born in Johannesburg, South Africa, on March 17, 1885, where his theatrical parents were on tour. After early stage experience, with his brother Charles, he joined the Fred Karno comedy company in the music halls of England and later toured America with them. He joined Keystone in Hollywood with Charles and, after a stint in two-reel comedies, was given the lead in THE SUBMARINE PIRATE which was a hit film. Other films made by Sydney included THE BETTER 'OLE, THE MAN ON THE BOX, THE PILGRIM, and THE GALLOPING FISH. He then took over the management of his brother's affairs and was seen in many of the Charlie Chaplin films. His greatest hit was in CHARLIE'S AUNT. Height 5 ft. 8 in. Brown hair and grey eyes. He died in 1965.

**CHASE, Charlie**—plate 237. Born in Baltimore, Maryland, on October 20, 1893. At the age of sixteen he was singing in movie theatres with illustrated lantern slides. He learned some dance steps as a song and dance man. In 1912, he was engaged by Mack Sennett to play the part of one of the famous Keystone cops. For several years he was a director of comedies for Hal Roach and then starred in a series of Hal Roach comedies. His film credits included STEPPING OUT, YOU CAN'T BUY LOVE, LEAPING LOVE, and MODERN LOVE. Height 6 ft. Brown hair and blue eyes. He died in 1940.

**CLARK, Marguerite**—plate 94. Born on February 72, 1887, in Avondale, Ohio. She was on the stage in musical comedy before making her screen *début* in 1909 in THE VALENTINE GIRL. Played many parts in the early days of the film industry and rose to fame by her performance in WILDFLOWER in 1915. For several years she rivalled Mary Pickford in popularity. Among her films were THE PRINCE AND THE PAUPER, BABY MINE, and THE GOOSE GIRL. Height 4 ft. 10 in. Dark brown hair and eyes. She died on September 25, 1940.

**CLAYTON,** Ethel—plate 78. Born in Champaign, Illinois, on November 18, 1890. After considerable success on the stage she commenced her screen career in 1913 and for many years was one of America's most popular stars. Her film credits include IF I WERE QUEEN, PRINCESS OR BROADWAY, WINDS OF YOUTH, an THE MANSION OF ACHING HEARTS. Height 5 ft. 6 in. Dark golden hair and blue eyes.

**CLAYTON, Marguerite**—plate 3. Born in Salt Lake City, Utah, on November 3, 1896, and educated at St. Mary's Academy there. in 1913, she went to Hollywood and following an interview with Broncho Billy Anderson was signed by him to play his leading lady in a series of Western for Essanay. Miss Clayton was Broncho Billy's leading lady in more than 300 of his two-reel Westerns and became famous not only for her beauty but for her riding feats. She later played co-starring roles in many films among them THE PALM BEACH GIRL and INSPIRATION. Height 5 ft. 3 in. Flaxen hair and blue eyes.

**CLIFFORD, Ruth**—plate 136. Born on July 17, 1900, in Pawtucket, Rhode Island. On leaving school in 1919 she entered films with the old Edison Company where she started as an extra and rose to be a leading lady. Moving to the Hollywood scene she starred in many successful films among them PONJOLA with Anna Q. Nilsson, THE LOVE HOUR, AS MAN DESIRES, THE DEVILS APPLE TREE, and ETERNAL WOMAN. Height 5 ft. 2 in. Light brown hair and blue eyes.

**CODY, Lew**—plate 207. Born on February 22, 1885, in Waterville, Maine, of French parents. His real name was Louis Joseph Cote. He made his film *début* in 1915 in a film called MATING. Originally identified with "villain" parts, he later became one of the screen's leading players of sophisticated light comedy roles. He came rapidly to the front following his role in Elinor Glyn's MAN AND THE MAID. Other of his films include ADAM AND EVIL, THE GAY DECEIVER, TEA FOR THREE, and ON ZE BOULEVARD. Famous as one of the leading wits of Hollywood and a noted after-dinner speaker. Height 5 ft. 11 in. Brown hair and blue eyes. Was married to Mabel Normand. His first wife was Dorothy Dalton, the screen star. He died in 1934.

**COMPSON, Betty**—plate 151. Born in Salt Lake City, Utah, on March 18, 1897. Made her screen *début* in Christie comedies and was elevated to stardom after her appearance in THE MIRACLE MAN. She became one of Paramount's leading players and enjoyed many years of uninterrupted success. Among her films were THE LITTLE MINISTER, THE GREAT GABBO, THE CASE OF SERGEANT GRISCHA, THE BARKER, and, the great spectacular, THE SPOILERS. She was married to Jame Cruze who produced THE COVERED WAGON, an early epic film. Height 5 ft. 3 in. Reddish-brown hair and blue eyes.

**COSTELLO, Dolores**—plate 164. She made her screen *début* as a child. The daughter of the screen's first matinee idol, Maurice Costello, she and her sister Helene were "in the movies" almost from babyhood. Born in Los Angeles on May 3, 1906, Dolores Costello was one of the screen's great beauties. She married John Barrymore. Among her films were THE SEA BEAST, NOAH'S ARK, BRIDE OF THE STORM, and OLD SAN FRANCISCO. Height 5 ft. 4 in. Blonde hair and blue eyes.

**COSTELLO, Maurice**—plate 13. Born on February 22, 1877, in Pittsburgh, Pennsylvania. He made his stage *début* in 1893 and was a noted star when the films claimed him in 1909. He signed with Vitagraph and remained with that company for many years. He was actually the first so-called "matinee idol" of the films and his handsome face was known around the world. Among his film credits were CAMILLE, A TALE OF TWO CITIES, THE BLACK FEATHER, SPIDER WEBS, THE SHAMROCK AND THE ROSE, and THE CRIMSON STAIN. Height 5 ft. 10 in. Black hair greying and blue eyes. He died in 1950.

**CRISP, Donald**—plate 73. Born in Glasgow, Scotland, on June 21, 1875. Made his stage *début* in New York in FLORADORA and after considerable success on Broadway came to the screen in 1906 with the old Biograph company under D. W. Griffith. In 1913 he turned director and became known as such for his films THE EYES OF THE WORLD and RAMONA. D. W. Griffith then claimed him for an important acting role in BROKEN BLOSSOMS with Lillian Gish and Richard Barthelmess. He later worked with Douglas Fairbanks, Sr. in THE BLACK PIRATE and DON Q. A long career of both acting and directing followed taking him well into the sound era. Height 5 ft. 9 in. Dark brown hair and eyes.

**CUMMINGS, Irving**—plate 62. Born on October 9, 1888, in New York City. After considerable experience as a stage actor, he made his screen *début* with the Pathe company. One of the pioneer film actors, he brought great talent and expertise to the silent screen. After a memorable acting career he turned to directing. Some of his silent era films included INFATUATION, EAST SIDE WEST SIDE, BEHIND THAT CURTAIN, NOT QUITE DECENT, and an early spectacular called THE JOHNSTOWN FLOOD. Later, in the sound era, he directed the great Warner Baxter success IN OLD ARIZONA. Black curly hair and brown eyes. Height 6 ft.

**CUNARD, Grace**—plate 35. Born in Paris, France, on December 12, 1899, of a French father and an English mother. Her parents emigrated to America and she was educated in Columbus, Ohio, where the family made their home. From a theatrical family, she made her stage *début* at thirteen and was still in her teens when she entered the films with the old Biograph company. She was best known for her roles in serial films in which she co-starred with Francis Ford, whom she later married. Best known films were THE BROKEN COIN, ELMO THE MIGHTY, LOVE AND LET LOVE, HEAVEN'S FREE, and UNTAMED. Black hair and brown eyes. Height 5 ft. 6 in.

## D

**DALTON, Dorothy**—plate 20. Born on September 22, 1893, in Chicago, Illinois. After considerable experience on the stage she made her film *début* as the heroine in PIERRE OF THE PLAINS in the early days of the motion picture. She starred in a great many pictures before 1917 including THE DISCIPLE, THE CAPTIVE GOD, and D'ARTAGNAN. Her films since then include THE DARK MIRROR and THE MARKET OF SOULS. She was at one time married to Lew Cody, the film star, and then to Arthur Hammerstein, the theatrical producer. One of the screen's great dramatic actresses. Height 5 ft. 6 in. Black hair and brown eyes.

**DANA, Viola**—plate 190. Born on June 28, 1898, in New York City. Her real name was Viola Flugrath. She became a Broadway hit in the title role of THE POOR LITTLE RICH GIRL. She made her screen *début* in 1915 with the Edison Company in New York. She starred in innumerable films including BRED IN OLD KENTUCKY, NAUGHTY NANNETTE, ONE SPLENDID HOUR, GLASS HOUSES, HER MAD ADVENTURE, and SALVATION JANE. Height 4 ft. 11 in. Brown hair and eyes. Married to Lefty Flynn, the cowboy star. She is the sister of Shirley Mason, also a film star.

**DANIELS, Bebe**—plate 167. Born on January 14, 1901, in Dallas, Texas, of a Spanish mother and a Scottish father. Her paternal great-grandfather was American consul in Buenos Aires. Made her first stage appearance at the age of four and worked with the David Belasco Stock Company. At the age of eight she made her screen *début* with the Selig Company and in her teens became a Mack Sennett girl. She was Harold Lloyd's leading lady in many of his films. She co-starred with Rudolph Valentino in MONSIEUR BEAUCAIRE and then in her own right did RIO RITA, LAWFUL LARCENY, LOVE COMES ALONG, THE PALM BEACH GIRL, ARGENTINE LOVE, and MISS BREWSTER'S MILLIONS. Height 5 ft. 5 in. with black hair and eyes. Spanish in appearance. Was married to film star Ben Lyon. She died in 1971.

**D'ARCY, Roy**—plate 121. Born in San Francisco, California, on February 10, 1894. His education was principally in Europe where he spent twelve years before he began his career as a tenor in musical shows on the New York stage. He made his film *début* as the Crown Prince in THE MERRY WIDOW. Many other important roles followed in LA BOHEME, BARDELYS THE MAGNIFICENT, VALENCIA, and KING OF THE KHYBER RIFLES. Height 5 ft. 10 in. Brown hair and eyes.

**DAVIES, Marion**—plate 179. Born on January 3, 1897, in Brooklyn, New York. Real name Marion Douras. Daughter of a New York judge. Her great beauty caught the attention of the producer of the stage success CHU CHIN CHOW, who placed her in the leading role in the show. She was later starred in the Ziegfeld Follies. She sat as a model for the famous American artists Harrison Fisher, Penrhyn Stanlaws, Montgomery Flagg, and Howard Chandler Christy, and her portrait appeared on the cover of virtually every magazine in America. She made her screen *début* in RUNAWAY ROMANY and got her first big chance in WHEN KNIGHTHOOD WAS IN FLOWER. Her big success in LITTLE OLD NEW YORK, the film in which she cut her hair short and played the part of a tomboy, assured her of stardom. Among her film credits are QUALITY STREET, THE RED MILL, HER CARDBOARD LOVER with Nils Asther, THE BEAUTIFUL REBEL, and PEG OF MY HEART. Height 5 ft. 5 in. Her hair was like spun gold and her eyes were blue. She died in Los Angeles in 1961.

**DEAN, Priscilla**—plate 205. Born on November 25, 1896, in New York City. She made her stage *début* at the age of four in RIP VAN WINKLE and her film *début* at the age of twelve in a picture produced by Lois Weber. She had several small parts in D. W. Griffith films and starred with Lee Moran and Eddie Lyons in a series of short comedies. Her great starring roles came when she joined Universal and included such films as UNDER TWO FLAGS, THE VIRGIN OF STAMBOUL, THE CRIMSON RUNNER, THE DANGER GIRL, and A CAFE IN CAIRO. Height 5 ft. 5 in. Dark brown hair and eyes. Married to film star Wheeler Oakman.

**de la MOTTE, Marguerite**—plate 212. Born on June 22, 1903, in Duluth, Minnesota. Began her professional career as a dancer. She was discovered by Douglas Fairbanks Sr. and made her screen *début* in one of his films. Among her screen credits are THE LAST FRONTIER, THE UNKNOWN SOLDIER, MEET THE PRINCE, and THE MAN IN THE IRON MASK in which she played the feminine lead opposite Douglas Fairbanks Sr. Height 5 ft. 2 in. Golden-red hair and blue eyes. She was married to film star John Bowers. She died in 1950.

**de PUTTI, Lya**—plate 98. Born in Budapest, Hungary, in 1904, of an Italian father and a Hungarian mother. She studied dancing from early childhood and as a young girl was with the Garden Ballet in Berlin. After considerable stage experience, she made her *début* in silent films in Germany and was an established star before going to Hollywood to play the leading role in D. W. Griffith's SORROWS OF SATAN in 1926. Other of her films included THE HEART THIEF, FATE GAVE ME 20 CENTS, BUCK PRIVATES, and THE INFORMER. Height 5 ft. 4½ in. Black hair and eyes. She died in 1931.

**de ROCHE, Charles**—plate 143. He was born in Paris in 1886 and was a star of stage and screen in France when Paramount enticed him to Hollywood. He made THE TEN COMMANDMENTS with an all-star cast directed by Cecil B. DeMille. Other films included MADAME SANS-GENE with Gloria Swanson, THE MARRIAGE MAKER, and THE CHEAT with Pola Negri. His real name was de Rochefort, but when Paramount signed him they dropped the "fort," and he starred in all his American films as Charles de Roche. Height 6 ft. Blonde hair and blue eyes. There is a theatre in Paris named for him.

**DESMOND, William**—plate 191. He was born on January 23, 1884, in Dublin, Ireland. Early stage work in Dublin preceded his American movie career. Arriving in New York as a young man, he obtained work almost immediately in films which later took him to Hollywood where his early successes were in Western dramas. He later made many popular films other than Westerns and was one of the screen's real "he-men." Among his film credits are THE SUNSET TRAIL, BLOOD AND STEEL, THE MEDLER, TONGUES OF SCANDAL, and NO DEFENSE. Height 5 ft. 11 in. Black hair and blue eyes. Died in 1949.

**DORSAY, Fifi**—plate 215. Born in Paris, France, on November 21, 1902. She was christened Yvonne, but chose the name of Fifi when she began her stage career in France. She came to Broadway as a dancer, working first in vaudeville and then in musical comedy. After an indifferent beginning in silent films, she came into prominence with the advent of sound in light comedy roles of the "French girl" type. Among her screen credits are included ON THE LEVEL, LUCKY IN LOVE, SHE WEARS THE PANTS, and THEY HAD TO SEE PARIS. Height 5 ft. 3 in., with dark brown hair and eyes.

**DRESSLER, Marie**—plate 240. Born in Coburn, Ontario, Canada, on November 9, 1869. Her real name was Lelia Koerber. She made her stage *début* in 1886 as Cigarette in UNDER TWO FLAGS. She became famous on both the London stage and on Broadway. She made her film *début* at about the same time Charlie Chaplin appeared in Hollywood and one of her most successful early films was with Chaplin in TILLIE'S PUNCTURED ROMANCE. Her other films included CAUGHT SHORT, THE GIRL SAID NO, BREAKFAST AT SUNRISE, LET US BE GAY, and her great triumph in the film ANNA CHRISTIE with Blanche Sweet. Height 5 ft. 6 in. with brown hair and grey eyes. She died in 1934.

## F

**FAIRBANKS SR., Douglas**—plates 55, 57. Born on May 23, 1883, in Denver, Colorado. Educated at Harvard. As a legitimate actor on Broadway, he became a popular favorite and did not go into screen work until 1914 when he made THE LAMB for the Fine Arts company. Known for his athletic prowess, he was starred in a long series of spectacular costume dramas where his athletic ability came into play. Among these films were THE MARK OF ZORRO, THE THIEF OF BAGDAD, THE BLACK PIRATE, ROBIN HOOD, THE GAUCHO, THE THREE MUSKETEERS, and THE MAN IN THE IRON MASK. He married Mary Pickford after divorcing his first wife, the mother of Douglas Fairbanks Jr., also a film star. Height 5 ft. 10 in. with dark brown hair and brown eyes. Died in 1939.

**FARNHAM, Dustin**—plate 95. Born on May 27, 1874, in Hampton Beach, New Hampshire. His father was a dramatic actor and his mother a singer. He spent fifteen years on the stage before entering films in 1913. His first film was SOLDIERS OF FORTUNE. Like his famous brother, William Farnham, Dustin became a popular Western star. His films included THE YOSEMITE TRAIL, THE MAN WHO WON, STRANGE IDOLS, and THE FLAMING FRONTIER, among many others made at the old William Fox Studio at Sunset and Western in Hollywood. Perhaps his greatest film was THE SQUAW MAN, directed by Cecil B. DeMille, made in 1913. Height 6 ft. Brown hair and eyes. He died in 1929.

**FARNHAM, William**—plate 23. Born on July 4, 1876, in Boston, Massachusetts, the son of theatrical parents, and a brother of film star Dustin Farnham. He is one of the veterans of the American screen and was universally popular for his roles in Westerns. He starred in one of the first great American classics of the screen, THE SPOILERS. In his later career he did considerable work in other than Westerns and co-starred with Norma Talmadge in DU BARRY. Other of his films included A BORDER INTRIGUE, LES MISERABLES, DES-

PERATE ADVENTURE, THE GAMBLING FOOL, and many others. Height 5 ft. 11½ in. Dark brown curly hair and blue eyes. He died in 1953.

**FARRAR, Geraldine**—plate 60. Born in Melrose, Massachusetts in 1882. She was educated in Europe and America for the operatic stage, and made her *début* in 1910 as Marguerite in FAUST. Before entering films she was a leading member of the Metropolitan Opera Company in New York. She was also at one time a member of the Berlin Opera Company where she scored great successes. She starred in many films in the silent era despite the fact that her beautiful voice could not be heard. Among her films were JOAN THE WOMAN, THE WOMAN GOD FORGOT, THE FLAME OF THE DESERT, MARIE ROSE, and THE STRONGER VOW. She was married to Lou Tellegen, star of stage and screen. Height 5 ft. 6 in. Dark brown hair and eyes. She never made a sound film, and died in 1967.

**FAWCETT, George**—pate 182. He was born in Roanoke, Virginia, on August 24, 1863. Educated at the University of Virginia. He made his stage *début* in 1886 in Hamlet and had an extensive career on both the New York and London stages before entering films in 1915. He became one of the truly "greats" of film character actors. Film credits include THE PRIVATE LIFE OF HELEN OF TROY, THE GREAT DIVIDE, THE MERRY WIDOW, ONCE A GENTLEMAN, MEN OF STEEL, SON OF THE SHEIK with Rudoph Valentino, and THE MAJESTY OF THE LAW, which was his first film. Height 5 ft. 9½ in. Grey hair and blue eyes.

**FAYE, Julia**—plate 184. Born in Richmond, Virginia, in 1903. She made her screen *début* with D. W. Griffith in INTOLERANCE. After a leading role in DON QUIXOTE, she played a succession of svelte society parts in OLD WIVES FOR NEW, FEET OF CLAY, FORBIDDEN FRUIT, and A FOOL'S PARADISE. She became a favourite of Cecil B. DeMille and he cast her in most of his films including THE KING OF KINGS. Height 5 ft. 3 in. with brown hair and eyes.

**FIELDS, W. C.**—plate 232. Born in Philadelphia, Pennsylvania, on February 10, 1879. His career covered the stage, musical comedy, vaudeville, and motion pictures. A great comedian, his first film was the role of the old showman in D. W. Griffith's SALLY OF THE SAWDUST in 1925. He again worked with Griffith in THAT ROYAL GIRL. Among his other films are included THE OLD ARMY GAME, SO'S YOUR OLD MAN, TWO FLAMING YOUTHS, and RUNNING WILD. With the advent of sound his films co-starring with Mae West became classics. Height 5 ft. 8½ in. Red hair and light blue eyes. Died in 1946.

**FINCH, Flora**—plate 7. "Flossie," as she was affectionatey known in private ife, was born in England in 1869 and was on the London stage in comedy before beginning her film career in America. She began as leading lady with John Bunny and remained such throughout his entire career between 1911 and 1915. After Bunny's death, she formed her own company, the Flora Finch Film Corporation, and starred for a time in her own comedies. In later years she appeared as a feature player in films made mostly at M-G-M. She had an important character role in THE CAT AND THE CANARY and also in QUALITY STREET. Height 5 ft. 3 in. Dark brown hair and grey eyes. She died in Hollywood on January 4, 1940.

**FISCHER, Margarita**—plate 144. Born in Portland, Oregon, on December 9, 1893, of theatrical parents. She made her stage *début* at the age of eight in her father's stock company. She entered films under contract to Selig and rose to stardom with that company. Among her films are included THE MANTLE OF CHARITY, REVELATION, THE GIFT OF GIVING, and K, THE UNKNOWN. She was married to Harry Pollard, the comedian of Essanay films who later became a director. She played the part of Eliza in his UNCLE TOM'S CABIN in 1927, just before the advent of sound pictures. Height 5 ft. 4½ in. Dark brown hair and eyes.

**FORD, Francis**—plate 34. Born in Portland, Maine, on September 15, 1883. As a youth, he fought in Cuba in the Spanish-American War. After five years on the stage, he entered films in 1910 and became perhaps the greatest male serial star of the screen. With his film actress wife, Grace Cunard, he made countless serials. He turned to directing and had an equally successful career in that field. Film credits include SO THIS IS ARIZONA, THUNDERING HOOFS, CRUISE OF THE HILLION, SIGN OF THE CACTUS, among many others. Elder brother of the famous director John Ford. Height 5 ft. 11 in. Black hair and grey eyes.

**FORD, Harrison**—plate 165. Born on March 16, 1892, in Kansas City, Missouri. Made his stage *début* in 1906 and his film *début* in 1915. He was one of the most popular leading men of his time, on Broadway, the London stage, and in films. Among his films were: THE SONG AND DANCE MAN, THE ROYAL GIRL, UP IN MABEL'S ROOM, THE NERVOUS WRECK, THE GIRL IN THE PULLMAN, PROUD FLESH, and SANDY. Height 5 ft. 10 in. Brown hair and eyes. He died in 1953.

**FRAZER, Robert**—plate 174. Born in Worcester, Massachusetts, on April 14, 1892. He was a star of the stage before making his *début* in films. His two greatest films were THE FEAST OF LIFE with Clara Kimball Young made in 1916, and MEN with Pola Negri in 1924. He was one of Hollywood's most popular leading men for many years. Among his film credits are included THE WOMAN I LOVE, SIOUX BLOOD, FROZEN JUSTICE, and THE DRAKE CASE. Height 6 ft. Dark brown hair and eyes.

**FREDERICK, Pauline**—plate 41, 43. Born in Boston, Massachusetts, on August 12, 1886. Her real name was Beatrice Libby. She made her stage *début* in 1902 as a chorus girl at the Knickerbocker Theatre in New York City. But drama was her forte and she was soon seen in some of the great Broadway successes including WHEN KNIGHTS WERE BOLD, INNOCENT, and MADAME X. She was a great star on Broadway at the time Famous Players brought her to Hollywood to star in THE ETERNAL CITY. BELLA DONNA, ZAZA, LA TOSCA, and RESURRECTION followed. She made MADAME X on the screen for Sam Goldwyn. She was directed by Lubitsch in THREE WOMEN, and with Warner Brothers made ON TRIAL and THE SACRED FLAME. The greatest performance of this great star was said to be ELIZABETH, THE QUEEN, which was done on the stage but not filmed. Height 5 ft. 4 in. Dark brown hair and eyes. She died in 1938.

## G

**GAUNTIER, Gene**—plate 12. Her real name was Genevieve Liggett and she was the most versatile of all the early stars. Born in Beaumont, Texas, on May 17, 1885, she commenced her screen career with Biograph and appeared in several one-reelers playing opposite D. W. Griffith, at that time an actor. She joined the Kalem Company in 1907 and became their sole leading lady as well as an assistant director and studio scriptwriter. It was said that Gene Gauntier wrote the script for every one of the 500 films in which she appeared. She also selected locations, supervised the sets, wrote the titles, edited the films, and handled the studio publicity. During her years with Kalem she was known to the public as "The Kalem Girl." She formed her own company in 1912 and made her own films until 1915 when she signed with Universal. She retired from the screen in 1918 and became a film critic for a newspaper syndicate. She was one of the real "greats" of the early films. Height 5 ft. 5 in. Dark brown hair and eyes.

**GISH, Dorothy and Lillian**—plate 31. See the following two profiles.

**GISH, Dorothy**—plate 33. Born on March 11, 1898, in Dayton, Ohio. Is the younger sister of Lillian Gish. She made her stage *début* at the age of four and had considerable theatrical experience before entering films in 1912 to become one of D. W. Griffith's great stars. To disguise her strong resemblance to her sister Lillian, she wore a black wig in all of her pictures. Actually, she had fair hair and blue eyes. She was 5 ft. tall. Following her work with Griffith which included the films HEARTS OF THE WORLD and ORPHANS OF THE STORM, Dorothy starred in NELL GWYN, TIPTOES, MADAME POMPADOUR, and LONDON, to name only a few. She was married to James Rennie, the English stage actor. She died in 1968.

**GISH, Lillian**—plate 32. Born on October 14, 1896, in Springfield, Ohio. Her real name was De Guiche and she is of French extraction. Her widowed mother travelled with a touring theatrical company to support her two daughters, Lillian and Dorothy. At the age of seven Lillian was a dancer with Sarah Bernhardt's American company. She was introduced to D. W. Griffith by Mary Pickford, whom she had known as Gladys Smith as a child. With her sister Dorothy, she worked for Griffith in small parts and was then featured in his film AN UNSEEN ENEMY. Her great chance came when Griffith cast her for the lead in THE BIRTH OF A NATION in 1915. Other famous films in which she starred include HEARTS OF THE WORLD, BROKEN BLOSSOMS, ORPHANS OF THE STORM, WAY

DOWN EAST, THE SCARLET LETTER, and THE WHITE SISTER. Height 5 ft. 2 in. with golden hair and blue eyes.

**GLASS, Gaston**—plate 112. Born in Paris, France, on November 6, 1895. He achieved great success on the French stage where he was at one time leading man for the great Sarah Bernhardt. He served in the French Air Force during the First World War. He went to New York after the war and was successful on the Broadway stage. In 1920 he was cast as the lead in the film HUMORESQUE. His sensitive and otherwise superb handling of this role brought him to film stardom. Other of his film successes included THE BROKEN WING, THE HERO, PURSUED, SHE GOT WHAT SHE WANTED, BEHIND CLOSED DOORS, and TIGER ROSE. Height 5 ft. 10 in. Brown hair and eyes.

**GLAUM, Louise**—plate 45. Born in Reno, Nevada, on February 12, 1886. Began her theatrical career as a member of the Belasco Stock Company. Entered films shortly thereafter, in 1914, and starred with William S. Hart in HELL'S HINGES, a great film of its day. Pioneered in many early films among them THE LEOPARD WOMAN, THE GIRL WHO DARED, and her famous starring role in WOLF WOMAN for Thomas Ince. Other films included FIFTY-FIFTY and THE TOAST OF DEATH. Height 5 ft. 5 in. Brown hair and blue eyes.

**GRAVES, Ralph**—plate 157. Born on June 9, 1900, in Cleveland, Ohio. He was hired as a boy actor by the old Essanay company and later played feature roles in Mack Sennett comedies. He was, however, a capable and talented dramatic actor and was cast in dramatic parts for most of his career. Among his screen credits are included THE SONG OF LOVE, FLIGHT, THE ETERNAL WOMAN, BACHELOR'S PARADISE, and BIG IDEAS. Height 6 ft. Fair hair and blue eyes.

**GRIFFITH, Corinne**—plate 96. Born on November 24, 1899, in Texarkana, Texas. Before beginning her screen career she was a professional dancer. Her fragile type of beauty had great appeal and after her triumph in DECLASSE she became established as a top star. Among her pictures were INFATUATION, THE LADY IN ERMINE, THE DIVINE LADY, SATURDAY'S CHILDREN, and THE GARDEN OF EDEN. She was the wife of Walter Morosco, the film director. Height 5 ft. 4 in. Golden brown hair and blue eyes.

## H

**HALE, Alan**—plate 224. Born on February 19, 1892, in Washington, D. C. Alan Hale's screen career dates back to the days of Biograph and Lubin. His inspired performances as a character actor can never be forgotten. He played leading roles in THE FOUR HORSEMEN OF THE APOCALYPSE, THE COVERED WAGON, GREAT EXPECTATIONS, OF HUMAN BONDAGE, THE LOST PATROL, and many others. He later turned to directing, but his real love was acting and he earned for himself a high place among the screen immortals. Height 6 ft. 1 in. Fair curly hair and blue eyes. Died in 1950.

**HALE, Creighton**—plate 166. Born in Cork, Ireland, on May 24, 1892, of theatrical parents. Began a stage career in early youth and toured America as a member of Lady Forbes-Robertson's company. He remained in America when given a contract with Pathe. He became known for his work with Pearl White in THE EXPLOITS OF ELAINE. Many prominent roles followed including RASPUTIN, ANNIE LAURIE, THE MARRIAGE CIRCLE, THE SHADOW ON THE WALL, and HOLIDAY. Perhaps his best was attained in THE CAT AND THE CANARY. Height 5 ft. 9 in. Fair hair and blue eyes. Died in 1965.

**HAMILTON, Neil**—plate 197. Born on September 10, 1889, in Lynn, Massachusetts. Studied at theological school for the priesthood but changed his mind and went on the stage. After several years of stage experience he made his film *début* with D. W. Griffith in THE WHITE ROSE. With Bobby Harron he was one of Griffith's top stars, appearing in AMERICA and ISN'T LIFE WONDERFUL. Among his film credits are BEAU GESTE, THE GOLDEN PRINCESS, THE STREET OF FORGOTTEN MEN, and THE MUSIC MASTER. Height 5 ft. 11 in. with dark brown hair and eyes.

**HARRIS, Mildred**—plate 49. Born in Cheyenne, Wyoming, on April 18, 1901. At the age of eleven she was hired by the Vitagraph Company and played child roles in a number of films including D. W. Griffith's ENOCH ARDEN. She appeared with Sir Herbert Tree in THE OLD FOLKS AT HOME, and was well on her way to stardom when she married Charles Chaplin at the age of eighteen. Among the films in which she starred or played leading roles are included THE ISLE OF RETRIBUTION, OUT OF THE PAST, THE MELODY MAN, SEA FURY, and SIDE STREET. Height 5 ft. 2 in. Blonde hair and blue eyes.

**HARRON, Robert**—plate 67. Born on April 24, 1896, in New York City's Greenwich Village. He was one of the most brilliant young screen actors of his day. He worked exclusively for D. W. Griffith productions, often with Lillian Gish or Mae Marsh. He played the youthful hero in THE BIRTH OF A NATION. With Richard Barthelmess, he was one of Griffith's two leading stars. He was cast in most of Griffith's films up until his untimely death when, it was said, he accidentally shot and killed himself on September 7, 1920. Height 5 ft. 11 in. Dark brown hair and eyes. Elder brother of John Harron.

**HART, William S.**—plate 44. Born in Newburgh, New York, on December 6, 1870. Bill Hart was a veteran of the early films and perhaps the greatest Western star of all time. Before making his screen *début* he was a Shakespearian actor on Broadway. His first films were for Thomas Ince. Then under his own banner, Hart-Artcraft he made WOLVES OF THE TRAIL, BLUE BLAZES RAWDEN, and many others. In 1920 he signed with Famous Player-Lasky where he made SAND, THE TOLL GATE, and TUMBLEWEEDS. His two greatest films were probably HELL'S HINGES and WILD BILL HICKOK. Height 6 ft. 1 in. Dark brown hair, greying, and blue eyes. Married to screen actress Winifred Westover. He died in Saugus, California in 1946.

**HAVER, Phyllis**—plate 156. Born on January 6, 1899, in Douglas, Kansas. She was a cinema pianist before she became a Mack Sennett girl. She was one of the original famous bathing beauties at the Sennett Studio. Like so many others of the Mack Sennett girls, she graduated into dramatic roles and starred with Emil Jannings in THE WAY OF ALL FLESH. Other film credits include UP IN MABEL'S ROOM, THE NERVOUS WRECK, HELL'S KITCHEN, SAL OF SINGAPORE, and CHICAGO. Height 5 ft. 6 in. Golden blonde hair and blue eyes. She died in 1960.

**HAYAKAWA, Sessue**—plate 77. Born on January 10, 1889, in Tokyo, Japan. Educated for the Japanese navy, but chose the stage instead, making his *début* with Madame Yacco, the Japanese Sarah Bernhardt. He later made a great success in Japanese versions of Shakespeare's plays. He came to America to practice his profession and was introduced to the screen by Thomas Ince. His first film was THE TYPHOON and after that he played a long series of Japanese and Oriental roles written especially for him. He was the first Oriental to become a star in his own right in America. Among his films were THE CHEAT with Fanny Ward, THE SECRET SIN, HONORABLE FRIEND, LOYALTY, and THE BRIDGE ON THE RIVER KWAI. Height 5 ft. 7 in. with black hair and eyes. Died in December 1973.

**HERSHOLT, Jean**—plate 80. Born in Copenhagen, Denmark, on July 12, 1886, the son of Henry and Claire Hersholt, famous stars of the Royal Theater in Copenhagen. As a youth he attended the Academy of Fine Arts and upon graduation became a portrait painter. But, following in his parents' footsteps, he turned to the stage and after considerable experience in the theatre went to Hollywood in 1915 and began his film career with Triangle. By 1917 he was under contract to Universal. He and the great Lon Chaney shared the same dressing room and experimented in make-up together. His first big break came when he was cast with Mary Pickford in TESS OF THE STORM COUNTRY. He next made GREED with Gibson Gowland under the direction of Erich von Stroheim. He enjoyed many years of success in such films as THE PAINTED VEIL, SEVENTH HEAVEN, GRAND HOTEL, and DINNER AT EIGHT. Height 5 ft. 11 in. Black hair and blue eyes. He died in 1956 in Beverly Hills.

**HIERS, Walter**—plate 234. Born on July 18, 1894, in Cordele, Mississippi. Was a stage comedian before making his screen *début* in 1918. He vied with Fatty Arbuckle for being the fattest man on the screen. His career reached its height when he was under contract to Paramount in the 1920s. Among his film credits were SIXTY CENTS AN HOUR, THE MAN FROM BLANKELEYS, HOLD THAT LION, FAIR WEEK, and HARD BOILED. Height 5 ft. 10 in. Brown hair and grey eyes.

**HOLMES, Helen**—plate 27. Born in Chicago, Illinois, on February 25, 1895. Educated at the Art Institute in Chicago. She inherited a ranch in California and learned to ride, shoot, and rope like a professional cowhand. She made her film *début* with the Kalem company where she became famous as a serial queen. Her first series THE

HAZARDS OF HELEN was made in 1914. Perhaps her most famous serial was THE RAILWAY GIRL, the episodes of which were filmed on a train with Miss Holmes performing highly dangerous stunts. Other films made by her include CROSSED SIGNALS, FAST FREIGHT, and THE LOST EXPRESS. Height 5 ft. 5 in. Dark brown hair and eyes.

**HOLMES, Stuart**—plate 150. Born in Chicago, Illinois, on March 10, 1887. He is the great grandson of the famous General von Moltke, German Field Marshall in the Franco-Prussian war. After studying art and sculpture, he decided on a stage career and made his screen *début* in 1925 after considerable stage experience. His first film was DICK TURPIN. His important role in THE FOUR HORSEMEN OF THE APOCALYPSE with Valentino started him on his career as one of the best-known "villains" on the screen. Other films include BELOVED BRUTE, NORTH STAR, BETWEEN FRIENDS, and STEELE OF THE ROYAL MOUNTED. Height 6 ft. Red hair and grey eyes.

**HORTON, Edward Everett**—plate 230. Born in Brooklyn, New York, on March 18, 1887. He began his stage career as a chorus boy and later went into stock. He made his screen *début* in 1922, but returned to the stage in 1928, thereafter dividing his time between stage and screen. One of America's most delightful comedians. Among his films to be remembered are RUGGLES OF RED GAP with Charles Laughton, ANGEL with Marlene Dietrich, DANGER—LOVE AT WORK, THE PERFECT SPECIMEN, THE GREAT GARRICK, and LOST HORIZON with Ronald Colman and H. B. Warner. Height 5 ft. 11 in. Brown hair and hazel eyes. Died in 1971.

## J

**JANNINGS, Emil**—plate 168. Born in Brooklyn, New York, on July 26, 1888, of German parents who returned with him to Germany when he was ten years old. At a very early age, he became an actor with a touring company. He made his *début* in silent films doing stunt work. More important roles followed until he achieved recognition by his performance in the title role of HENRY THE EIGHTH. More starring roles followed in OTHELLO, THE LAST LAUGH, and PETER THE GREAT, all made in Germany. His greatest successes, however, were in America where he made THE WAY OF ALL FLESH, THE STREET OF SIN, THE PATRIOT, and BETRAYAL. Height 6 ft. Blonde with blue eyes. He died in 1950.

**JOHNSON, Arthur**—plate 24. Born in Philadelphia, Pennsylvania, on January 12, 1880. Together with Bronco Billy Anderson, he was the first actor to star regularly in motion pictures. He was an original member of the old Biograph Company where he made several films with Mary Pickford when she was a girl of fourteen and went by the name of Dorothy Nicholson. Many of his films were made with Florence Lawrence as his co-star, the most important of which was A DRIVE FOR A LIFE, which was directed by D. W. Griffith. For the last six years of his life he was the leading male star of the Lubin Company. Among his many films was THE ADVENTURES OF DOLLY directed by Griffith, THE UNCHANGING SEA, THE GIBSON GODDESS, SONG OF A SHIRT, IN OLD CALIFORNIA, HER TWO SONS, and RESURRECTION which co-starred Florence Lawrence. Height 6 ft. 1 in. Slender with black hair and brown eyes. He was a fine light comedian as well as a talented dramatic actor. He died in 1916 at the height of his career at the age of thirty-six.

**JOY, Leatrice**—plate 133. Born on November 7, 1899, in New Orleans, Louisiana. Real name was Leatrice Zeidler. She entered films as an extra in Mary Pickford's PRIDE OF THE CLAN made in 1918. She was "discovered" by Cecil B. DeMille and was starred in his production of HELL'S HIGHROAD. He then cast her importantly in his great spectacular THE TEN COMMANDMENTS. By then she had attained stardom. Other film credits include THE ANGEL OF BROADWAY, THE WEDDING SONG, THE BELLAMY TRIAL, and A MOST IMMORAL LADY. Height 5 ft. 3 in. Black hair and brown eyes. She was at one time married to film star John Gilbert and has a daughter by that marriage.

**JOYCE, Alice**—plate 22. Born on October 1, 1890, in Kansas City, Missouri. She was an artist's model before making her screen *début* in 1910 in a film for Kalem called THE ENGINEER'S SWEETHEART. She remained with Kalem as a leading lady until 1915 at which time she joined the Vitagraph company. Alice Joyce became one of the most popular actresses on the screen with pictures such as THE GREEN GODDESS with George Arliss, DANCING MOTHERS, BEAU GESTE, SORRELL AND SON, and STELLA DALLAS. Height 5 ft. 7 in. Dark brown hair and eyes. She died in 1955.

**K**

**KEENAN, Frank**—plate 18. This veteran of stage and screen was born in Iowa in 1858. He was for many years one of America's greatest stage stars before making his film *début* early in film history. He is still remembered for his role in THE BELLS, the stage version of which was played by Sir Henry Irving. Among Frank Keenan's films were GATES OF BRASS, THE GILDED BUTTERFLY, THE SILVER GIRL, SMOULDERING EMBERS, and THE DIXIE HANDICAP. The co-starring of Frank Keenan and Charles Ray in THE COWARD in 1915 was a great triumph for both. Height 5 ft. 11 in. Brown hair and grey eyes.

**KERRIGAN, J. Warren**—plate 25. Born on July 25, 1891, in Louisville, Kentucky. Chose the stage for his career and while playing the lead in THE ROAD TO YESTERDAY in Chicago, was spotted by an Essanay producer and persuaded to transfer his talents to the screen. Was later leading man for the Biograph company. He was a great screen idol of his day. Two of his most successful films were THE COVERED WAGON and CAPTAIN BLOOD. Other films included THE LAST NOTICE, THE LIGHT OF HEAVEN, and END OF THE ROAD. Height 5 ft. 11 in. Dark wavy hair and brown eyes. Died June 9, 1947.

**KERRY, Norman**—plate 148. Born on June 11, 1889, in Rochester, New York. With a successful stage career already established, he was put under contract to Universal upon urging by Western star Art Acord, a close friend. His great success in Universal's THE MERRY-GO-ROUND won him stardom and some of his great successes include THE LOVE THIEF, THE HUNCHBACK OF NOTRE DAME, LOVE ME AND THE WORLD IS MINE, THE WOMAN FROM MOSCOW, and ANNIE LAURIE. Height 6 ft. 2 in. Dark brown hair and eyes. Died January 12, 1956, in Hollywood.

**KIRKWOOD, James**—plate 154. Born on February 22, 1883, in Grand Rapids, Michigan. After a long career on the legitimate stage he was persuaded by D. W. Griffith to take up screen work and became a director for the old Biograph Company. He directed his first film in 1909 and subsequently many of Mary Pickford's early films in which he also acted. When he was under contract to Universal as an actor and starred in many films of his own. Among his film credits are included THAT ROYAL GIRL, THE SPOILERS, THE EAGLE'S MATE, LOVERS' ISLAND, and THE MILLION DOLLAR MYSTERY. Height 6 ft. Red hair and blue eyes. At one time was married to film star Lila Lee.

**L**

**LAMARR, Barbara**—plate 159. Born in Richmond, Virginia, on September 3, 1898. Before entering motion pictures was a leading dancer and musical comedy actress. She made her stage *début* at the age of seven. Rose to stardom with her film role in THE THREE MUSKETEERS with Douglas Fairbanks, Sr. Like Theda Bara, she was famous for her "vamp" roles. Film credits include THE PRISONER OF ZENDA, THE ETERNAL CITY, THE SHOOTING OF DAN McGREW. Height 5 ft. 3 in. Black hair and eyes. Was married to Jack Daugherty. Died January 30, 1926, in Hollywood.

**LA PLANTE, Laura**—plate 142. Born November 1, 1904, in St. Louis, Missouri. She was trained as a violinist but became interested in the screen. She obtained a small part in a Christie comedy in 1919. She continued in films gaining experience until four years later she was given a contract with Universal at which studio she attained stardom. Her first films were as the heroine in Westerns. She then moved to dramatic comedy and here she gained her fame and popularity in such films as SKINNER'S DRESS SUIT, SILK STOCKINGS, and THE LOVE TRAP. Her big break came in SHOW BOAT followed by a second big hit in THE CAT AND THE CANARY. Height 5 ft. 2 in. Golden hair and blue eyes. She married her director, William Seiter.

**LA ROCQUE, Rod**—plate 180, 181. Born in Omaha, Nebraska, on November 29, 1898, of French-English parentage. He came to the attention of Cecil B. DeMille who placed him in the cast of THE TEN COMMANDMENTS. His work with Mae Murray in THE FRENCH DOLL brought him further recognition and he was soon a star in his own right. Among his films were THE

DELIGHTFUL ROGUE, BEAU BANDIT, JAZZMANIA, THE RESURRECTION, and ONE ROMANTIC NIGHT. Height 6 ft. 2 in. with black hair and brown eyes. Married to film star Vilma Banky. Died in 1971.

**LAWRENCE, Florence**—plate 4, 5. Born in Hamilton, Ontario, Canada, on September 22, 1886. She made her stage *début* at the age of four and became known throughout Canada and the United States as "Baby Flo, The Child Wonder Whistler." She was making films in 1908, and was actually the first female movie star as before her time the studios did not allow the names of the players to be used. In the very early days they were all anonymous. Under contract to Biograph, Florence Lawrence became known as "The Biograph Girl." Her salary was $25.00 a week. Before signing with Biograph she made ROMEO AND JULIET for Vitagraph. Paul Panzer played Romeo. She made REDEMPTION under the direction of D. W. Griffith. For several years she was easily the most valuable property in motion pictures. It was Carl Laemmle who made her famous as the first star of the cinema under her own name. Among her films were included THE LITTLE REBEL, THE HOYDEN, THE MENDED LUTE, THE RESURRECTION, and a series of popular two-reel comedies known as THE JONESY PICTURES. Height 5 ft. 4 in. Light brown hair and blue eyes. She died by her own hand in 1939.

**LEWIS, Mitchell**—plate 40. Born in Syracuse, New York, in 1877. As an officer in the U. S. Navy, he fought in the Spanish-American War. After the war, while on the Broadway stage he was selected to play the lead in the film version of Rex Beach's THE BARRIER. Acclaimed for this film, he stayed on in Hollywood in the early days of the industry. He was cast in another great film, MADAME X, with Pauline Frederick, and then followed successes in THE BRIDGE OF SAN LUIS REY, GOLD MADNESS, TELL IT TO THE MARINES, and ONE STOLEN NIGHT. Height 6 ft. 1 in., with black hair and eyes.

**LINDER, Max**—plate 213. Born in Bordeaux, France, on December 16, 1885. Was world-renowned as a film comedian. After achieving a reputation on the French stage, he made his *début* on the screen with the Pathe company. In 1907 and 1908, he was perhaps the most famous film artist in the world. In 1916 he joined the Essanay company in Hollywood and made a series of light comedies for them. He then returned to France and the French screen, but was in Hollywood again in 1919 to produce his own films released through the Robertson-Cole Studio. Back in Paris in 1925, he died by suicide together with his twenty-one-year-old wife. His first films in America included MAX COMES ACROSS, MAX WANTS A DIVORCE, and MAX AND HIS TAXI. Later, under his own company in Hollywood, he made SEVEN YEARS BAD LUCK, BE MY WIFE, and THE THREE MUST-GET-THERES. Height 5 ft. 6 in. Dark hair and brown eyes. He died in 1925.

**LLOYD, Harold**—plate 239. Born on April 20, 1893, in Omaha, Nebraska. He joined a theatrical stock company at an early age and while touring the country became stranded in California in 1914. He secured "extra" work with the old Edison company and in 1916 was "discovered" by Hal Roach and starred in a series of films in which he became known as Lonesome Luke. This was the beginning of his triumphs as the famous comedian with the horn-rimmed glasses. Among his best known films were SAFETY LAST, GRANDMA'S BOY, GIRL SHY, THE FRESHMAN, SPEEDY, FEET FIRST, and WELCOME DANGER. Height 5 ft. 9 in. Black hair and blue eyes. Married Mildred Davis who was his leading lady in films. He died in 1971.

**LOCKWOOD, Harold**—plate 135. Born in Brooklyn New York, in 1891. Stage work in musical comedy in New York before making his screen *début* in 1910 with the old Nestor Company. Often co-starred with May Allison and became a contender with Wallace Reid as the country's leading matinee idol. Screen credits include HEARTS ADRIFT, WILDFLOWER, THE GREAT ROMANCE, TESS OF THE STORM COUNTRY with Mary Pickford, and THE GREATER GLORY. Height 5 ft. 11½ in. Dark brown hair and blue eyes. Had a son, also called Harold Lockwood, who worked in films.

**LONG, Walter**—plate 170. Born in 1884 in Milford, New York. One of the best known "villains" in American films. He came to fame with D. W. Griffith for his role in THE BIRTH OF A NATION. He was the tough, ugly, powerfully-built bully type. Among his film credits are BLOOD AND SAND, RAFFLES, THE RIDIN' KID FROM POWDER RIVER, STEEL PRE-

FERRED, and JIM THE CONQUEROR. Height 5 ft. 11 in. Brown hair and grey eyes.

**LOVE, Bessie**—plate. 155. Born in Midland, Texas, on September 10, 1898. Her real name was Juanita Horton. During her high school days in Los Angeles, she played a small part in the D. W. Griffith production of INTOLERANCE. She later became leading lady to Douglas Fairbanks Sr., and worked in a number of his films. For a period of time she turned to musical comedy on the stage but returned to the screen in THE SONG AND DANCE MAN. Other of her films include THE LOST WORLD, BROADWAY MELODY, GOOD NEWS, DRESS PARADE, and YOUNG APRIL. She was one of the smallest stars on the screen, being under 5 ft. and slender. Fair hair and brown eyes.

**LOVE, Montague**—plate 88. Born in Hampshire, England, in 1887. Educated at Cambridge University. He made his stage *début* as a youth in Edmund Breeze's company of THE LION AND THE MOUSE. His film *début* was in the George Archainbaud production of THE CROSS BEARER. After his film success in the title role of RASPUTIN he was lured to Hollywood where he became one of the best known villains in American pictures. Among his films were CHARMING SINNERS, DON JUAN, KING OF KINGS for DeMille, SON OF THE SHEIK with Valentino, BULLDOG DRUMMOND with Ronald Colman, and MIDSTREAM. Height 6 ft. 1 in. Brown hair and blue eyes. He died in 1943.

**LYTELL, Bert**—plate 139. Born in New York City on February 24, 1888, of prominent theatrical parents. After a brilliant career on Broadway, he made his film *début* in 1918 in THE LONE WOLF. His heyday in films came during his work under contract to Jesse Lasky and Paramount. Among his many films were LADY WINDEMERE'S FAN, SHIP OF SOULS, THE IDLE RICH, THE LONE WOLF RETURNS, and STEELE OF THE ROYAL MOUNTED. Height 5 ft. 10 in. Dark brown hair and eyes. Married to film star Claire Windsor. He died in 1954.

## M

**MacDERMOTT, Marc**—plate 26. Born in Goulburn, New South Wales, Australia, on February 6, 1873. He began his stage career in Sydney. Came to London to play the principal supporting role with Mrs. Patrick Campbell in the stage production of THE SECOND MRS. TANQUERAY, and was her leading man when she toured America. He remained in America and began film work at the Edison Company. He was with the Edison Company for six years as a leading man and worked with many of the leading actresses in the early days of the silent films. Among his virtually legion films were INTRIGUE, RANSON'S FOLLY, THE NEW MOON, RESURRECTION, THE TEMPTRESS, THE LOVE THIEF, and HE WHO GETS SLAPPED with Lon Chaney. Height 6 ft. 1½ in. Brown hair and grey eyes. Died in 1929.

**MacDONALD, J. Farrell**—plate 109. Born in Waterbury, Connecticut, in 1875, of Irish parents. Educated at Yale University. After substantial stage experience he was prevailed upon by D. W. Griffith to work in films. This was at the time when Griffith was directing for the old Biograph Company in New York and Mary Pickford was just starting her screen career. MacDonald played with Miss Pickford in one of her first starring films, RAGS. He was a top character actor in America for many years. Some of his many films include THE IRON HORSE, SUNRISE, EAST SIDE WEST SIDE, SHOW BOAT, SLAVE SHIP, and TOPPER. Height 5 ft. 10 in. Brown hair and blue eyes. He died in 1952.

**MacDONALD, Katherine**—plate 82. She was born in Pittsburgh, Pennsylvania, on October 15, 1894, and without previous stage experience became one of America's leading film actresses. She was called "The American Beauty." Known for her sensitive and talented interpretation of dramatic roles, her services were always in demand. Among her many films were THE WOMAN CONQUERS, OLD LOVES FOR NEW, THE SCARLET LILY, HEADIN' SOUTH with Douglas Fairbanks Sr., THE WOMAN THOU GAVEST ME, and RIDDLE GAWNE with Bill Hart and Lon Chaney. Height 5 ft. 7 in. Golden blonde hair and blue eyes. Died in 1956.

**MacDONALD, Wallace**—plate 64. Born in Mulgrave, Nova Scotia, in 1891. After a successful stage career in which he played the handsome leading man, he made his film *début* in the early days of the silent films. He played the male lead opposite many of the popular female stars of the day. He was adept in smooth, sophisticated parts but could work just as convincingly in Western films and light comedy. Among his films were DARK SKIES, FANCY BAGGAGE, MADAME SPHINX with Alma Rubens, SPOTLIGHT SADIE with Mae Marsh, and THE BEST BET. Height 5 ft. 10½ in. Dark brown hair and eyes.

**MacGRAIL, Walter**—plate 195. Born in Brooklyn, New York, on July 4, 1889. One of the best-known villains in American films. He made his film *début* in the silent era after considerable stage experience and was much in demand from the very beginning. He was with Pearl White in THE PERILS OF PAULINE, in PLAYTHINGS OF DESTINY with Anita Stewart and THE BAD MAN with Holbrook Blinn. His other films included FORBIDDEN WATERS, PRISONERS OF THE STORM, OLD SAN FRANCISCO, HAVOC, MEN WITHOUT WOMEN, and COMBAT. Height 5 ft. 11 in. Black hair and blue eyes.

**MacLEAN, Douglas**—plate 118. Born in Philadelphia, Pennsylvania, on January 12, 1896. The son of a minister, he was educated as a civil engineer. But the stage was his real love and he was very fortunate to be cast in a play called ROSALIND with Maude Adams on Broadway. He later played a leading role with Alice Brady. In Los Angeles, he continued his stage work with the Oliver Morosco Stock company. He made his film *début* with Mary Pickford in a film called CAPTAIN KIDD JUNIOR. He then produced and starred in a film called GOING UP. It was such a phenomenal success that every studio in Hollywood sought his services. One success after another followed—SEVEN KEYS TO BALDPATE, THE CARNATION KID, THE YANKEE CONSUL, NEVER SAY DIE, and LET IT RAIN, to name only a few. He was acclaimed as the top star of light comedy. Height 5 ft. 9½ in. Brown hair and eyes. He died in 1967.

**MAIN, Marjorie**—plate 238. Her real name was Mary Tomlinson and she was born in Acton, Indiana, on February 24, 1890. She was one of the great comediennes of all time. In 1925 she was working in silents with W. C. Fields. She furnished the delightful comedy relief in TAKE A CHANCE with James Dunn and June Knight. She also distinguished herself in CRIME WITHOUT PASSION and DEAD END, but her most famous films were the MA KETTLE series in which she starred in the title role. Height 5 ft. 6 in. Brown hair and eyes.

**MARSH, Mae**—plates 66, 193. Born on November 9, 1897, in Madrid, New Mexico. She was educated in a convent in San Francisco and began earning a living as a telephone operator. While visiting the old Biograph studio where her sister Margaret played small parts, she was seen by D. W. Griffith who persuaded her to embark upon a screen career. Her first film was made in 1912 and was called THE ESCAPE. It starred Blanche Sweet and Henry B. Walthall. Griffith teamed her with Bobby Harron and together they made JUDITH AND BETHULIA, HOME SWEET HOME, and Griffith's great spectacle INTOLERANCE. Among her other films were POLLY OF THE CIRCUS, SPOTLIGHT SADIE, and THE WHITE ROSE which Griffith directed with Miss Marsh, Ivor Novello, Carol Dempster, and Neil Hamilton as the stars. The greatest performance of her career was in THE BIRTH OF A NATION, made by Griffith in 1915. Height 5 ft. 3 in. Auburn hair and grey eyes. She died in 1968.

**MARMONT, Percy**—plate 70. "Perc" was born in London, England, on November 26, 1883. Before achieving success on the American screen, he was a popular stage star in London. He was brought to America by director Maurice Tourneur in 1913. His first film was ROSE OF THE WORLD. His greatest role was that of Mark Sabre in IF WINTER COMES. In personal life he was one of the most popular actors in Hollywood—and also one of the best. Other film credits include INFATUATION, MANTRAP, YELLOW STOCKINGS, LADY OF THE LAKE, and THE SHOOTING OF DAN McGREW. Height 6 ft. with fair hair and grey eyes.

**MARSHALL, Tully**—plate 100. Born in Nevada City, Nevada, on April 13, 1864. Educated at the University of Santa Clara in California and made his stage *début* in San Francisco. His stage career was a distinguished one. He worked with the great Modjeska in Shakespeare, and with E. H. Southern, among other great stage stars. He came to the screen in the film version of PAID IN FULL in 1915. His Jim Bridger, the old scout in THE COVERED WAGON is probably the finest performance ever presented on the screen. Other film credits include INTOLERANCE, HE WHO GETS SLAPPED, ALIAS JIMMY VALENTINE, TWINKLETOES, and THE HUNCHBACK OF NOTRE DAME. Height 5 ft. 9½ in. Grey hair and eyes. Died in 1943.

**MASON, Shirley**—plate 187. Born in Brooklyn, New York, in 1901. Her real family name is Flugrath and she is the younger sister of Edna Flugrath and Viola Dana, both of whom were screen stars. She was on the stage at four with William Faversham and was a thoroughly experienced actress before signing a film contract with Fox, at which studio she remained for six years. She made PASSION with Clifford Bruce in 1917, followed by THE STARDUST TRAIL, SWEET ROSIE O'GRADY, and THE SCARLET HONEYMOON. In 1920 she scored a hit in TREASURE ISLAND with Lon Chaney. Other film credits include SCANDAL PROOF, MUST YOU GO, and DARK SKIES. Height 5 ft. Brown hair and grey eyes.

**MAYO, Frank**—plates 85, 173. Born in New York City in 1886 of theatrical parents. He spent several years on the stage, including three in England before making his screen *début* in DAVY CROCKETT. His grandfather, Frank Mayo, was famous for the stage version. In 1917, he had a great hit in THE INTERLOPER. THE BRUTE BRAKER and AFRAID TO FIGHT followed, and in 1923 a big spectacular SOULS FOR SALE with Barbara Lamarr and Richard Dix and directed by Lubitsch. Other film credits include THE FLAMING HOUR, THE FIRST DEGREE, SIX DAYS, and THEN CAME THE WOMAN. Height 5 ft. 11 in. Brown hair and grey eyes. Was married to Dagmar Godowsky.

**MEIGHAN, Thomas**–plate 145. Born on April 9, 1888, in Pittsburgh, Pennsylvania, of Irish parents. The stage claimed him as a youth and fame came in THE COLLEGE WIDOW which he played both on Broadway and the London stage. He starred in BROADWAY JONES in London and then made his first film there called DANDY DONOVAN with Gladys Cooper. Returning to America he then devoted his entire career to film work and attained his greatest success with Jesse Lasky and Paramount. His films include THE MIRACLE MAN, THE ADMIRABLE CRICHTON, THE CITY OF SILENT MEN, TIN GODS, and WOMAN PROOF. Height 6 ft. Black hair and blue eyes. Was married to stage star Frances Ring. Died in 1936.

**MENJOU, Adolphe**—plate 186. Born on February 18, 1890, in Pittsburgh, Pennsylvania. He had a French father and an Irish mother. He was educated to become a mechanical engineer, but joined a theatrical society at college and became interested in acting. After five years with stock companies and in vaudeville, he made his screen *début* in 1912 with Vitagraph. Served in the first World War and was discharged as a Captain. Came into film prominence with his role in A WOMAN OF PARIS. During his years with Paramount, he was at his best, loved by the public for his suave, sophisticated roles. His film credits include THE FRONT PAGE, one of his greatest, BELLA DONNA, THE SORROWS OF SATAN, THE ACE OF CADS, A FAREWELL TO ARMS, and THE MARRIAGE CIRCLE. Height 5 ft. 10 in. Dark brown hair and blue eyes. Married actress Veree Teasdale. Died in 1963.

**McCOY, Tim**—plate 198. Born in Wyoming on April 10, 1893. A great authority on the American Indian and called by them the "White Eagle." His first interest in films came as a consultant for the epic film THE COVERED WAGON. He organised the Indian participation in the film and supervised their appearance. He also appeared in person in a prologue at the principal theatres where THE COVERED WAGON was being shown. A film career followed in which he starred in many Westerns, among them WAR PAINT, THE INDIANS ARE COMING, CALIFORNIA, and SKIES WEST. Height 5 ft. 11 in. Light brown hair and blue eyes. Was at one time a colonel in the U. S. Army.

**McKIM, Robert**—plate 69. Born in San Jacinto, California, on August 26, 1887. A well-known villain in films who made his *début* in 1915 in THE DISCIPLE with William S. Hart. Most of his films fell into the class of "greats," including THE MARK OF ZORRO with Douglas Fairbanks Sr., THE SPOILERS with William Farnham, MONTE CRISTO, THE BAT, THE THRILL SEEKERS, and THE WINNING OF BARBARA WORTH. Height 6 ft. Black hair and brown eyes.

**MILLER, Marilyn**—plate 104. Born in Evansville, Indiana, on September 1, 1900. Real name was Marilyn Reynolds and her mother was a famous stage performer. With her mother, stepfather, and two sisters, she appeared as a child dancer. The family was billed as "The Five Columbians." A top act, the company toured America and Europe. Back in New York, Marilyn rose to stardom in musical comedy and at the height of her career became star of Ziegfeld Follies. She made her film *début* in the famous SALLY. She was at one time the wife of Jack Pickford. Height 5 ft. 5 in. Blonde with blue eyes. She died in 1936.

**MINTER, Mary Miles**—plate 63. Born on April 1, 1898, in Shreveport, Louisiana. Her real name was Juliet Shelby. She began her theatrical career at the age of five with Arnold Daly in his stage production of CAMEO KIRBY. At seventeen, she was signed by Metro Pictures and appeared in that studio's screen production of BARBARA FRIETCHIE. Among her film credits are included DRUMS OF FATE, THE HEART SPECIALIST, THE EYES OF JULIA DEEP, SOUTH OF SUVA, THE AMAZING IMPOSTER, and her greatest, THE TRAIL OF THE LONESOME PINE. Height 5 ft. 2 in. Golden hair and blue eyes.

**MONTANA, Bull**—plate 228. Born on May 18, 1887, in Milano, Italy. Real name of "the Bull" was Luigi Montagna. He emigrated to the United States as a young man and became a pugilist. Douglas Fairbanks Sr. witnessed one of his fights in New York and decided he had a "face for films." Fairbanks brought the Bull to Hollywood and used him in a current film he was making called IN AGAIN OUT AGAIN, starring Fairbanks and Arlene Pretty. Bull was a born comedian and was soon famous. He worked in THE FOUR HORSEMEN OF THE APOCALYPSE and SON OF THE SHEIK with Valentino, and THE THREE MUST-GET-THERES with Max Linder. In 1923, he starred for Metro Pictures in two films, ROB 'EM GOOD and THE TWO TWINS. He was a supporting actor for comedy relief and many other films. Bull was 5 ft. 10 in. tall. Brown hair and eyes. Died in Hollywood in 1950.

**MOORE, Colleen**—plate 169. Born in Port Huron, Michigan, on August 19, 1900. Real name Kathleen Morrison. Discovered for the screen by D. W. Griffith and made her film *début* with the old Triangle company. Her popularity was formidable in the Twenties when, after her success in FLAMING YOUTH, she became known as the "flaming youth" girl. She typified the youth of the day. In SO BIG, she revealed herself as a fine dramatic actress, and in Ivor Novello's LILAC TIME she was superb. Other of her films include LOVE NEVER DIES, WE MODERNS, THE DESERT FLOWER, and THE BAD BOY made with Bobby Harron in 1917. TWINKLETOES was another of her delightful films. Height 5 ft. 3 in. Black hair and brown eyes. Was married at one time to John McCormack.

**MOORE, Matt**—plate 140. Born in Meath, Ireland, in 1888, and emigrated to America with his family in 1898. With his two brothers, Owen and Tom, he became one of the three famous Moores in motion pictures. He made his film *début* in 1912, and popularity caught up with him when he played the leading role in AMBROSE APPLEJACK'S ADVENTURE. Following a long series of films in the early days of silent films, he co-starred with Marion Davies in TILLIE THE TOILER. Other films include MARRIED ALIVE, THE JAZZ BRIDE, EARLY TO WED, DRY MARTINI, and TWENTY THOUSAND LEAGUES UNDER THE SEA. In his early days in films he worked with both Florence Lawrence and Mary Pickford. Height 5 ft. 10 in. Red hair and blue eyes.

**MOORE, Owen**—plate 30. Born on December 12, 1887, in Meath, Ireland. Came to America with his family at age eleven. Worked first on the stage and then began his film career in 1909 with Biograph. He worked in several films with Mary Pickford, whom he later married. He made IN SWIFT WATER with Florence Lawrence, and PRETTY MRS. SMITH with Fritzi Scheff. Then NEARLY A LADY with Elsie Janis. He made ESCAPE for D. W. Griffith with Bobby Harron and Blanche Sweet, and MY VALET with Mabel Normand. Other film credits include THE ROAD TO MANDALAY, EAST OF BROADWAY, OUTSIDE THE LAW, REPORTED MISSING, and A STAR IS BORN. Height 5 ft. 11 in. Brown hair and eyes. Brother of Tom and Matt Moore. Following his divorce from Mary Pickford he married Ziegfeld star Kathryn Perry.

**MOORE, Tom**—plate 123. Born in 1886 in Meath, Ireland, and was fourteen when his family emigrated to America. Like his younger brothers, Matt and Owen, he was in the Broadway theater before entering films in 1910. He joined the Kalem company and made NINA OF THE THEATER with Allice Joyce. 1915 found him at Pathe where he made WHOSE GUILTY with Anna Q. Nilsson, followed by THE CINDERELLA MAN with Mae Marsh. He made ONE NIGHT IN ROME with Laurette Taylor and countless other films among them THE SONG AND DANCE MAN, THE LOVE THRILL, ON THIN ICE, and A KISS FOR

CINDERELLA. Height 5 ft. 10 in. Brown hair and blue eyes. Was married to Renee Adoree.

**MOORE, Victor**—plate 221. Born in Hammonton, New Jersey, February 24, 1876. Had a lengthy career on the stage before entering films, and for many years he appeared with Emma Littlefield, his wife, in vaudeville. He came to the screen as a character actor of no mean ability, delighting film audiences with his comic grimaces and nervous hesitancy. He made a great many films, both silent and sound. Among them was MAKE WAY FOR TOMORROW, LOUISIANA PURCHASE, MEET THE MISSUS, WE'RE ON THE JURY, and SHE'S GOT THAT SWING. One of his first films was made in 1915. It was called SNOBS and co-starred him with Anita King. In 1916, he made a very memorable film called THE CLOWN. Height 5 ft. 8 in. Brown hair and eyes. He died in 1962.

**MORAN, Polly**—plate 229. Born in Chicago, Illinois, on June 28, 1884. She ran away from home when a young girl and found her way to the vaudeville stage as a comic. She became well-known as a performer on the American stage and toured Europe and South Africa before entering films in 1915. Her first film was with Mack Sennett in THE JANITOR with Charlie Murray. Played important parts in many films in comic or character parts. Among her film credits are CAUGHT SHORT, BRINGING UP FATHER, WAY OUT WEST, and THE DIVINE WOMAN, which starred Greta Garbo. Height 5 ft. 5½ in. Medium brown hair and blue eyes.

**MORENO, Antonio**—plate 90. Born in Madrid, Spain, in 1888. He emigrated to New York in 1902 and got his start on the Broadway stage with the Maude Adams company. He entered films in 1914 with Vitagraph as a leading man and in 1915 was elevated to stardom after making THE ISLAND OF REGENERATION and ALADDIN FROM BROADWAY, both films with Edith Storey. THE TRAIL OF THE LONESOME PINE with Ernest Torrence and Mary Miles Minter was a big success for him, and MARE NOSTRUM with Alice Terry followed. He made MY AMERICAN WIFE with Gloria Swanson, and STORY WITHOUT A NAME with Agnes Ayres. Other films included THE IRON TEST, THE BORDER LEGION, and he co-starred with Clara Bow in IT. Height 5 ft. 10 in. Black hair and eyes. Married Daisy Danziger, a Los Angeles society girl. He died in 1967.

**MULHALL, Jack**—plate 201. Born in Wappingers Falls, New York, on October 7, 1891. Graduated from Columbia University in New York. Was playing stock when he met Rex Ingram who introduced him to the Edison company where he made his screen *début* in COLD CASH. He went from Edison to Biograph when that company included Mary Pickford, the Gish sisters, Henry B. Walthall, and Blanche Sweet. He worked with all of them. 1920 found him at Paramount where he made ALL OF A SUDDEN PEGGY with Marguerite Clark. Other of his films include ROAD TO PARADISE, MAN CRAZY, TWIN BEDS, THE GOLDEN CALF, and ORCHIDS AND ERMINE. Height 5 ft. 10 in. Brown hair and blue eyes.

**MURRAY, Mae**—plate 172. Born on May 10, 1893, in Portsmouth, Virginia, of Belgian and Austrian parents. Her real name was Marie Adrienne Koenig. She began a stage career at fourteen in musical comedy. She rose to be a star dancer in the Ziegfeld Follies. She made her screen *début* in 1916 in TO HAVE AND TO HOLD. She starred in many films and was one of the most exotic of screen celebrities. Her film credits include PEACOCK ALLEY, THE MERRY WIDOW, FASCINATION, MADEMOISELLE MIDNIGHT, LOVE SONG, and VALENCIA. Among her husbands were director-producer Robert Z. Leonard and Prince Midivani. Height 5 ft. 5 in. Golden blonde hair and blue eyes. Noted for her "bee-stung" lips. She died in 1965.

## N

**NALDI, Nita**—plate 208. Born in New York City on April 4, 1899. Her parents were Italian. Trained in voice and dancing, she entered musical comedy on the New York stage at an early age and rose to fame in the Ziegfeld Follies. She entered films and appeared with Rudolph Valentino in BLOOD AND SAND. She was featured in DeMille's THE TEN COMMANDMENTS and co-starred with Richard Barthelmess in EXPERIENCE. Other of her films included THE MOUNTAIN EAGLE, THE MIRACLE OF LIFE, GLIMPSES OF THE MOON, REPORTED MISSING, and PRATERNIZZI, a film made in Vienna in 1926. Miss Naldi was the "amazon" type—big, dark, and beautiful. She was 5 ft. 8 in. tall. Her hair and eyes were black. She died in 1961.

**NAZIMOVA, Alla**—plate 50. Born May 22, 1879, at Yalta in the Crimea, Russia. Her real name was Alla Mazimoff. Had a successful stage career in Russia, London, and on Broadway before making her screen *début* in 1916 in WAR BRIDES. Followed THE MADONNA OF THE STREETS, THE RED LANTERN, and THE REDEEMING SIN. She became Metro's best moneymaker. Her CAMILLE with Rudolph Valentino was a great triumph. She made Ibsen's THE DOLL HOUSE, SALOME, MADAME PEACOCK, and THE BRAT, to name a few. All were top quality and top box-office. Height 5 ft. 4 in. Black hair and violet eyes. She was married to Charles Bryant, the English actor. Died in 1945.

**NEGRI, Pola**—plates 222, 223. Born on December 30, 1897, in Lipna, Poland. Real name was Appollonia Chalupez. Began her stage career at the age of 16 in Warsaw. Later became a member of the Imperial Russian Ballet in St. Petersburg. Her aptitude for the violin then induced her to become a professional violinist and as such she toured Europe. At the outbreak of the Russian revolution she went to Germany and was cast in films by director Ernst Lubitsch. Her great success in LOVE AND PASSION, DU BARRY, and GYPSY BLOOD led to an American contract. FORBIDDEN PARADISE with Rod LaRocque, LILY IN THE DUST, EAST OF SUEZ, HOTEL IMPERIAL, ONE ARABIAN NIGHT, and THE CHEAT with Jack Holt and Charles de Roche were among her American films. Was married first to Polish Count Domski, and then to Prince Serge Midivani. Height 5 ft. 4 in. Black hair and grey eyes.

**NILSSON, Anna Q.**—plate 119. Born on March 30, 1894, in Ystad, Sweden. While visiting relatives in America as a young girl she sought and secured work in motion pictures with the old Kalem Company in 1911. She subsequently became one of the best known and admired actresses on the American screen. Three of her greatest films were the Cecil B. DeMille production of ADAM'S RIB with Milton Sills, THE SPOILERS also with Milton Sills, and PONJOLA. Other film credits include THE ISLE OF LOST SHIPS, THE MASKED WOMAN, MIDNIGHT LOVERS, THE GREATER GLORY and SUNSET BOULEVARD. Height 5 ft. 7 in. Golden hair and blue eyes. Died in 1974.

**NORMAND, Mabel**—plate 84. Born on November 16, 1894, in Boston, Massachusetts. She joined the Vitagraph company in 1909 under the name of Mabel Fortescue and made her screen *début* in the BETTY series for that studio. After a stretch with Biograph, she became one of the leading Keystone players and "Queen" of the Mack Sennett lot. She made a series of films with Fatty Arbuckle, and with Charlie Chaplin did TILLIE'S PUNCTURED ROMANCE. Her greatest role came in the film MICKEY after which Sam Goldwyn starred her in MOLLY O, SUZANNA, and EXTRA GIRL. She was married to film star Lew Cody. Height 5 ft. 3 in. Black hair and brown eyes. She is still classed as one of the all-time "greats." She died in 1930.

**NOVAK, Eva**—plate 128. Born on April 11, 1898, in St. Louis, Missouri. Began her film career with small parts in 1920 and rose to stardom for her work in Western drama. She is the sister of Jane Novak who was already a film star when Eva entered films. Included in her film credits are WESTWARD HO, RIDERS WEST, RED SIGNALS, DUTY'S REWARD, and DIXIE FLYER. Height 5 ft. 5 in. Golden blonde hair and grey eyes.

**NOVAK, Jane**—plate 129. Born on January 12, 1896, in St. Louis, Missouri. She began a stage career at the age of twelve and had a great deal of theatrical experience before entering films in 1917. She made ROADS OF DESTINY with John Bowers and Pauline Frederick, REDSKIN with Richard Dix, and a long series of films including THE LURE OF THE WILD, DANGEROUS VIRTUE, ONE INCREASING PURPOSE, and WHAT PRICE LOVE. She and her sister Eva starred together in a film called THE MAN LIFE PASSED BY directed by Victor Schertzinger. Height 5 ft. 7 in. Blonde with blue eyes.

**NOVARRO, Ramon**—plate 218, 219, 220. His real name was Ramon Samanyagos and in 1922 Rex Ingram pulled him out of the extra line and gave him a role in THE PRISONER OF ZENDA. He became one of the screen's greatest performers. Born in Durange, Mexico, on February 6, 1899, he was the eldest of ten children. With a superlative singing voice he originally intended to sing operatically. His unexpected chance in films changed his mind and he rose quickly to stardom. He made SCARAMOUCHE, WHERE THE PAVEMENT ENDS, THE STUDENT PRINCE, THE ARAB, THE PAGAN, BEN HUR with Francis X. Bushman and

May MacAvoy, and MATA HARI with Garbo. He spoke several languages. Height 5 ft. 10 in. Black hair and eyes. He died in 1968.

## O

**OAKLAND, Vician**—plate 68. Born in Oakland, California, on September 3, 1889. She began her theatrical career as a very young girl and worked mostly in musical comedy. She was a star in the Ziegfeld Follies before she made her *début* in films in 1924 in MADONNA OF THE STREETS. Among her film credits are WEDDING BELLS with Raymond Griffith, THE TIME, THE PLACE, AND THE GIRL, and her big role as Mrs. Selby in UNCLE TOM'S CABIN. Height 5 ft. 6 in. Fair hair and blue eyes. Was married to stage comedian John T. Murray. Died in 1958.

**O'BRIEN, Eugene**—plate 158. Born in Colorado in 1884, he had many years of stage experience when he entered films in 1915. He began his screen career with Essanay. He made COME OUT OF THE KITCHEN with Marguerite Clark. Then followed POPPY with Norma Talmadge. He made THE SAFETY CURTAIN for Selznick, and then again with Norma Talmadge THE VOICE OF THE MINARET, and SECRETS. His other films included INNOCENCE, FLAMES, CHANNING OF THE NORTHWEST, and FINE MANNERS. Height 6 ft. Medium brown hair and blue eyes.

**O'BRIEN, George**—plate 202. Born in San Francisco, California, on September 3, 1900, son of the then Chief of Police of San Francisco. Served in the First World War in a sub chaser and was a heavyweight boxer in the Navy's Pacific fleet. Following the war, he met Tom Mix, the great cowboy star, who introduced him to films at the Fox studio. His big chance came with the filming of THE IRON HORSE, a great spectacular in which he played the leading role. Another of his important films was SUNRISE. Other film credits include HAVOC, THE BLUE EAGLE, THE DEVIL'S MASTER, THE LAST OF THE DUANES, and NOAH'S ARK. Height 5 ft. 11 in. Brown hair and eyes. Handsome and powerfully built without appearing too muscular.

**OLMSTEAD, Gertrude**—plate 206. Born in Chicago, Illinois, on November 2, 1897. After winning a beauty contest, she came to the attention of Universal and was put under contract by that studio. After a period of bit playing, she was gradually given leading roles. Following her success in THE BELOVED ROGUE, she was starred or co-starred in many films, among them CALIFORNIA STRAIGHT AHEAD, MONTE CARLO, SONNY BOY with Al Jolson, CAMEO KIRBY with John Gilbert, THE HIT OF THE SHOW, and PUPPETS. She was married to film director Robert Z. Leonard. Height 5 ft. 2 in. Medium brown hair and grey eyes.

**O'MALLEY, Pat**—plate 51. Born in Forest City, Pennsylvania, on September 3, 1892, the son of Irish emigrants. Began his professional career with a circus and became an accomplished tight-rope walker. His film *début* was made in the early days of the silent screen with the old Edison company. He then moved to Kalem where he rose to stardom. One of his early starring roles was with Ruth Stonehouse in THE PAPER DOOR. During his long career in films, he co-starred with most of the top stars of his day. He made MY OLD DUTCH with Florence Turner, ALIBI, THE MAN I LOVE, THE SLAVE and, perhaps his most memorable O'MALLEY OF THE MOUNTED. Height 5 ft. 11 in. Dark brown hair and blue eyes.

## P

**PALLETTE, Eugene**—plate 225. Born in Winfield, Kansas, on July 18, 1889. Educated at Culver Military Academy. With some stage experience behind him, he made his film *début* in the very early days of the silent era. He had an important role in INTOLERANCE, a D. W. Griffith epic, and in 1916 co-starred with Norma Talmadge in a series of two-reel films. He served in the American army during World War I. Returned to films at the end of the war and became one of America's most famous character actors. Among his films are included THE CANARY MURDER CASE, THE DUMMY, THE VIRGINIAN, THE BORDER LEGION, and SLIGHTLY SCARLET. Height 5 ft. 9 in. Brown hair and blue eyes. In later years weighed over 270 pounds. He died in 1954.

**PANGBORN, Franklin**—plate 231. Born in Newark, New Jersey, on January 23, 1896. Had a long successful career on the stage before entering films. Worked with both Pauline Frederick and Alla Nazimova on Broadway and became famous for his light comedy roles. His first important part in motion pictures was in EXIT SMILING. Other film credits include THE NIGHT BRIDE, GETTING GERTIE'S GARTER, THE REJUVENATION OF AUNT MARY, and NOT SO DUMB. One of America's best character actors. Height 5 ft. 10½ in. Brown hair and blue eyes. He died in 1958.

**PANZER, Paul**—plate 21. Born on November 3, 1873, in Wurtzberg, Bavaria. After considerable stage experience in both Europe and America, he made his screen *début* in 1908. One of the pioneers of the early screen, he co-starred with virtually all the leading stars of the day at one time or another in his career. In what was undoubtedly the first screen version of ROMEO AND JULIET, he played Romeo to the Juliet of Florence Lawrence. He was with Pearl White in THE PERILS OF PAULINE, in BELOW ZERO with Eva Novak, and THE REDSKIN with Richard Dix. Six feet tall, he had dark brown hair and eyes.

**PETERS, House**—plate 146. Born in Bristol, England, in 1880, he was educated in engineering and became a mining engineer in South Africa. He served in the Boer War after which he returned to London and began a career in the theatre. Successful as a leading man on the London stage and then on Broadway, he was claimed by Hollywood. In motion pictures, his rugged, virile personality met with great popularity. He co-starred with Ethel Clayton in THE GREAT DIVIDE in 1915, and firmly established himself with ROSE MARIE and THE STORM. Other film credits include COMBAT, COUNSEL FOR THE DEFENSE, and HEAD WINDS. Height 6 ft. 1½ in. Dark brown hair and grey eyes. He died in 1967.

**PHILBIN, Mary**—plate 149. Born in Chicago, Illinois, on July 16, 1904. She was discovered by Erich von Stroheim who was impressed by a photograph of Miss Philbin in a magazine where she was entered in a beauty contest. He obtained a contract for her with Universal in 1920, and for 18 months she played minor parts. Then von Stroheim cast her as the heroine in his film THE MERRY-GO-ROUND, and she was acclaimed as the movie discovery of the year. A highly successful film career followed and among her films are included STELLA MARIS, LOVE ME AND THE WORLD IS MINE, THE DRUMS OF LOVE, THE LAST PERFORMANCE, and THE SHANNONS OF BROADWAY. Height 5 ft. 2 in. Fair hair and blue eyes.

**PICKFORD, Jack**—plate 102. Born on August 18, 1896, in Toronto, Canada. His real name was Smith and he is a younger brother of film star Mary Pickford. After attending St. Francis Military Academy in New York, he joined his sister in films. He was just 17 when he made HOME SWEET HOME with James Kirkwood and Donald Crisp. He made SEVENTEEN and then GREAT EXPECTATIONS with Louise Huff. Perhaps his greater role was in TOM SAWYER. Other of his films included BROWN OF HARVARD, EXIT SMILING, ALL SQUARE, and HIS MAJESTY BUNKER BEAN. He was married to Olive Thomas, who died of poisoning in Paris, Marilyn Miller, and then Mary Mulhern. They were all Ziegfeld girls. Height 5 ft. 7 in. Brown hair and eyes.

**PICKFORD, Mary**—plate 54, 56. Born on April 18, 1893, in Toronto, Canada. Real name Gladys Smith. Played child roles on the stage before starting her screen career in 1909 in a comedy produced by D. W. Griffith. She was known then under the name of Dorothy Nicholson and had only a small part in the film. She impressed Griffith, however, and he starred her in his next picture called THE VIOLIN MAKER OF CREMONA. Many successful films in rapid succession soon won the hearts of the public and Mary became affectionately known as "America's Sweetheart." Among her most famous films were TESS OF THE STORM COUNTRY, LITTLE ANNIE ROONIE, DADDY LONGLEGS, SPARROWS, POLLYANNA, DOROTHY VERNON OF HADDON HALL, and COQUETTE. Her first husband was film star Owen Moore, whom she divorced to marry Douglas Fairbanks, Sr. and, later, Buddy Rogers. Height 5 ft. Golden hair and blue eyes.

**POWER, SR., Tyrone**—plate 97. Born in London, England, on May 2, 1869. Emigrated to America with his family when a child. Made his stage *début* in New York in 1884. After a long and distinguished career on Broadway and on the London stage, he entered films with Selig in 1915. His first film was JOHN NEEDHAM'S DOUBLE. Other of his films included FOOTFALLS, BRAVEHEART, BRIDE OF THE STORM, and THE BIG TRAIL. He was scheduled for the starring role in THE MIRACLE MAN but died before the film was started. He was the father of Tyrone Power, great star of the sound era. Height 5 ft. 11 in. Grey hair and brown eyes. Died in 1919.

**PREVOST, Marie**—plate 65. Borne in Sarnia, Canada, in 1898, of French ancestry. Educated in a convent in Montreal. Entered films as a Mack Sennett bathing beauty, and within six months was playing leading roles in Mack Sennett comedies. She later starred in serious roles and made a tremendous hit in THE MARRIAGE CIRCLE in 1924. She gained the enviable reputation of being one of the best light comedy actresses in American films. Some of her starring vehicles were UP IN MABEL'S ROOM, GETTING GERTIE'S GARTER, LADIES OF LEISURE, SWEETHEARTS ON PARADE, and THE NIGHT BRIDE. Height 5 ft. 5 in. Dark hair and blue eyes. Was married to film star Kenneth Harlan. She died in 1937.

**PRICE, Kate**—plate 183. Born in Cork, Ireland, in 1877. She was a leading character actress on the stage before making her *début* in films in 1908. With the old Vitagraph company her first film was JACK FAT AND JIM SLIM. She starred in the KATE series for Vitagraph and then joined Keystone comedies. In later years she played straight character roles. Among her films were QUALITY STREET, THE SEA TIGER, GODLESS GIRL, DINTY with Colleen Moore, ORCHIDS AND ERMINE, and the Irish wife role in THE COHENS AND THE KELLYS with Charlie Murray, Vera Gordon, and George Sidney. A big and heavy woman, she weighed over 200 pounds. Height 5 ft. 11 in.

**PURVIANCE, Edna**—plate 48. Born in Nevada in 1896. She was a typist in San Francisco until 1915. On a trip to Hollywood, she visited a friend at the Essanay studio, was seen by the casting director and asked to make a screen test. Chaplin, with Essanay at the time, saw the test and chose her for his leading lady in THE CHAMPION. She was Chaplin's leading lady for several years. THE ADVENTURER, THE VAGABOND, THE IMMIGRANT, and THE GOLD RUSH, were among the films she made with him. In 1923, she made A WOMAN OF PARIS with Adolphe Menjou. Chaplin directed but did not feature in the film. Height 5 ft. 4 in. Blonde and blue eyes. She died in 1958.

## R

**RAY, Charles**—plate 114, 115. Born on March 15, 1891, in Jacksonville, Illinois. With a background of stage experience, he entered films in 1909 under Thomas H. Ince. His first picture was a civil war drama called THE FAVORITE SON. His biggest early hit was in THE COWARD with veteran actor Frank Keenan. Some of his early films included PEGGY with Billie Burke, HOME with Bessie Barriscale, FORTY FIVE MINUTES FROM BROADWAY, THE CLODHOPPER, and VANITY. He later specialised in country yokel roles in such successful films as PEACEFUL VALLEY, STRING BEANS, and NINE O'CLOCK TOWN. His best-known pictures of later years included THE COURTSHIP OF MILES STANDISH, GETTING GERTIE'S GARTER, GARDEN OF EDEN, THE GIRL I LOVE, and THE AUCTION BLOCK. Height 6 ft., with brown hair and eyes. He died in 1943.

**REID, Wallace**—plate 116, 117. Born in New York City on April 15, 1890, the son of Hal Reid, a well-known dramatic critic. Educated at the New Jersey Military Academy, he was first a journalist and then went on the New York stage. He joined Vitagraph in 1911 and worked in THE DEERSLAYER with Florence Turner. He made THE TEST with Frank Lloyd for Nestor in 1914. His big break came when D. W. Griffith cast him for a part in THE BIRTH OF A NATION. He made ENOCH ARDEN with Lillian Gish and CARMEN with Geraldine Farrar. He was Paramount's leading male star and for many years led all film popularity polls. His best remembered films are THE AFFAIRS OF ANATOLE, VALLEY OF THE GIANTS, DON'T TELL EVERYTHING with Gloria Swanson, NICE PEOPLE with Bebe Daniels and Conrad Nagel, THE DANCING FOOL, and PETER IBBETSON. Height 6 ft. 1 in. Fair hair and blue eyes. Married to film star Dorothy Davenport. A son and a daughter. Died January 18, 1923.

**RHODES, Billie**—plate 93. One of the most charming of early comediennes who became "The Nestor Girl" in 1914, soon after joining the company. She had made her film *début* the year before with Kalem. Typical of her hundred or more Nestor comedies was WHEN MARY TOOK THE COUNT, and WHAT COULD A POOR GIRL DO? with Lee Moran. Other films included A SEMINARY SCANDAL, SOME NURSE, and BEWARE OF BLONDES with Cullen Landis. She made PERILS OF THE SEA with the distinguished actor Carlyle Blackwell and shortly thereafter signed with Robertson-Cole. Among her films at that studio was THE BLUE BONNET. After proving herself to be a comedienne equally versatile and delightful as Mabel Normand, she retired from the screen at the height of her career. She was born in Salem, Oregon, on May 8, 1894. Height 5 ft. 2 in. Dark brown hair and eyes.

**ROBERTS, Theodore**—plate 216, 217. Born in San Francisco, California, on October 2, 1861. He was one of the veterans of the screen and perhaps the most famous character actor of the silent era. A close friend of Cecil B. DeMille, he played in virtually all the DeMille pictures including THE TEN COMMANDMENTS. Other film credits include MASK OF THE DEVIL, GOLD BRAID, THE CAT'S PAJAMAS, THE GIRL OF THE GOLDEN WEST, PUDDIN' HEAD WILSON, and THE AFFAIRS OF ANATOLE. Height 6 ft., with grey hair and blue eyes.

**ROGERS, Charles "Buddy"**—plate 214. Born on August 13, 1904, in Olathe, Kansas. Entered films via the Paramount school of film acting in 1925. His first picture was FASCINATING YOUTH. The title of that film describes Buddy very well—tall, dark, and handsome. His greatest success was WINGS with Clara Bow and Richard Arlen. His other films included YOUNG EAGLES, CLOSE HARMONY, RIVER OF ROMANCE, ABIE'S IRISH ROSE, and MY BEST GIRL with Mary Pickford, whom he later married. Height 6 ft. 1 in. Black wavy hair and brown eyes.

**ROLAND, Gilbert**—plate 131. Born in Chihuahua, Mexico, on December 11, 1903, of Spanish parents. His real name was Louis Antonio Damasco Alonsa. His father was a famous bull-fighter in Seville and continued his profession in Mexico. Gilbert Roland came to Hollywood in 1924 and, without previous theatrical experience, made his screen *début* in THE LADY WHO LIED. He then did some "doubling" for his countryman Ramon Novarro in THE MIDSHIPMAN. A strikingly handsome young man, he was given the leading role opposite Clara Bow in THE PLASTIC AGE in 1926. This was followed by the male lead in two of Norma Talmadge's films, CAMILLE and THE DOVE. Other starring vehicles included THE ROSE OF THE GOLDEN WEST with Mary Astor, THE WOMAN DISPUTED, THE LOVE MART with Billie Dove, and NEW YORK NIGHTS. Height 5 ft. 11 in. Black hair and brown eyes.

**ROLAND, Ruth**—plate 71. Born in San Francisco, California, in 1893. She was on the stage from the age of four and entered films at seventeen. She became known as "The Serial Queen" with the Kalem company. Among the film serials in which she starred were THE ADVENTURES OF RUTH, THE TIGER'S TRAIL, and HANDS UP. With Pathe, she then embarked upon a serial called WHO PAYS? with Henry King. Other of her films included THE RED CIRCLE with Philo McCullough, THE NEGLECTED WIFE, and THE MASKED WOMAN. Height 5 ft. 5 in. Auburn hair and blue eyes. She died in 1937.

**RUBENS, Alma**—plate 113. Born in San Francisco, California, in 1897. Before entering films she had considerable stage experience, including musical comedy. Her first film was THE HALF BREED with Douglas Fairbanks Sr. Perhaps her greatest film was HUMORESQUE in which she co-starred with the French star Gaston Glass. Other of her films included ENEMIES OF WOMEN with Lionel Barrymore, UNDER THE RED ROBE, THE GILDED BUTTERFLY, THE HEART OF SALOME, THE SHOW BOAT, and SIBERIA. She was the wife of screen star Ricardo Cortez. Height 5 ft. 6 in. Black hair and eyes. Died in 1931.

**RUSSELL, William**—plate 75. Born on April 12, 1886, in New York City. Was a child actor and as a young man became successful on Broadway in the portrayal of strong dramatic roles. Made his film *début* in 1911 in THE ROMAN SLAVE, a Biograph picture directed by D. W. Griffith. He made THE GARDEN OF LIES with Jane Cowl, A DIAMOND IN THE SKY with Lottie Pickford and Irving Cummings, and scored a great triumph in ANNA CHRISTIE with Blanche Sweet. Among his other films are THE BLUE EAGLE, THE ESCAPE, MADONNA OF AVENUE A, THE CRUSADER, and BEFORE MIDNIGHT. He also made a series of Westerns. Married to film star Helen Ferguson. Height 6 ft. 2 in. Black hair and eyes. Died in 1968.

## S

**ST. JOHN, Al**—plate 233. Born in Santa Ana, California, in 1894. He literally rode to success on the screen in the early silent era, for it was his antics on a bicycle that first attracted attention to this young man who was to become one of the screen's most popular comedians.

Among his films are included THAT'S MY MEAT, A FACE IN THE FOG, MIDNIGHT PHANTOM, THE OUTCASTS OF POKER FLAT, and PRIVATE AFFAIRS. Nineteen-thirteen found him already in films working in Keystone comedies with Ford Sterling, Charlie Murray, Hank Mann, Mack Swain, and Fatty Arbuckle. He was one of the original Keystone cops. Height 5 ft. 9 in. with fair hair and blue eyes. Died in 1963.

**SALISBURY, Monroe**—plate 132. Born in Wheeling, West Virginia, on May 8, 1879, he had many years of stage experience before entering films in the very early day of the industry. He was in THE SQUAW MAN with Dustin Farnham and Winifred Kingston in 1914, and, in the same year, starred with Bessie Barriscale in ROSE OF THE RANCHO. In 1915, he made THE GOOSE GIRL with Marguerite Clark, followed by RAMONA. With Universal he made a number of films, many of which were made in "snow" country. He was a convincing interpreter of rugged life in the Far North. Height 5 ft. 11½ in. Dark brown hair and eyes.

**SCHILDKRAUT, Joseph**—plate 106. Born in Vienna, Austria, on March 22, 1895, of a Hungarian father and a Romanian mother, and with grandparents who were Spanish and Turkish. Educated in music and dramatics and traveled all over the world with his famous actor father. He attained fame on the New York stage before D. W. Griffith signed him for the lead with the Gish girls in ORPHANS OF THE STORM. He had already made one film, his first, called THE SONG OF LOVE with Norma Talmadge. He was one of the stars in DeMille's THE KING OF KINGS. Other film credits include THE MISSISSIPPI GAMBLER, MEET THE PRINCE, NIGHT RIDE, another film with Norma Talmadge called THE DUST OF DESIRE, and SHOW BOAT. Height 5 ft. 11 in. Black hair and brown eyes. He died in 1964.

**SEMON, Larry**—plate 236. Born in West Plains, Missouri, on Arril 16, 1890, of theatrical parents. His father was known to theatergoers as Zera the Great—a famous magician. Larry went to art school and became a cartoonist on the New York Sun. When his comedy ideas caught the attention of Vitagraph, they signed him as a comic. His best known pictures were THE WIZARD OF OZ, THE PERFECT CLOWN, SIMPLE LIFE, UNDERWORLD, SPUDS, and THE GIRL IN THE LIMOUSINE. Height 5 ft. 2 in. Light brown hair and blue eyes. He died on October 8, 1928, at the age of thirty-eight and at the peak of his career as one of America's most popular comedians.

**SHERMAN, Lowell**—plate 53. Born in San Francisco, California, on October 11, 1885. Before entering films he was one of the leading actors on the Broadway stage. He was the star of David Belasco's GIRL OF THE GOLDEN WEST. D. W. Griffith brought him to the screen in his WAY DOWN EAST with Lillian Gish and Richard Barthelmess. He played a leading role in MONSIEUR BEAUCAIRE with Valentino, and a long series of films followed including LAWFUL LARCENY, EVIDENCE, CONVOY, and SATAN AND SABLES. Height 6 ft. Dark hair and eyes. Was married to screen star Pauline Garon. Died in 1934.

**SIEGEMANN, George**—plate 110. Born in New York City in 1878. He was educated at Boston University. After a long and successful stage career he made his film *début* with D. W. Griffith. His role in THE BIRTH OF A NATION was highly praised and Griffith then cast him in "heavy" parts in his two spectacles, INTOLERANCE and HEARTS OF THE WORLD. He usually played the villain and he looked the part. His film credits include THE MERRY-GO-ROUND, SCARAMOUCHE, OLIVER TWIST, HOTEL IMPERIAL, THE CAT AND THE CANARY, and THE MAN WHO LAUGHS—all famous titles in film history and George Siegemann helped to make them so. Height 6 ft. 2 in., with dark hair and eyes. He died in 1929.

**SPARKS, Ned**—plate 227. Born in St. Thomas, Canada, on June 17, 1884. In 1903, took part in the Alaskan gold rush but, failing to find gold, he took a job in a Dawson City dance hall as an entertainer. This was the beginning of his stage career which continued for many years before he entered films. His character parts in American films delighted audiences. His "dead pan" face and his eternal cigar highly enhanced his comedy roles. His comedy was the sophisticated type delivered with suave expertise. Among his films were THE CANARY MURDER CASE, DOUBLE CROSS ROADS, NOTHING BUT THE TRUTH, STREET GIRL, and LOVE COMES ALONG. Height 5 ft. 10 in. Black hair and brown eyes. Very slenderly built. He died in 1957.

**STANDING, Wyndham**—plate 61. Born on August 23, 1880, in London, England. Son of Herbert Standing, the well-known English actor. Made his stage *début* in 1899, and for some years worked with Sir Henry Irving. Made his screen *début* in Hollywood in 1914 and played in more than one hundred American films. He co-starred with most of the great stars of the day and among his films are included PAID IN FULL, EARTHBOUND, THE JOURNEY'S END, BILLY THE KID, and with Elsie Ferguson in ROSE OF THE WORLD. Height 6 ft. 1 in. Brown hair and grey eyes.

**STARKE, Pauline**—plate 122. Born on January 10, 1900, in Joplin, Missouri. She started in films in 1916 in small parts and it was not until she made THE SHOES THAT DANCED in 1918, that she attained recognition. Her fragile type of beauty was her great appeal and, together with her sensitive ability to act, brought her stardom. One of her greatest films was HELL'S KITCHEN. Other film credits include WAR PAINT, CAPTAIN SALVATION, STREETS OF SHANGHAI, and LOVE'S BLINDNESS. Height 5 ft. 4 in. Brown hair and grey eyes.

**STEWART, Anita**—plate 91. Born on February 17, 1896, in Brooklyn, New York. Educated at the same school and was friendly with the Talmadge sisters. She was trained for a musical career, but entered pictures upon the urging of her brother-in-law, Ralph Ince, the film producer. She made her screen *début* in an Ince film for Vitagraph called THE WOOD VIOLET. She worked with Earle Williams in TWO WOMEN and again in MY LADY'S SLIPPER. In 1919, she made VIRTUOUS WIVES with Conway Tearle, and in that same year scored with a great hit of its day IN OLD KENTUCKY. Other films include PLAYTHINGS OF DESTINY with Walter McGrail, THE COMBAT with Wilfred Lytell, and BAREE, SON OF KAZAN, in which she played an Indian girl. Height 5 ft. 5 in. Dark brown hair and eyes. Died in 1961.

**STEWART, Roy**—plate 189. Born on October 17, 1884, in San Diego, California. Was one of the pioneers of Western drama. He co-starred with Mary Pickford in one of her early films and went on to cowboy stardom in such successes as IN OLD ARIZONA, THE VIKING, THE GREAT DIVIDE, FIGHTING WESTWARD, THE DEVIL DODGER with Gilbert Roland, and PONY EXPRESS. He then surprised everyone by appearing in white tie and tails with Kathlyn Williams and Leatrice Joy in JUST A WIFE for Selznick. A very fine actor. Height 6 ft. 2 in. Black hair and brown eyes.

**STONE, Lewis S.**—plate 83. Born on November 15, 1879, in Worcester, Massachusetts. Attended Barnard Military Academy and served in the Spanish American War in 1898. He had a long career in the legitimate theatre before entering films in 1915. His first film was HONOUR'S ALTAR in which he co-starred with Bessie Barriscale. Several starring roles with the Essanay company followed after which he returned to the Army as a Major in the First World War. He returned to films after the war and to a long and very successful career. Among his film credits are HELD BY THE ENEMY with Jack Holt, THE PRISONER OF ZENDA, SCARAMOUCHE, THE TRIAL OF MARY DUGAN, and his famous role of the Judge in the ANDY HARDY series. Height 5 ft. 10 in. Grey hair and blue eyes. Died in 1953.

**STONEHOUSE, Ruth**—plate 74. Born in Elkhart, Indiana, in 1894. She had stage experience as a classical dancer before entering films. Her first studio was Essanay and in 1911 she made THE PAPERED DOOR with Pat O'Malley. She was the top star at Essanay for a number of years. She co-starred with Francis X. Bushman in THE SPY'S DEFEAT and in BLOOD WILL TELL. Other credits included PEG OF THE RING, BROKEN BARRIERS, PARLOR BEDROOM AND BATH, and ERMINE AND RHINESTONES. She had an important role in BLOOD AND SAND with Rudolph Valentino. Height 5 ft. 3 in. Blonde and blue eyes.

**STOREY, Edith**—plate 38. One of the pioneers of motion pictures. She was born on January 21, 1888, in Chicago, Illinois, and was a professional in the theater when she entered films with the old Melies company. With Norma Talmadge and Lillian Walker, she made a delightful early film called THE TROUBLESOME STEPDAUGHTERS. Under contract to Vitagraph, she made THE ISLAND OF REGENERATION with Antonio Moreno. Another film with Antonio Moreno followed called ALADDIN FROM BROADWAY. Among her many other films was AN ENEMY OF THE KIND with E. H. Sothern, THE CHRISTIAN with Earle Williams, DUST OF EGYPT, and AS THE SUN WENT DOWN. Height 5 ft. 6 in. Black hair and brown eyes.

**SUMMERVILLE, Slim**—plate 241. Born on July 12, 1892, in Albuquerque, New Mexico. Was a coffin maker, a lumberjack, a bricklayer, and a furniture maker before starting his film career in the old Keystone days. He became one of America's most beloved comedians and scored highly in such films as THE CHINESE PARROT, ALL QUIET ON THE WESTERN FRONT, THE KING OF JAZZ, FIFTY ROADS TO TOWN, and TIGER ROSE. He was 6 ft. 3 in., tall and slender. Brown hair and eyes. Real name was George Summerville. Died in 1946.

**SWANSON, Gloria**—plate 196. Born in Chicago, Illinois, on March 27, 1899. Her father was a sea captain and Gloria spent many years travelling with him. She received an offer to work in films from Essanay and made her first film with them. She then joined Keystone and appeared in Mack Sennett comedies. She was one of the original Mack Sennett bathing girls. Her big break came with Jesse Lasky and Paramount where she was the studio's leading female star for many years. Her films include THE AFFAIRS OF ANATOLE with Wallace Reid, MADAME SANS-GENE, SADIE THOMPSON, BLUEBEARD'S EIGHTH WIFE, MALE AND FEMALE, and DON'T CHANGE YOUR HUSBAND. She was married to Wallace Beery and, later, to the Marquis de Falaise. Height 5 ft. 3 in. Reddish brown hair and blue eyes.

**SWEET, Blanche**—plates 14, 15. Born on June 18, 1896, in Chicago, Illinois. She made her first stage appearance at the age of three in THE BATTLE OF THE STRONG. She was just fourteen when she made her screen *début* with Vitagraph in a film called A CORNER OF THE WHEAT. At that time she went by the name of Daphne Wayne. In 1912, she made two films with Henry B. Walthall—JUDITH AND BETHULIA and THE AVENGING CONSCIENCE. She was teamed with Thomas Meighan in two films THE SECRET SIN and THE SOWERS. Among her films with D. W. Griffith was THE ESCAPE with Owen Moore and Bobby Harron. Other of her legion of films were QUINCY ADAMS SAWYER with Lon Chaney, THE PALACE OF THE KING, RAGAMUFFIN, SIMPLE SOULS, BLUEBEARD'S SEVEN WIVES with Ben Lyon, and THE UNPARDONABLE SIN. Undoubtedly her greatest film was ANNA CHRISTIE with William Russell, George Marion, and Marie Dressler. Height 5 ft. 3 in. Golden hair and blue eyes. She was married to Marshall Neilan.

## T

**TALMADGE, Constance**—plate 52. Born in Brooklyn, New York, on April 19, 1897. She was sixteen when she made her *début* with the old Vitagraph company in 1914. Her first big part was in the D. W. Griffith fllm INTOLERANCE. She made LESSONS IN LOVE with Kenneth Harlan, THE DANGEROUS MAID, EAST IS WEST, THE GOLDFISH, THE HONEYMOON with Earle Fox, and WEDDING BELLS with Harrison Ford. More hits followed, among them THE DUCHESS OF BUFFALO, VENUS, and HER SISTER FROM PARIS. She became one of America's top box-office attractions. Height 5 ft. 6 in. Blonde with brown eyes. She was a sister of Natalie and Norma Talmadge, both screen stars.

**TALMADGE, Natalie**—plate 199. Born on June 17, 1898, in Brooklyn, New York. A sister of Constance and Norma, she was given a small part in INTOLERANCE by D. W. Griffith which gave her a start on a film career. She became associated with Fatty Arbuckle in his comedies and played the lead opposite him in THE BELL BOY. Later, she was under contract to First National where she starred in a series of films. THE PASSION FLOWER was perhaps her best film. Other film credits included OUR HOSPITALITY, LOVE IS BEAUTIFUL, and ONCE AND FOREVER. She was married to the famous film comedian Buster Keaton. Height 5 ft. 6 in. with brown hair and eyes. She died in 1969.

**TALMADGE, Norma**—plates 130, 160. Born on May 2, 1895, in Niagara Falls, New York. Made her screen *début* in 1910 with Vitagraph. Her first important film for them was A DIXIE MOTHER with Carlyle Blackwell. She played in more than 250 films in her career and was undoubtedly one of the greatest stars of the silent screen. Screen credits include CAMILLE, SECRETS, ASHES OF VENGENCE, THE GARDEN OF ALLAH, THE DOVE, KIKI, and SMILING THROUGH. Height 5 ft. 4 in. Dark brown hair and brown eyes. Was a sister of Natalie and Constance Talmadge. Married to film producer Joseph Schenck. Later married to Georgie Jessel. Died in 1957.

**TAYLOR, Estelle**—plate 200. Born in Wilmington, Delaware, in 1899, she was a stage celebrity before entering films. She came into prominence in a film called WHILE NEW YORK SLEEPS with Marc MacDermott. Another film BLIND WIVES, also with Marc MacDermott followed. Then Cecil B. DeMille selected her for an important role in THE TEN COMMANDMENTS. Followed MONTE CRISTO with John Gilbert, and a co-starring part with John Barrymore in DON JUAN. A very beautiful and talented actress, she was 5 ft. 5 in. tall and had dark brown hair and eyes. Married to pugilist Jack Dempsey. She died in 1958.

**TELLEGEN, Lou**—plate 59. Born in Athens, Greece, in 1881, of Greek and Dutch parents. He was educated in Holland and began his professional career on the Paris stage. He became a *protégè* of the great Sarah Bernhardt and was her leading man. He persuaded her to appear in a film when motion pictures were first produced in France. He later toured America with her. He remained in America and became a naturalised citizen. When Jesse Lasky brought Sarah Bernhardt to America to make QUEEN ELIZABETH, Tellegen was chosen as her leading man in the film. He made a great many films, among them MARRIED ALIVE, THREE BAD MEN, GREATER THAN MARRIAGE, and WOMANPOWER. Married first to Geraldine Farrar, the opera singer and film star, and then to Nina Romano, and later to Katarine Casanova, a Ziegfeld Follies beauty. Height 6 ft. 2 in. Brown hair and eyes. He died in 1934.

**TERRY, Alice**—plate 171. Born in Elkhart, Indiana, in 1899. Her real name was Alice Taafe. She made NOT MY SISTER with William Desmond and Bessie Barriscale in 1916, and then her big break came when she was chosen for the lead opposite Rudolph Valentino in THE FOUR HORSEMEN OF THE APOCALYPSE. She also made THE CONQUERING POWER with Valentino. Then, another great role in THE PRISONER OF ZENDA with Ramon Novarro. She co-starred with Novarro in two other films—WHERE THE PAVEMENT ENDS and THE ARAB. She made THE GREAT DIVIDE with Conway Tearle and Wallace Beery, and MARE NOSTRUM with Antonio Moreno, among many films including SCARAMOUCHE, THE GARDEN OF ALLAH, and THE THREE PASSIONS. Married to film director Rex Ingram. Of Welsh extraction with auburn hair and blue eyes. Height 5 ft. 2 in.

**THOMAS, Olive**—plate 103. Born in Charleroc, Pennsylvania, on October 16, 1898. Had a dancing career and rose to fame in the Ziegfeld Follies. She was acclaimed by the artist Harrison Fisher, as the most beautiful woman in the world. She made her film *début* in 1918 and remained in films until her untimely death in Paris from food poisoning two years later. She was married to film star Jack Pickford who was with her when she died. Her films included OUT YONDER, UPSTAIRS AND DOWN, THE SPITE BRIDE, and FOOTLIGHTS AND SHADOWS. Height 5 ft. 2 in. Brown hair and blue eyes.

**TINCHER, Fay**—plate 107. Born in Topeka, Kansas, on July 27, 1889. Fay Tincher created a new type of screen character which might be described as the "gum-chewing" girl. She was actually the first female commedienne in films. After an important role in D. W. Griffith's film THE BATTLE OF THE SEXES, she went exclusively into comedy roles and made a long succession of screen comedies. She made a total of over 300 films in the early days of the silent era—mostly two-reelers. Height 5 ft. 5 in. Dark brown hair and eyes.

**TURNER, Florence**—plate 19. Born in New York City on January 6, 1887. Began a stage career in her early youth and at eighteen had already built a reputation as a fine dramatic actress. She appeared with Sir Henry Irving on the New York stage in ROBESPIERRE. She made her film *début* with Vitagraph in 1907 and, together with Florence Lawrence, was the first actress to be known as a film star. The early matinee idol Maurice Costello was very often her leading man. One of her early films was ST. ELMO. Then came THE DEERSLAYER with Harry Morey. Other film credits include FOOLS GOLD, EAST IS EAST, JEALOUSY, and A TALE OF TWO CITIES. She also made a number of films in England and appeared on the London stage. Height 5 ft. 2 in. Dark brown hair and eyes. Died in Hollywood in 1946.

## V

**VALENTINO, Rudolph**—plates 161, 162, 163. Born on May 10, 1895, in Castellaneta, Italy. His mother was French and his father was a captain in the Italian cavalry. Educated in a military academy in Italy. He emigrated to New York at the age of eighteen where he became an exhibition ballroom dancer and won great fame and popularity as such. He became acquainted with film star Norman Kerry in New York and Kerry persuaded him to try the Hollywood films. In Hollywood, Kerry introduced him to the film writer June Mathis who secured for him the part of Julio in THE FOUR HORSEMEN OF THE APOCALYPSE. The film became one of the greatest box-office smashes of all time and Valentino found himself a star. Among his films were THE SHEIK, BLOOD AND SAND, THE EAGLE, COBRA, THE SAINTED DEVIL, SON OF THE SHEIK, MONSIEUR BEAUCAIRE, and CAMILLE. He died in 1926 at the age of thirty-one. Height 5 ft. 11 in. Black hair and brown eyes.

## W

**WALKER, Lillian**—plate 29. Born in Brooklyn, New York, on April 21, 1888. Of Swedish descent, her real name was Lillian Wolke. After getting her start as an actress on the stage, she made her film *début* in the early days of silent pictures. In 1912, she made THE TROUBLESOME STEPDAUGHTER with Norma Talmadge and Edith Storey for Vitagraph. This studio then teamed her with Earle Williams and they made a series of films together. Among her film credits are included KITTY MACKAY, THE BLUE ENVELOPE with Adolphe Menjou, THE NEW SECRETARY, and THE MILLION DOLLAR REWARD. Height 5 ft. 2 in. Blonde hair and blue eyes.

**WALSH, George**—plate 152. Born on March 16, 1892, in New York City. Was well known on the Broadway stage when he made his film *début* in 1915. Being very handsome in a completely masculine way and with a splendid body, he became known as an athletic star. He made DON QUIXOTE with Fay Tincher and De Wolf Hopper in 1915. ROSITA with Mary Pickford was one of his big films, as was VANITY FAIR with Eleanor Boardman and Mabel Ballin. Other of his films included THE PRINCE OF BROADWAY, THE LOVE TEST, SLAVE OF DESIRE with Bessie Love and Carmel Myers, MAN OF QUALITY, THE BEAST, ISLE OF DESIRE, and THE SHARK. Height 5 ft. 11½ in. Dark brown hair and eyes.

**WALTHALL, Henry B.**—plate 79. Born on March 16, 1879, in Shelby City, Alabama. Educated in law, but went on the stage immediately after graduation. Was induced to act for the screen by D. W. Griffith and played featured parts in several Griffith films before being cast for the role of "The Little Colonel" in THE BIRTH OF A NATION. This film made him a top star. He costarred with Kathlyn Williams in SINGLE WIVES and with Lois Wilson in HIS ROBE OF HONOR. He made THE BARRIER with Lionel Barrymore and THE ROAD TO MANDALAY with Lon Chaney. Other film credits included GHOSTS, THE RAVEN, THE STRANGE CASE OF MARY PAGE, THE UNKNOWN PURPLE, THE SCARLET LETTER, and THE BRIDGE OF SAN LUIS REY. Height 5 ft. 6 in. Black hair greying and brown eyes. Died in June 1936.

**WALTON, Gladys**—plate 120. The girl who made UNTAMEABLE and THE GIRL WHO RAN WILD was born on May 30, 1896, in Nashville, Tennessee. She had beauty, charm, and a wonderful smile that delighted film-goers. Actually, she was a forerunner of Clara Bow. Among her films were TOP O' THE MORNING, PINK TIGHTS, both for Universal, JUST FOR TWO, WAY UP NORTH, and her unforgettable role in SECOND HAND ROSE. Height 5 ft. 4 in. Brown hair and eyes.

**WARD, Fanny**—plate 76. Born in St. Louis, Missouri, on June 22, 1875. She made her stage *début* at the age of fifteen and achieved success in musical comedy. She went to London in 1894 where she was a West End favourite for many years. In 1900, she married Joseph Lewis, a multi-millionaire. She became noted for her diamonds and when she returned to the stage her diamonds were valued in the millions. Returning to America, she made her film *début* in 1913 in THE MARRIAGE OF KITTY. Several years of film success followed and, although between forty and fifty years of age, she could pass for early twenties on the screen. Among her films were THE CHEAT, SALLY TEMPLE, THE SCHOOL FOR HUSBANDS, COMMON CLAY, and TENNESSEE'S PARTNER. Just 5 ft. tall. Fair hair and blue eyes.

**WARNER, H. B.**—plate 37. Born in London, England, on October 26, 1876. Son of the famous English actor Charles Warner. After a long stage career in England, he came to Broadway in 1905 to star in the stage play MERELY MARY with Eleanor Robson. He remained to become a favourite of both the American stage and screen. Jesse Lasky signed him in 1914 and he began a truly fabulous screen career. To name a few of the greats —the role of Jeseus in Cecil B. DeMille's THE KING OF KINGS, ZAZA with Gloria Swanson, THE DIVINE LADY with Corinne Griffith, THE TEMPTRESS with Greta Garbo, ONE HOUR BEFORE DAWN with Anna Q. Nilsson, his great role in SORRELL AND SON, and in LOST HORIZON with Ronald Colman. Other of his films included THE BEGGAR OF CAWNPORE, THE DANGER TRAIL, THE MAN WHO TURNED WHITE, and CHANCE MEETING. Height 6 ft. 1 in. with fair hair and blue eyes.

**WASHBURN, Bryant**—plate 137. Born in Chicago, Illinois, on April 28, 1889. Real name was Dwight Ludlow. After a successful acting career on the Chicago and New York stages, he joined the films in 1911. Under contract to Essanay, he played leading roles with that studio for six years. Perhaps his first important film was THE PROMISED LAND with Marguerite Clayton. BLIND VIRTUE, SKINNER'S DRESS SUIT, and HONEYMOON FLATS followed. Perhaps his greatest was RUPERT OF HENTZAU in which he played the title role with an all star cast including Bert Lytell, Elaine Hammerstein, and Lew Cody. He made TIL I COME BACK TO YOU, a war picture with Monte Blue, SIX BEST CELLARS with Wanda Hawley, and IT PAYS TO ADVERTISE with Lois Wilson and Walter Hiers. Height 5 ft. 11 in. Curly dark brown hair and brown eyes. Married Mabel Forest and has a son and a daughter.

**WHITE, Pearl**—plate 10. Born on March 4, 1889, in Greenridge, Missouri. She made her stage *début* at the age of six as little Eva in UNCLE TOM'S CABIN. At thirteen, she joined a travelling circus and became a bareback rider. Her first films were with the Powers Film Company in New York, where she made her first movie in 1910. The following year she joined the Lubin company in Philadelphia for a brief period and then returned to New York to do a series of comedies for the Crystal Film Company. In 1914, she joined Pathe where she made her famous serial THE PERILS OF PAULINE. Crane Wilbur was her leading man and Paul Panzer supported. This was followed by THE EXPLOITS OF ELAINE in thirty-six parts. She made seven other serials and then a number of feature films for Pathe and Fox. Her final serial PLUNDER was made in 1922. In France, she made THE PERILS OF PARIS and a feature film called TERROR. She remained in Paris and made it her home. Undoubtedly the greatest box-office attraction in the early American cinema, Pearl White never set foot in California. All her films were made either in the East or in France. Height 5 ft. 6 in. Honey blonde hair and blue eyes. She died on August 4, 1938.

**WILBUR, Crane**—plate 11. Born in Athens, New York, on July 28, 1887. His first love was the stage where he spent twelve years and gained top stature on Broadway before entering films. He made his film *début* in the very early days of the motion picture, starting with Pathe in New York. One of the veterans of the screen, he co-starred with Pearl White in many of her serials, and worked with most of the other great stars of the time. One of his best feature films was a Civil War tale called THE HEART OF MARYLAND in which he was supported by Catherine Calvert. Other films included ROAD OF STRIFE, THE CORSAIR, THE FINGER OF JUSTICE, and ALL LOVE EXCELLING. Dark brown hair and eyes. Height 5 ft. 10½ in.

**WILLIAMS, Earle**—plate 28. Born on February 28, 1880, in Sacramento, California. Made his stage *début* in 1901 and had ten years of theater before entering films in 1911. One of his first films was THE ARTIST'S MADONNA with Lillian Walker. Two films co-starring Anita Stewart followed—THE GODDESS and MY LADY'S SLIPPER. His next was THE SKYROCKET with Peggy Hopkins Joyce. He made THE SEAL OF SILENCE, THE MAN FROM DOWNING STREET, ARSENE LUPIN, THE FORTUNE HUNTER, and A ROGUE'S ROMANCE with Rudolph Valentino. Other films included THE ANCIENT MARINER, and DIPLOMACY. Height 5 ft. 11 in. Black hair and blue eyes. He died in 1927.

**WILLIAMS, Kathlyn**—plate 9. Born in Butte, Montana, on November 20, 1885. She was a stage actress of considerable stature before she made her first film in 1910 for Selig called THE FIRE CHIEF'S DAUGHTER. She made a series of films including A MANSION OF MYSTERY with Harold Lockwood for Selig. She came on strong with William Farnham in THE SPOILERS and followed with THE NE'ER-DO-WELL. She made two films with Wallace Reid—CLARENCE and BIG TIM-

BER, and JUST A WIFE with Roy Stewart and Leatrice Joy. Some of her other films were CONRAD IN HIS QUEST FOR YOUTH, SWEET LADY PEGGY, REDEEMING LOVE, and THE HIGHWAY OF HOPE. It must be mentioned that back in the early days of her film career Selig starred her in the "first" movie serial ever made, called THE ADVENTURES OF KATHLYN. Height 5 ft. 6 in. Golden blonde hair and blue eyes. Died on September 23, 1960.

**WOLHEIM, Louis**—plate 178. Born in New York City on March 28, 1880. Educated at Cornell University where he played football on the university team. After obtaining B.A. and M.A. degrees he became a professor of mathematics at Cornell. He was coaxed onto the New York stage by Lionel Barrymore and achieved great success in Eugene O'Neill's THE HAIRY APE. Began his career as a pugilist in a film called LITTLE OLD NEW YORK. Other film credits include WHAT PRICE GLORY, THE WOLF SONG, ALL QUIET ON THE WESTERN FRONT, HELL'S ANGELS, and SORRELL AND SON. Height 5 ft. 10 in. Brown hair and eyes. He was the screen's ugliest and meanest villain. Died in 1931.

## Y

**YOUNG, Clara Kimball**—plate 81. Born in Chicago, Illinois, on February 19, 1882. Her parents were show people and she was a descendant of Mrs. Siddons, the famous English actress. She was on the stage at the age of three and her entire life was spent in the theatre, either on the stage or in films. Vitagraph signed her in 1912 and starred her with Hal Reid (father of Wallace Reid) in CARDINAL WOLSEY. She then made MY OFFICIAL WIFE, BEAU BRUMMEL, and TRILBY. Other film credits included CAMILLE, THE DEEP PURPLE with Milton Sills, THE EYES OF YOUTH with Valentino, ENTER MADAME with Elliott Dexter, THE WOMAN OF BRONZE with John Bowers, and THE CLAW with Jack Holt and Milton Sills. Black hair and eyes. Height 5 ft. 4 in. Married to James Young the actor-director. She died in 1960.

Top Row Left to Right: Lionel Barrymore, Irene Castle, John Barrymore.
Bottom Row Left to Right: Joan Crawford, William Boyd, Mary Astor.

Top Row Left to Right: Ricardo Cortez, Constance Bennett, Ralph Graves.
Bottom Row Left to Right: Richard Dix, Pauline Starke, George Brent.

**Top Row Left to Right: Gary Cooper, Lupe Velez, C. Aubrey Smith.**
**Bottom Row Left to Right: May MacAvoy, Victor McLaglen, Dolores Del Rio.**

**Top Row Left to Right: Mae West, Warner Baxter, Marlene Dietrich.**
**Bottom Row Left to Right: Clark Gable, Bette Davis, Ronald Colman.**

Top Row Left to Right: Maurice Costello, Florence Lawrence, Broncho Billy Anderson.
Bottom Row Left to Right: Pearl White, John Bunny, Flora Finch

**Top Row Left to Right: William Farnham, Florence Turner, Francis X. Bushman.**
**Bottom Row Left to Right: Mae Marsh, Robert Harron, Ruth Roland.**

**Top Row Left to Right: Larry Semon, Charlie Murray, Walter Hiers**
**Bottom Row Left to Right: Ford Sterling, Bobby Vernon, Buster Keaton.**

Top Row Left to Right: Betty Blythe, Charles Ray, Ethel Clayton.
Bottom Row Left to Right: Frank Mayo, Fay Tincher, Theodore Roberts.

# PART TWO

**1 Wallace Reid**

2 **Wallace Reid**

**3 Wallace Reid**

4 Mary Brian

**5 Jack Finch**

**6 Reginald Denny**

**7 Corrine Griffith**

**8 Herbert Rawlinson**

**9 Lila Lee**

**10 Ann Dvorak**

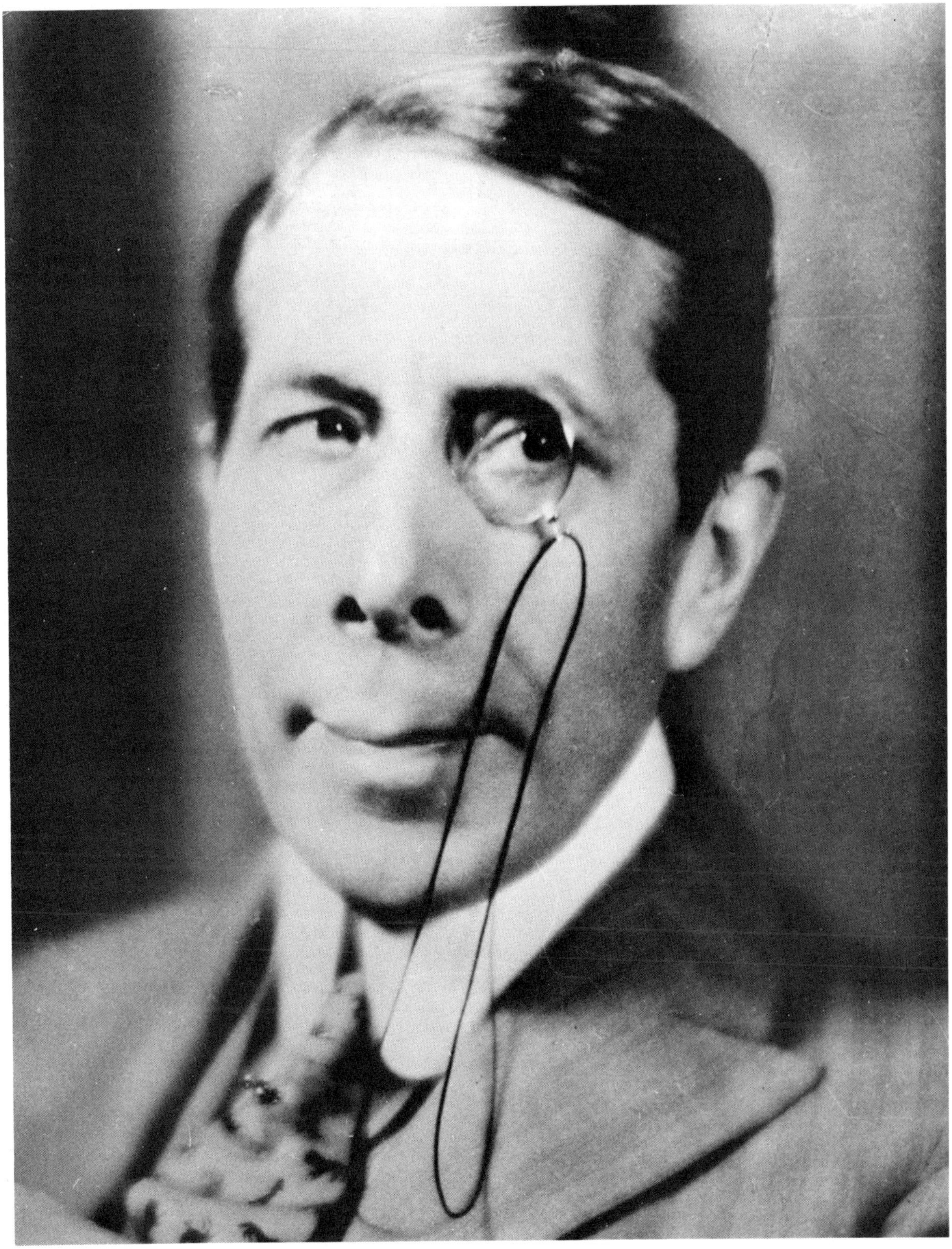

**11 George Arliss**

**12 Lois Wilson**

**13 Jack Holt**

**14 Lily Damita**

**15 Lloyd Hughes**

**16 Florence Vidor**

**17 Alex B. Francis**

**18 Betty Bronson**

19 John Harron

**20 Ivan Lebedeff**

**21 Mary Astor**

22 Claire Windsor

23 Robert Warwick

24 **Ethel Barrymore**

**25 Ivor Novello**

**26 Lionel Barrymore**

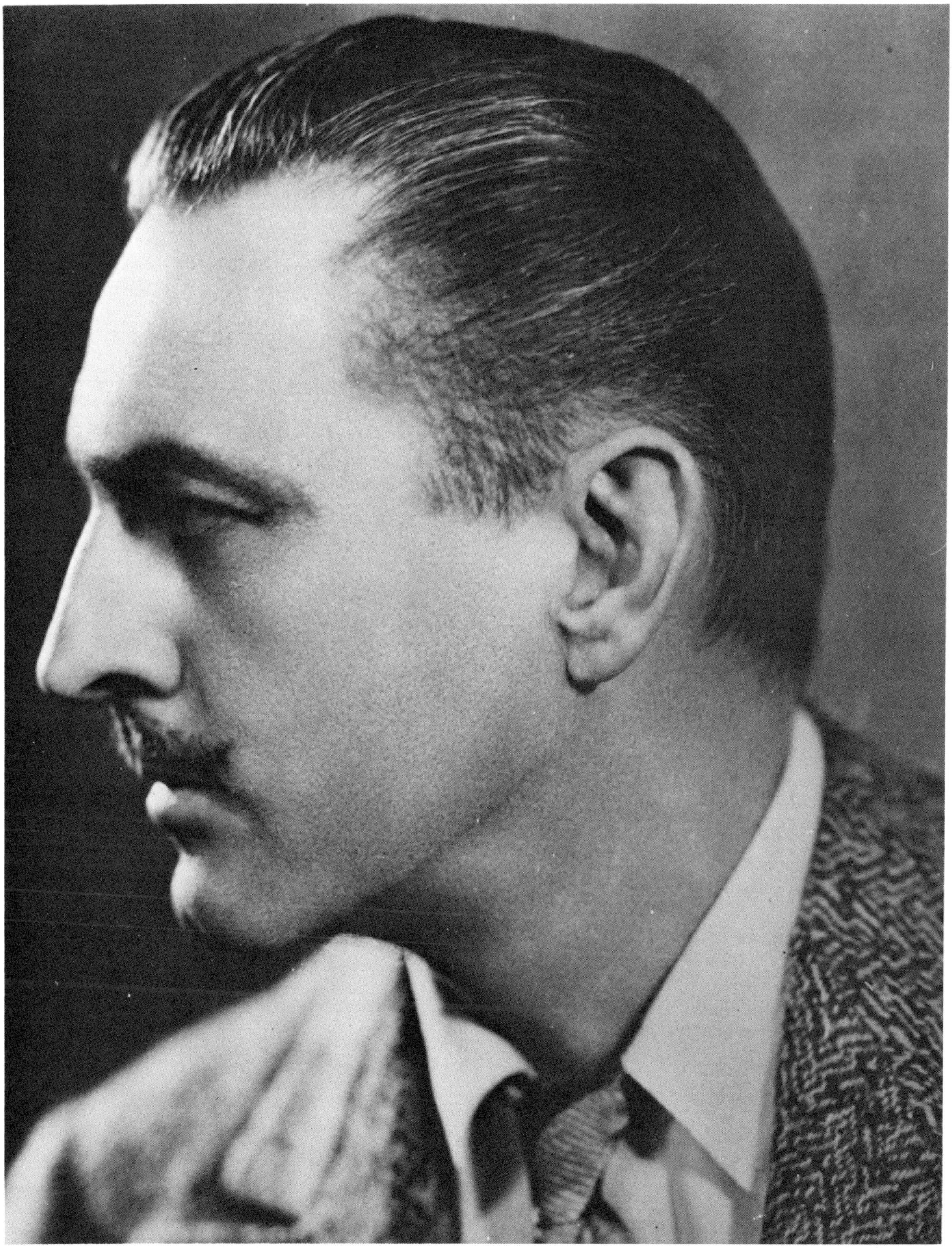

**27 John Barrymore**

28 **Mildred Davis**

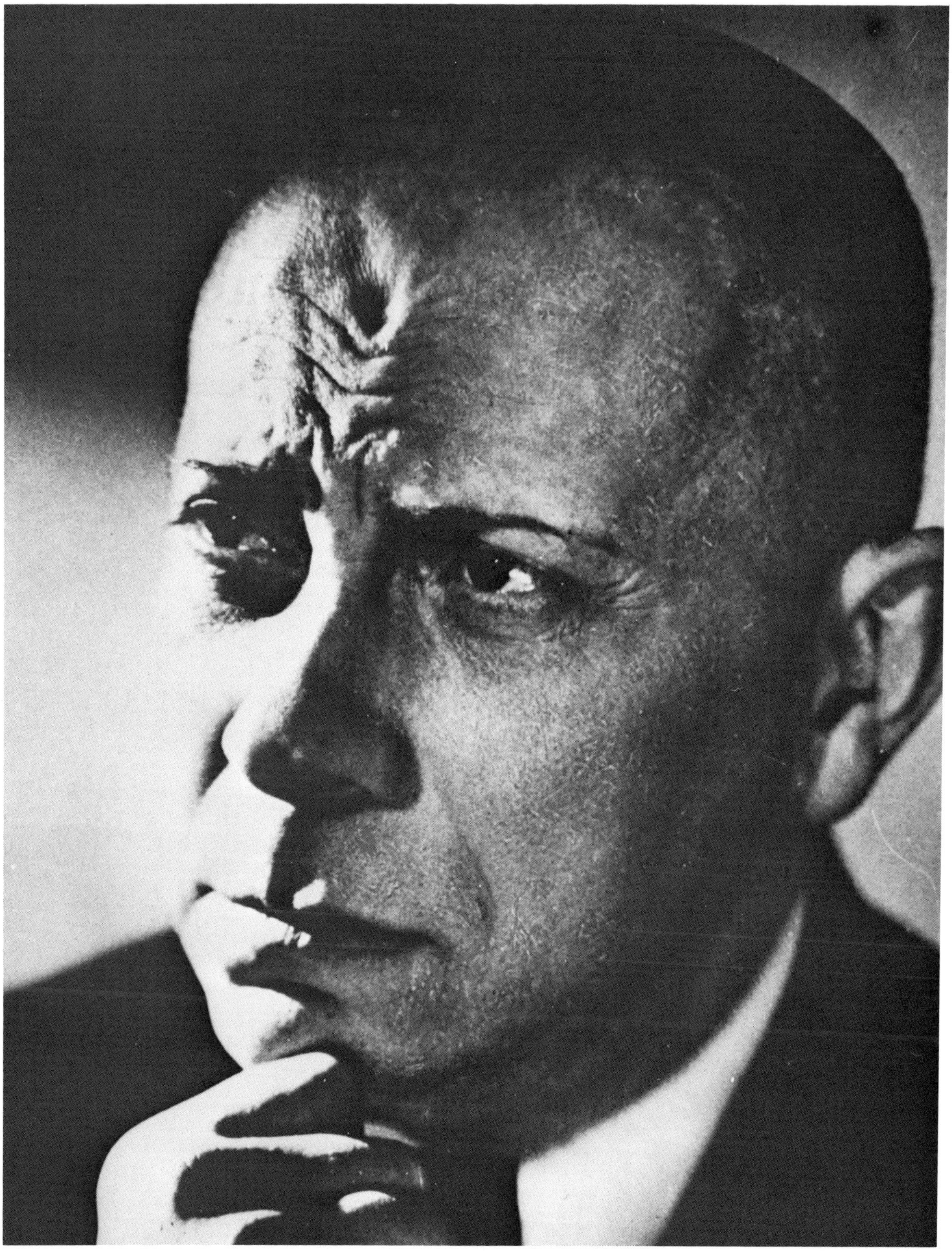

**29 Eric von Stroheim**

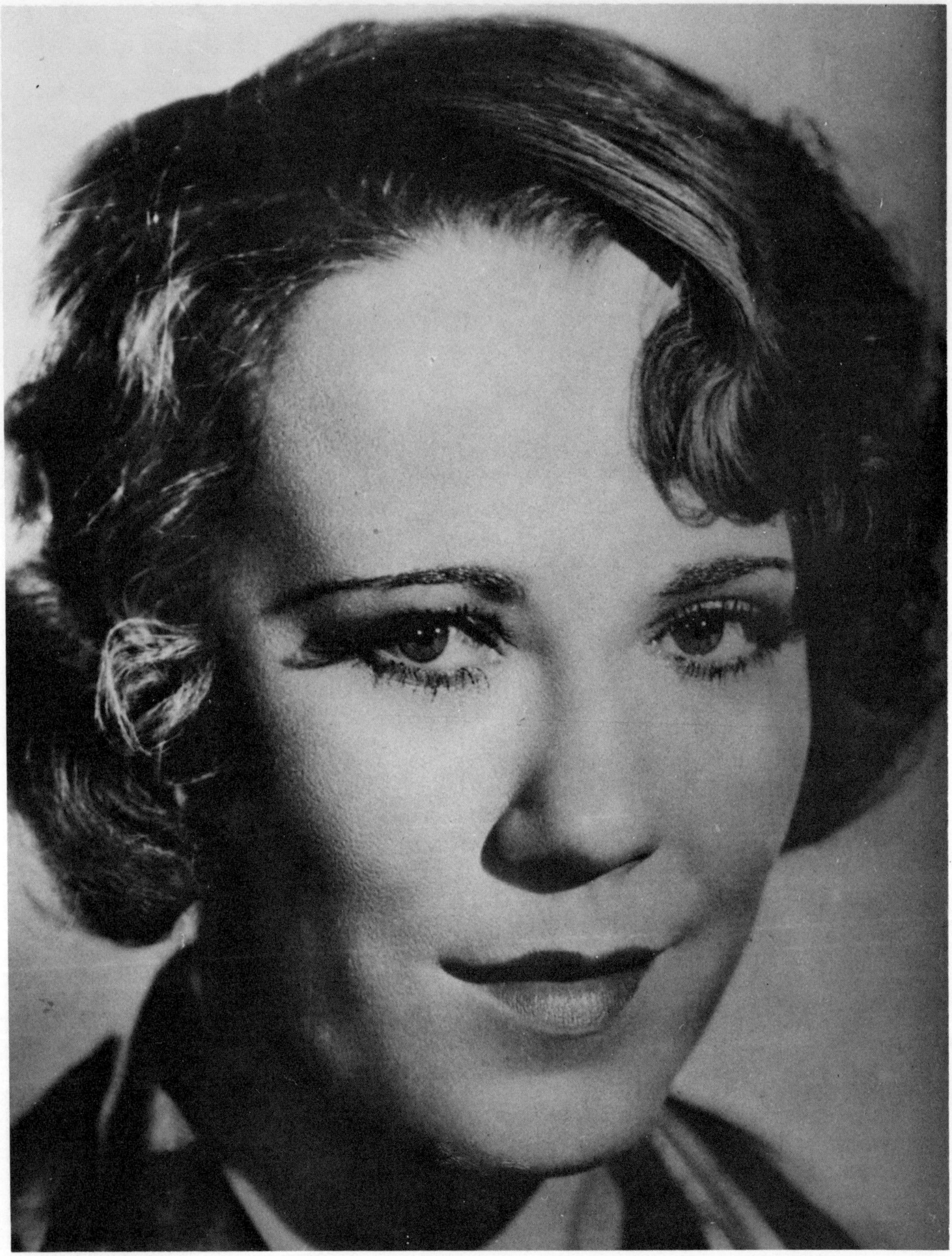

**30 Louise Fazenda**

**31 Harry Carey**

**32 William S. Hart**

33 William S. Hart

**34 Tom Mix**

**35 Tom Mix**

**36 Jack Hoxie**

**37 Gene Autry**

**38 Hoot Gibson**

**39 Tex Ritter**

**40 Walter Miller**

**41 Ken Maynard**

42 Fred Thompson

**43 Tim Holt**

**44 Roy Rogers**

**45 Buck Jones**

**46 Anna May Wong**

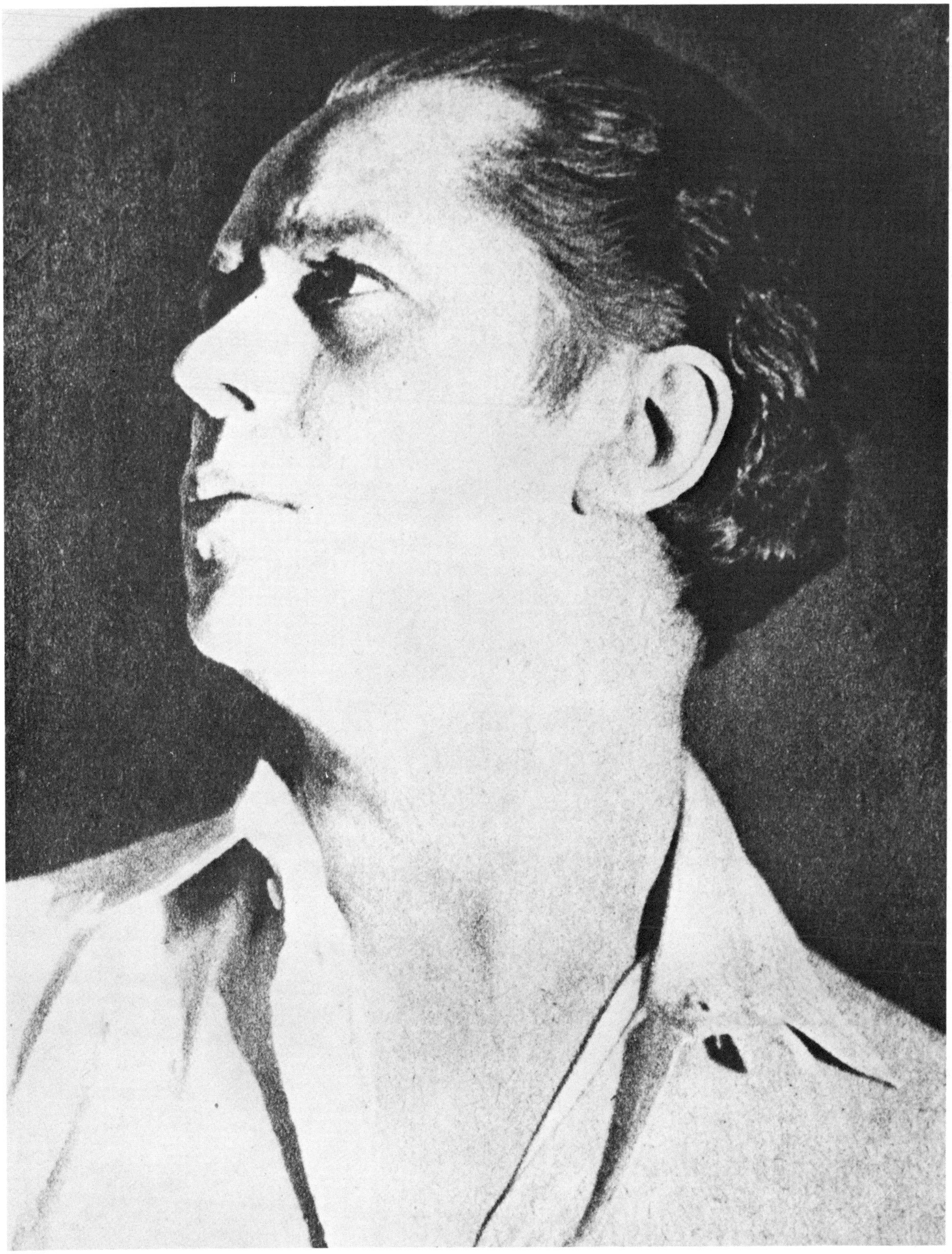

**47 Theodore Kosloff**

**48 Billie Dove**

**49 Leslie Fenton**

**50 Madge Evans**

**51 Malcolm MacGregor**

**52 Noel Coward**

**53 Eleanor Boardman**

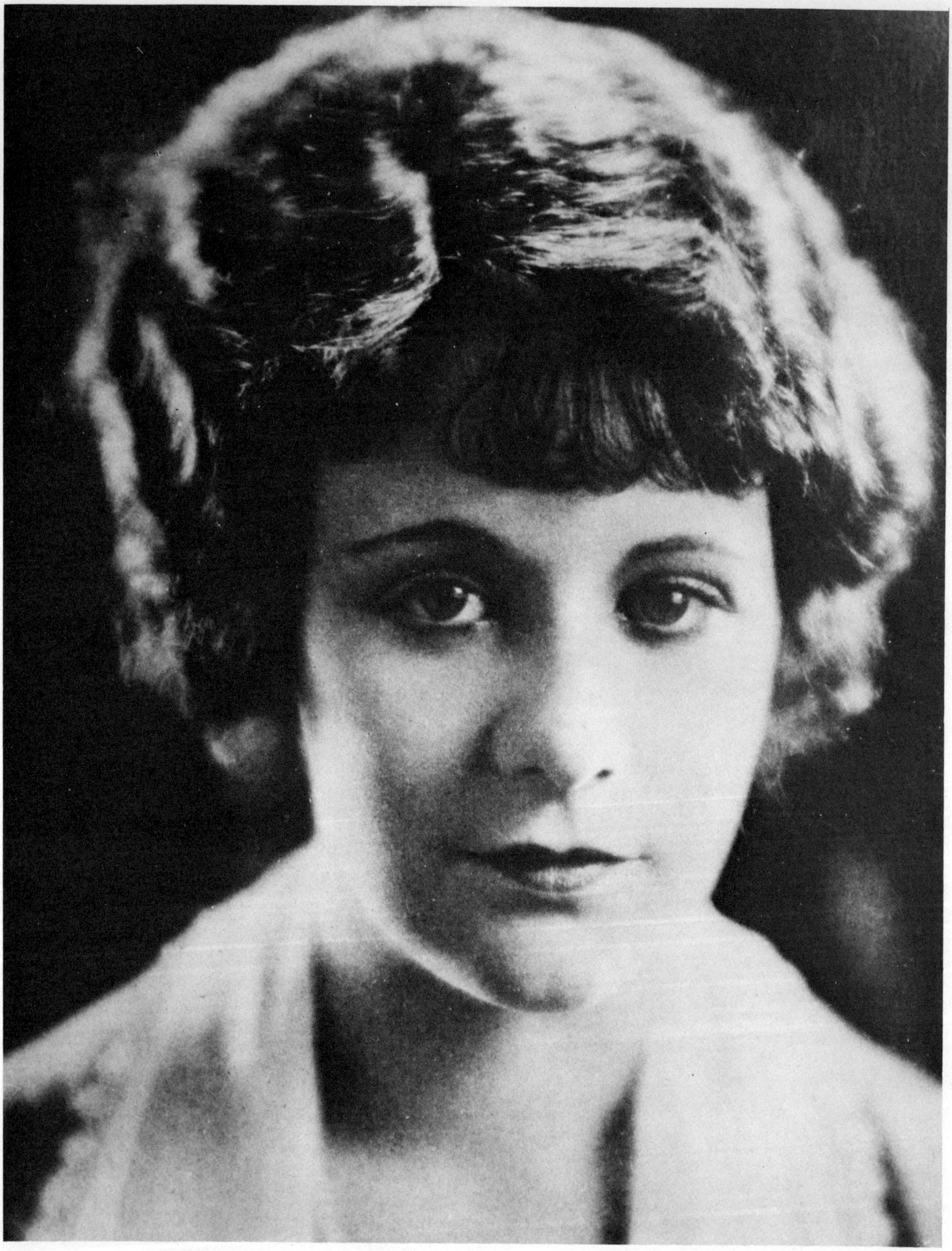

**54 Virginia Valli**

**55 Ross Alexander**

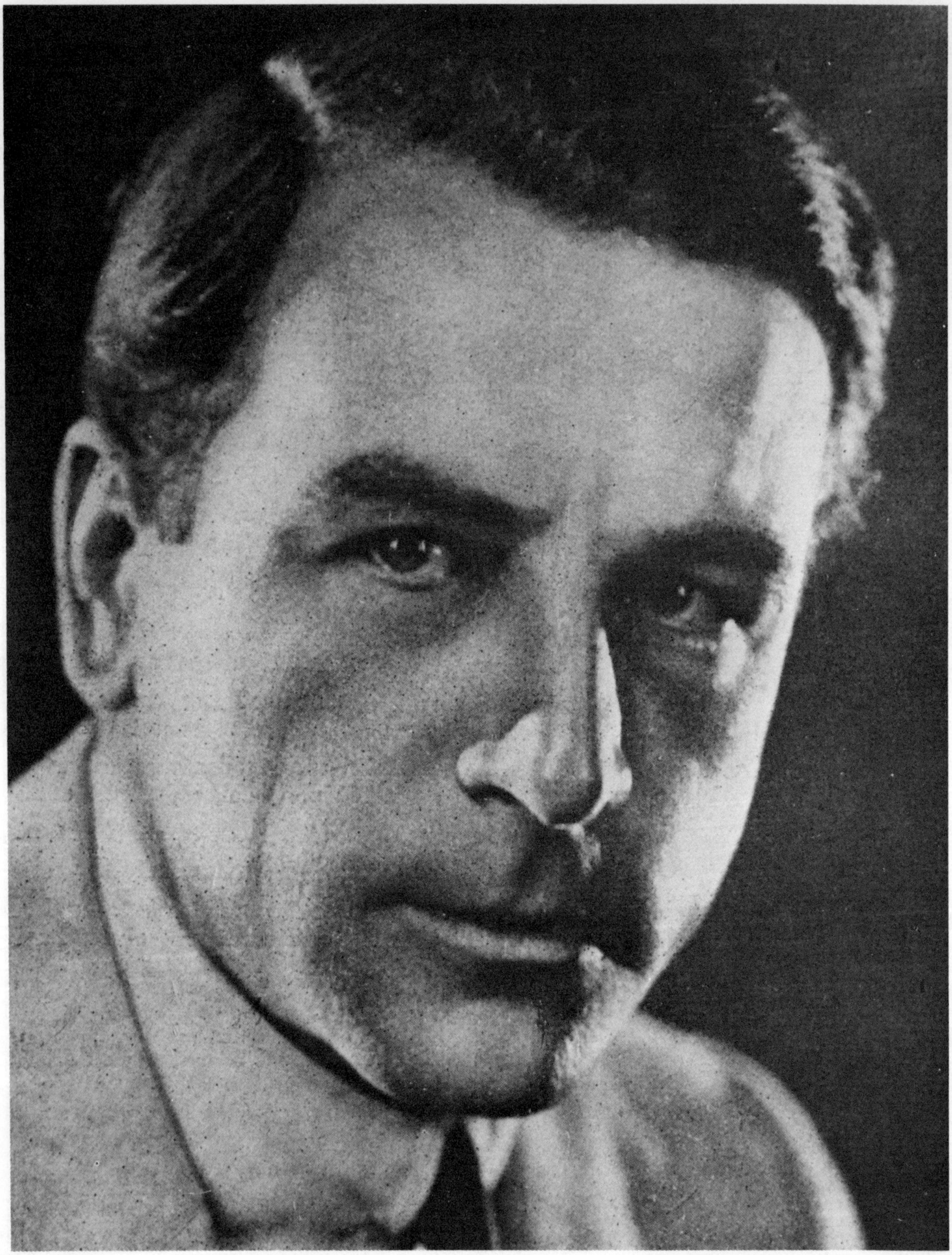
**56 Milton Sills**

**57 Doris Kenyon**

58 William Haines

**59 Elinor Fair**

**60 Conway Tearle**

**61 Elaine Hammerstein**

62 Richard Arlen

**63 Clara Bow**

**64 Ernest Torrence**

**65 Ernest Torrence**

**66 Madge Kennedy**

67 Lee Moran

**68 Dorothy Mackaill**

**69 Victor Varconi**

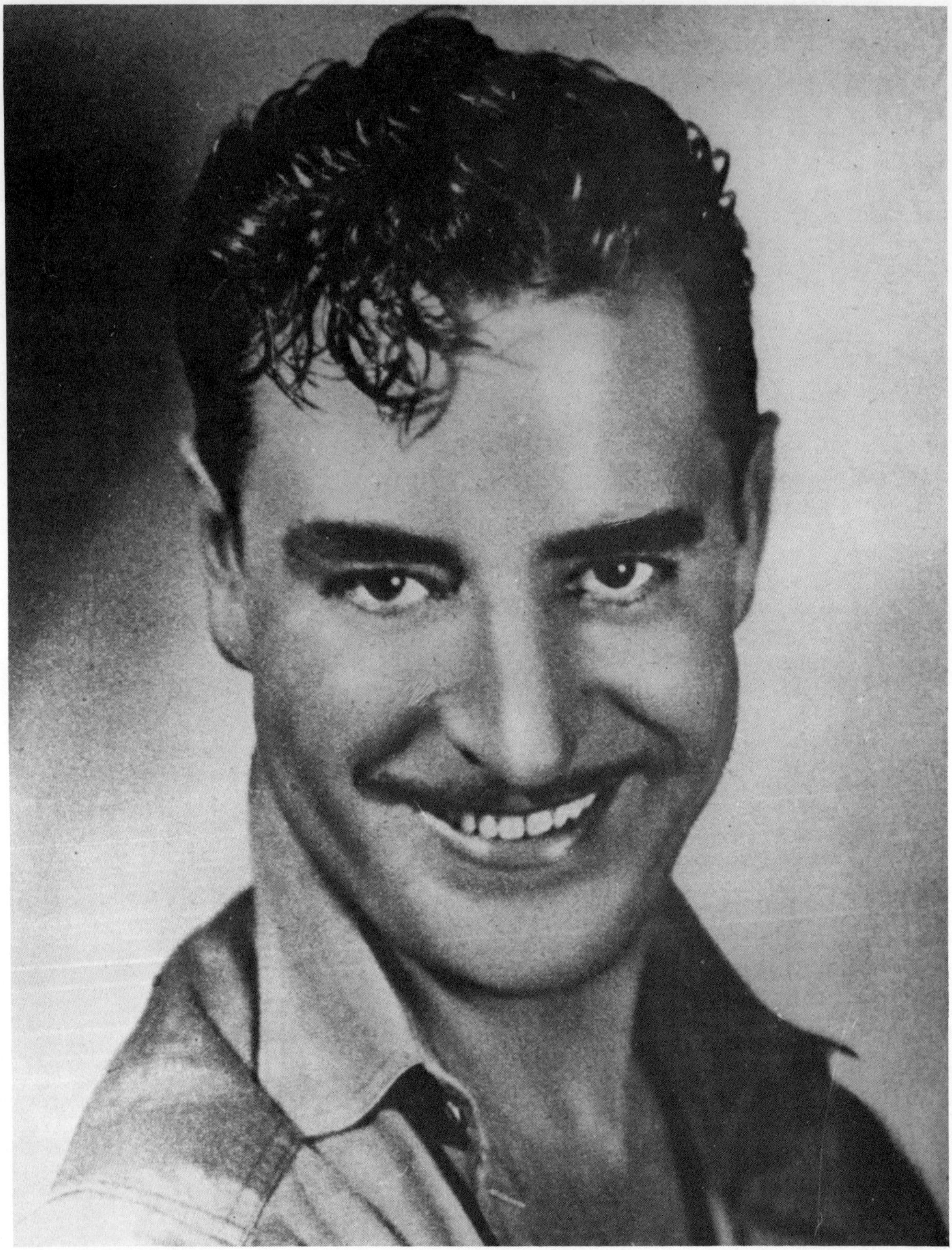

**70 John Gilbert**

**71 Greta Garbo**

**72 John Gilbert**

**73 Greta Garbo**

**74 David Torrence**

**75 Diana Wynyard**

**76 Wallace Beery**

**77 Wallace Beery**

**78 Charles Farrell**

**79 Elsie Ferguson**

**80 Janet Gaynor**

**81 Charles Bickford**

82 Douglas Fairbanks, Jr.

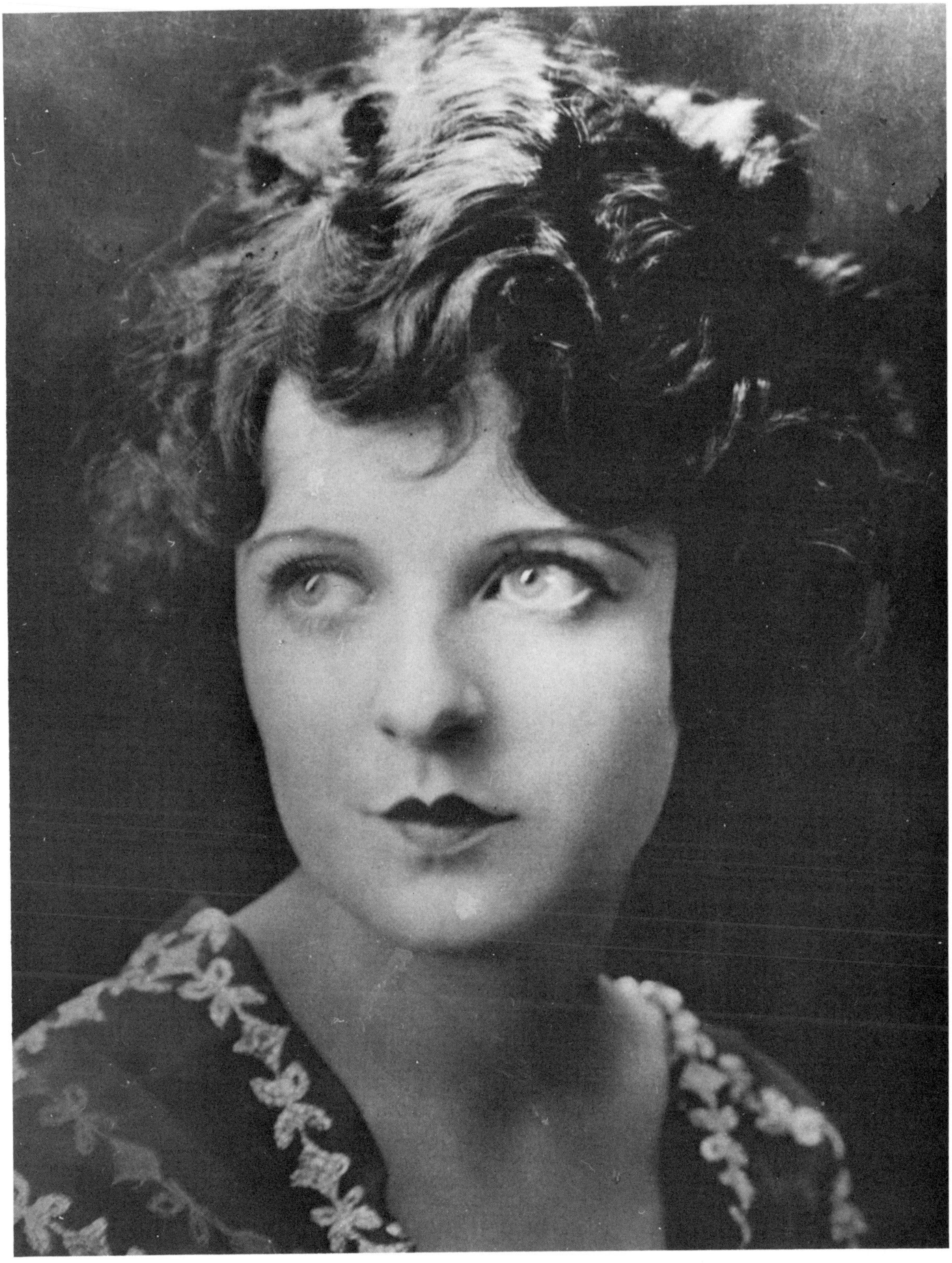

83 May MacAvoy

84 C. Aubrey Smith

**85 Buela Bondi**

**86 Norma Shearer**

87 Robert Agnew

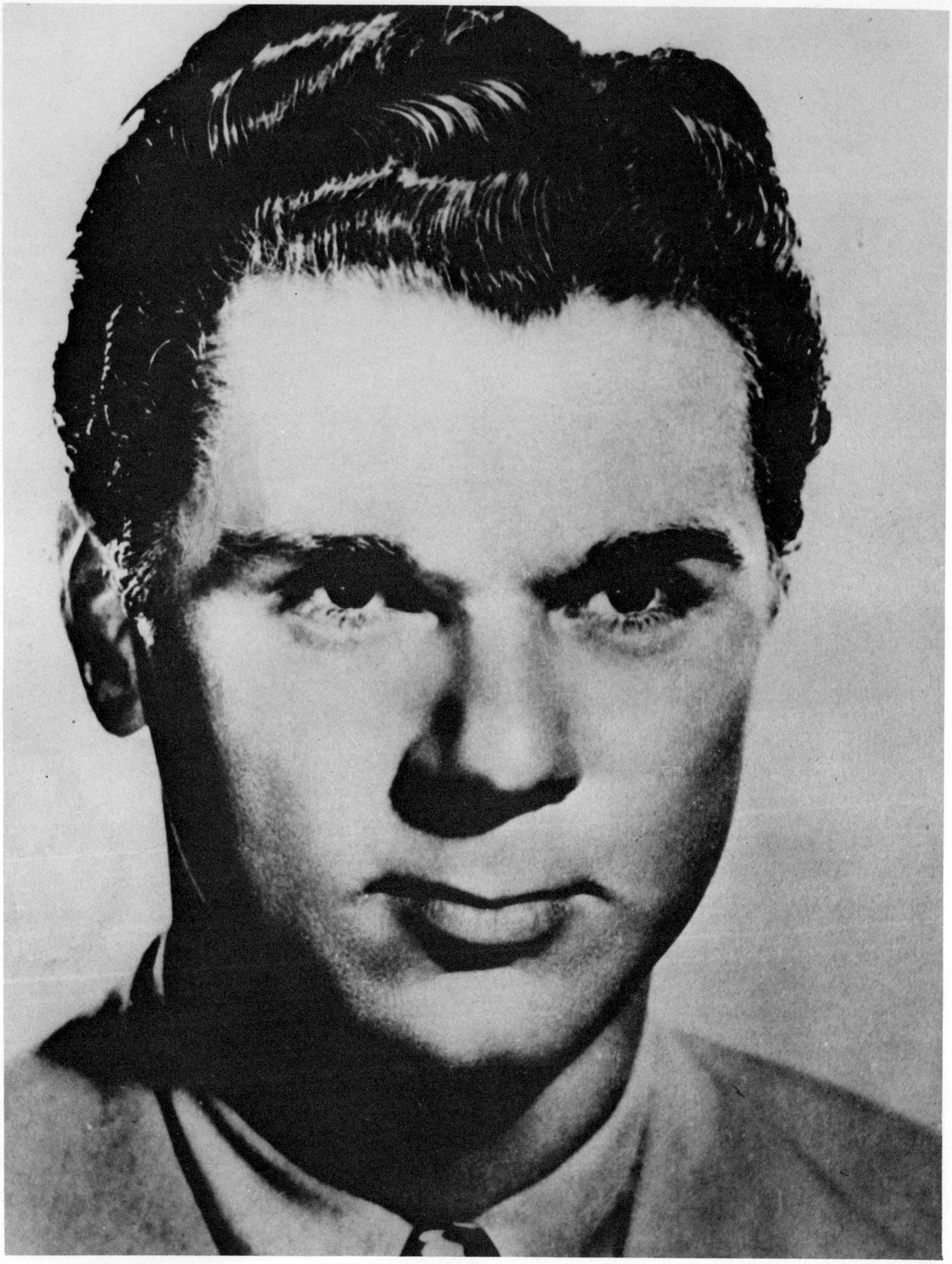

88 Jackie Cooper

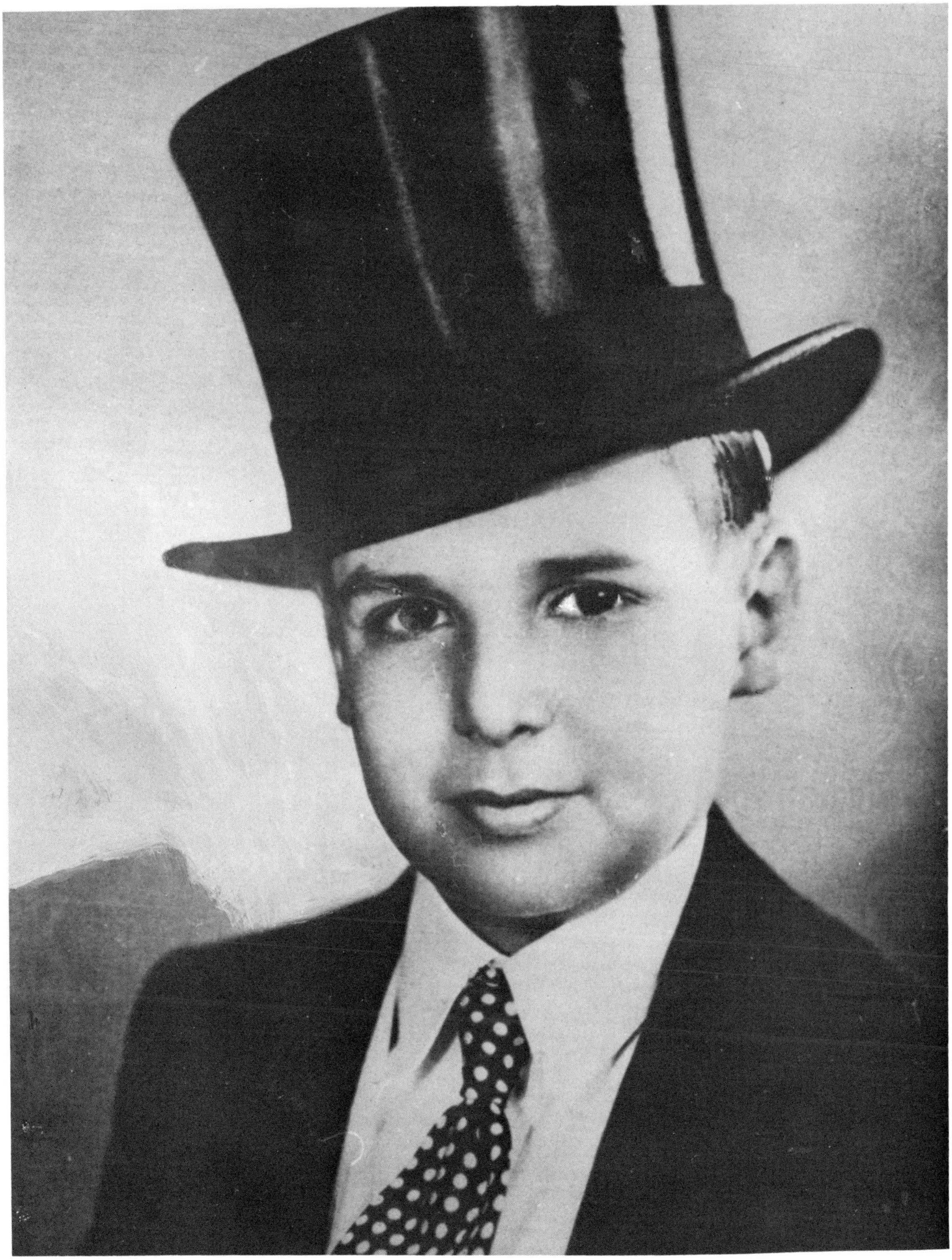

**89 Jackie Cooper**

**90 Renee Adoree**

**91 Phillips Holmes**

**92 Ricardo Cortez**

**93 Constance Bennett**

94 Don Alvarado

**95 Agnes Ayres**

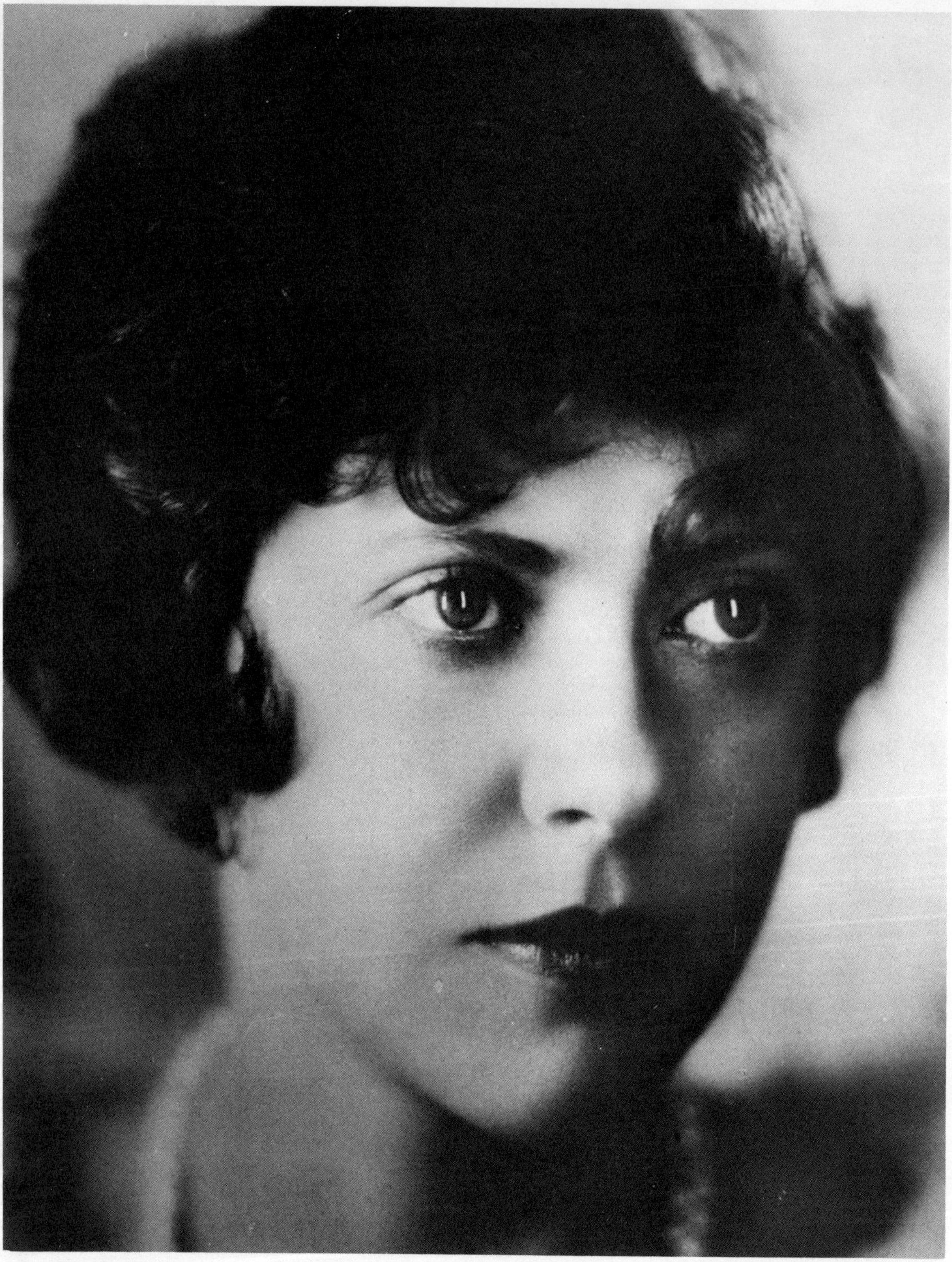

**96 Ruth Chatterton**

**97 Ralph Forbes**

**98 Elliott Dexter**

**99 Gloria Swanson**

**100 Bela Lugosi**

**101 Dolores del Rio**

**102 Jack Oakie**

**103 Patsy Ruth Miller**

**104 Carmel Myers**

**105 Clive Brooke**

**106 Noah Beery**

**107 Marjorie Rambeau**

**108 Zasu Pitts**

**109 Lloyd Hamilton**

**110 Bobby Vernon**

**111 Chester Conklin**

**112 Charlie Murray**

**113 Ben Turpin**

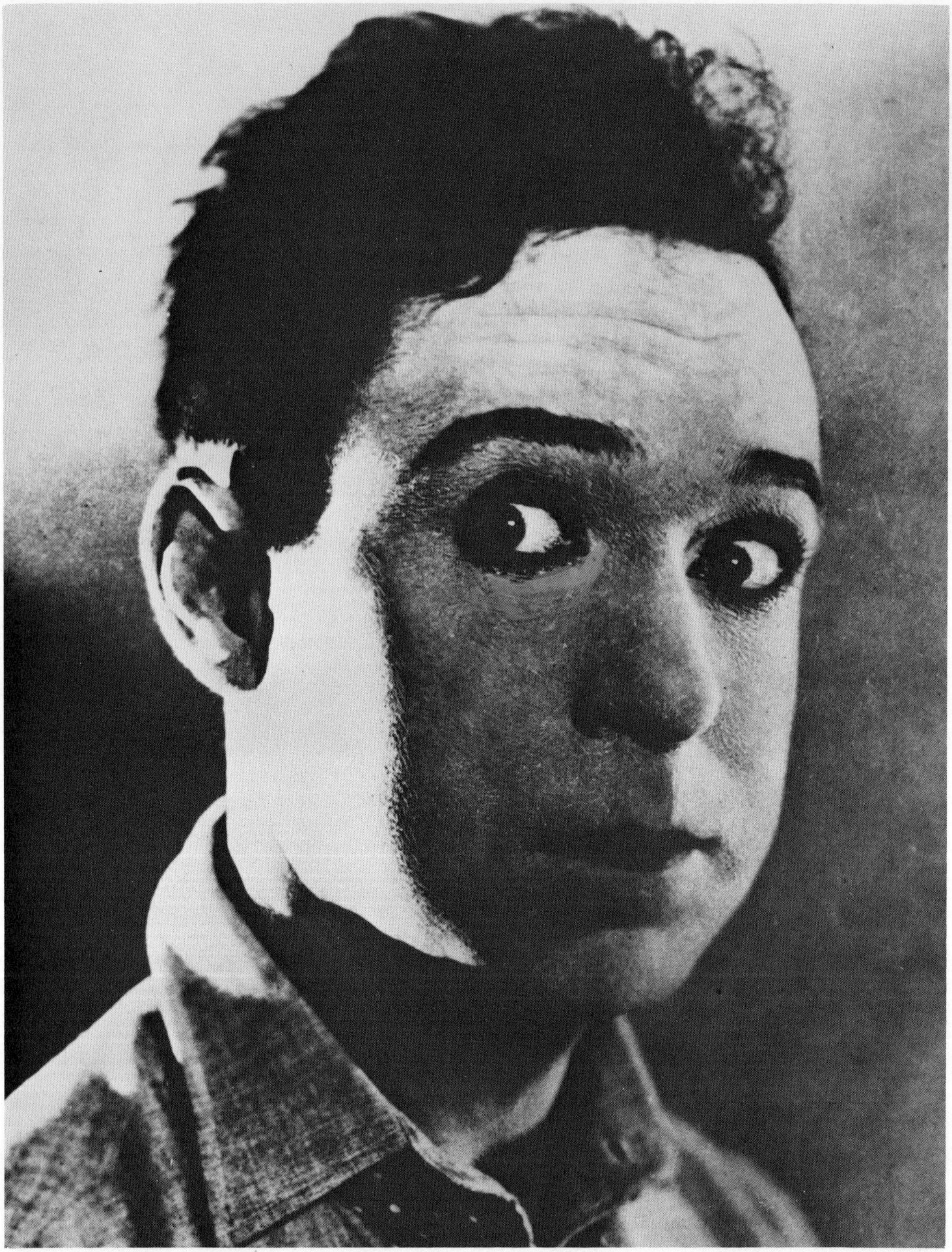

114 Harry Langdon

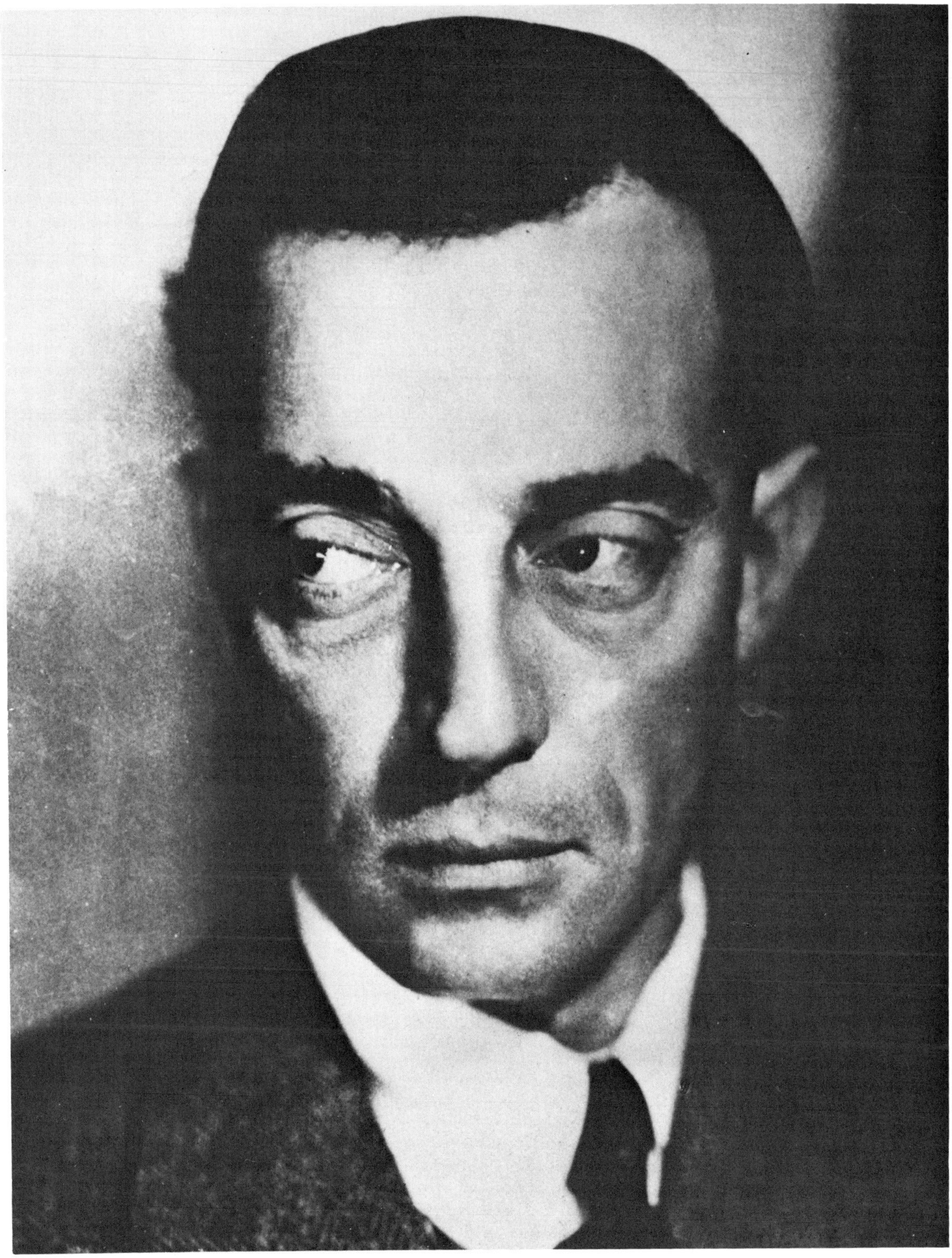

**115 Buster Keaton**

**116 Harry "Snub" Pollard**

**117 Mack Swain**

**118 Ford Sterling**

**119 Ford Sterling**

**120 Jimmy Finlayson**

121 Clyde Cook

**122 Victor Potel**

**123 Victor Potel**

**124 Barton MacLane**

**125 Jane Darwell**

**126 Jacqueline Logan**

**127 Regis Toomey**

128 Ronald Coleman

**129 Benita Hume**

**130 Elissa Landi**

**131 Walter Huston**

**132 Richard Dix**

**133 Wanda Hawley**

**134 Lilyan Tashman**

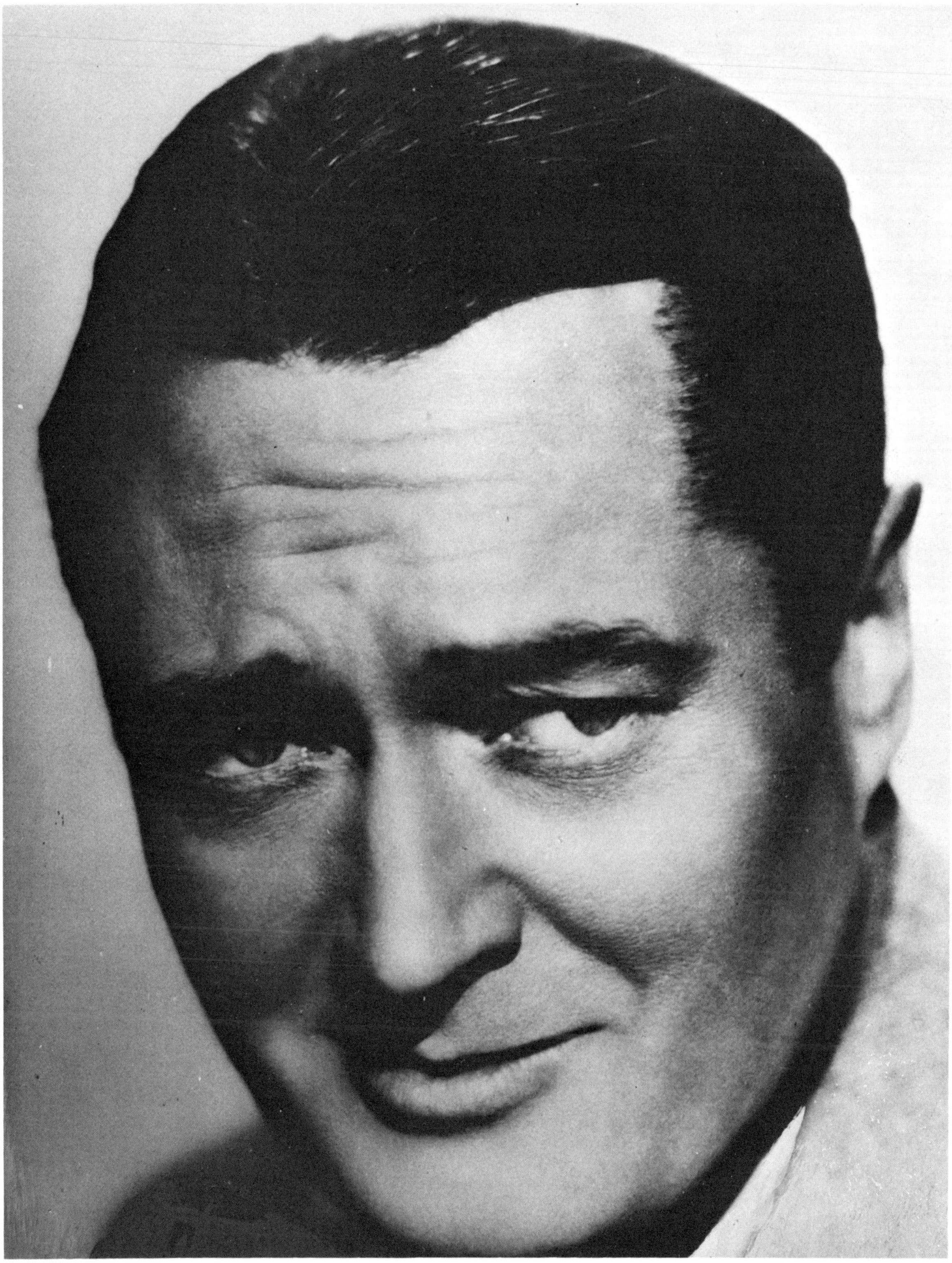

**135 Edmund Lowe**

**136 Esther Ralston**

**137 Johnny Mack Brown**

**138 Irene Rich**

**139 Will Rogers**

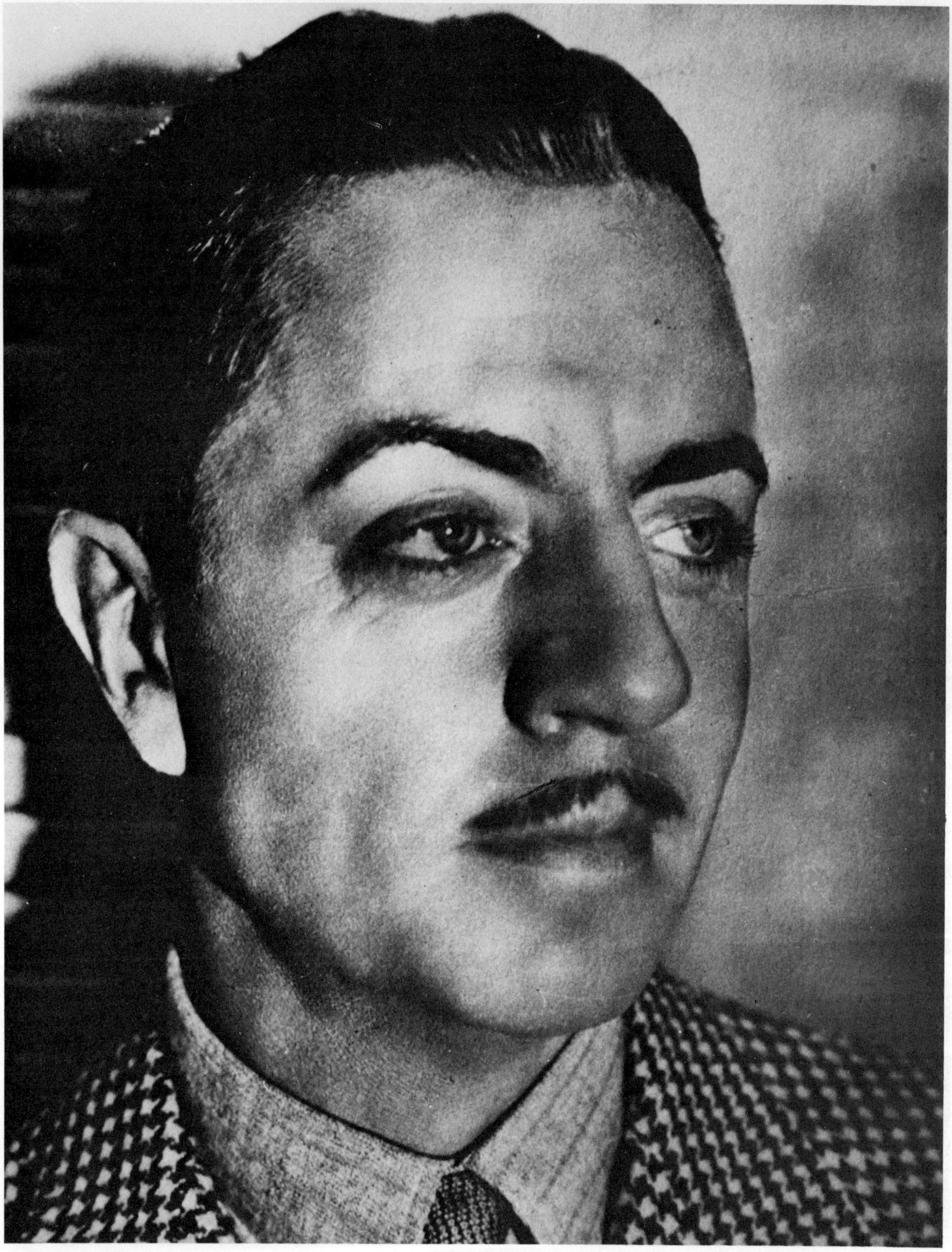

**140 William Powell**

**141 Carol Lombard**

**142 Wallace Ford**

**143 Evelyn Brent**

**144 Una Merkel**

**145 Chester Morris**

**146 Sally Eilers**

**147 James Dunn**

**148 Simone Simon**

**149 Louis Calhern**

**150 May Robson**

**151 Claude Gillingwater**

152 Raymond Hatton

153 Louis Hayward

**154 John Bowers**

**155 Nancy Carroll**

**156 Basil Rathbone**

**157 Jack Buchanan**

**158 Camilla Horn**

**159 Conrad Nagel**

**160 Boris Karloff**

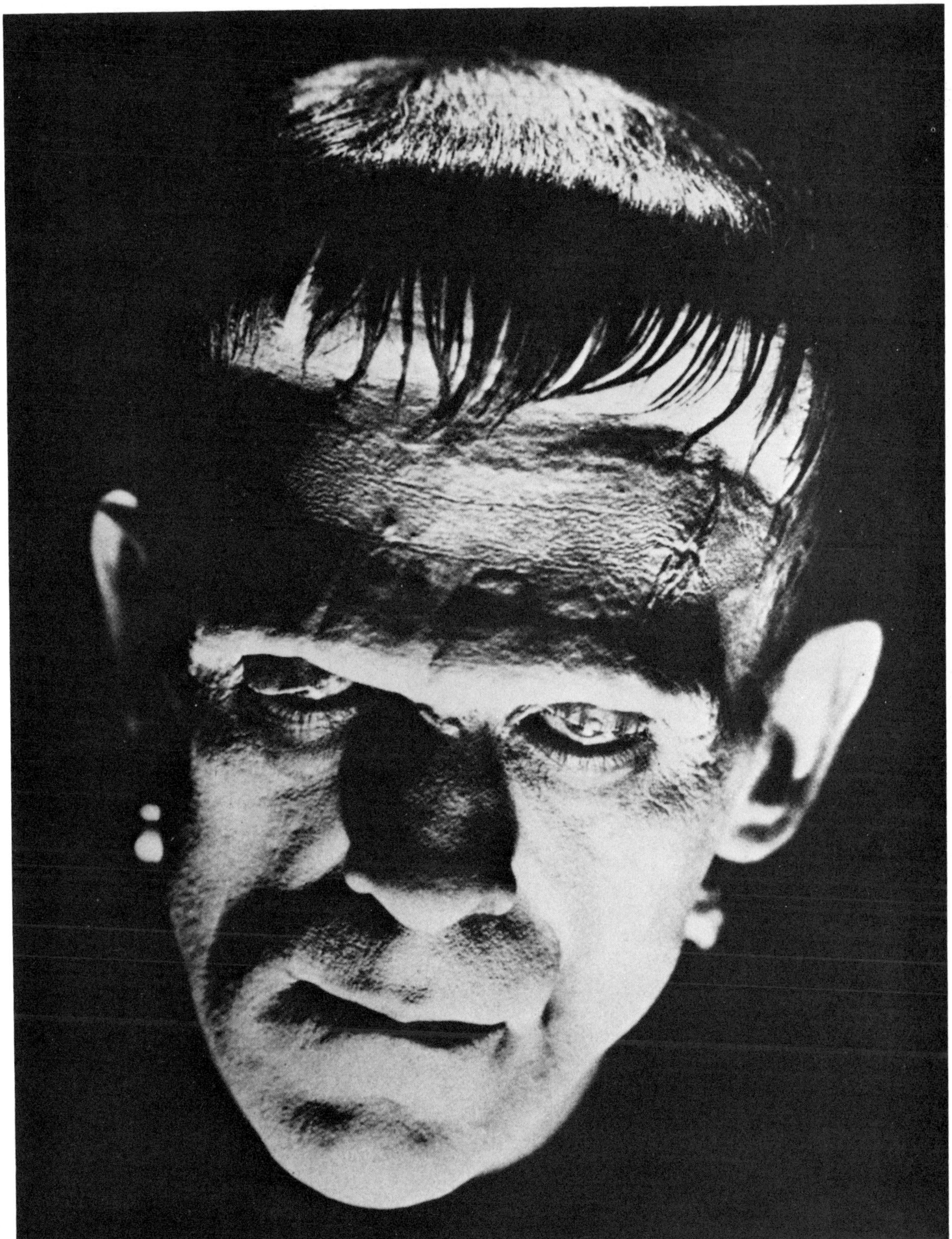

**161 Boris Karloff**

162 Paul Kelly

**163 Myrna Loy**

**164 Dorothy Sebastian**

165 Glenn Tyron

**166 George Brent**

**167 Joan Crawford**

168 Francis Lederer

**169 Raymond Griffith**

**170 Lupe Velez**

**171 Ian Hunter**

172 Warner Oland

**173 Sidney Toler**

**174 Brian Aherne**

175 Walter Pigeon

**176 Marion Nixon**

**177 James Hall**

178 Kenneth Harlan

**179 Joan Bennett**

180 Sally O'Neil

**181 Warren William**

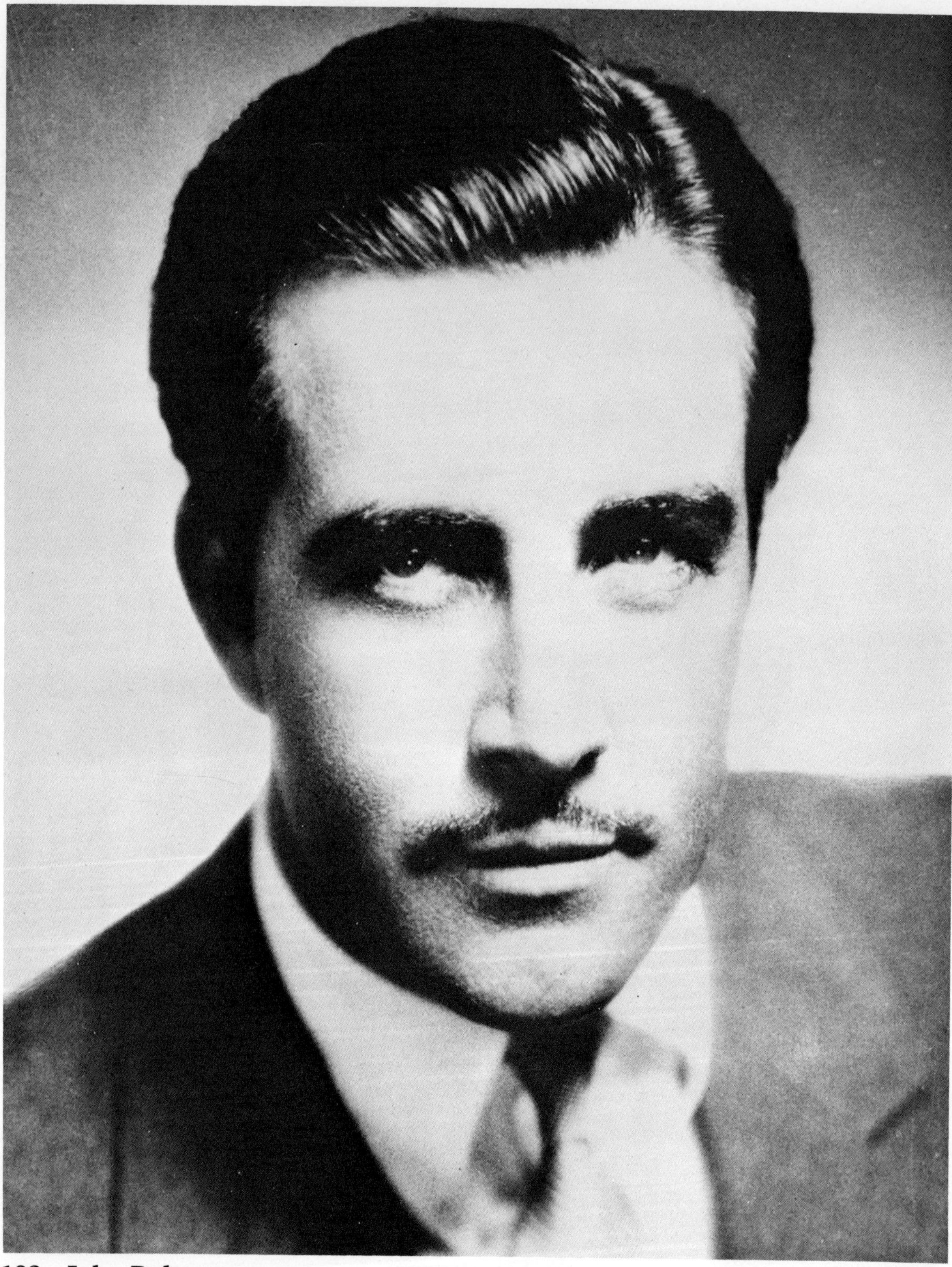

182 John Boles

**183 Jean Parker**

**184 Edward Arnold**

185 Robert Armstrong

**186 Marion Davies**

**187 John Miljan**

**188 Rosalind Russell**

**189 Lew Ayres**

**190 Jean Harlow**

**191 Gary Cooper**

**192 Gary Cooper**

**193 Jean Harlow**

**194 Virginia Bruce**

**195 Leslie Howard**

196 Helen Hayes

197 Frederick March

198 Fay Wray

**199 Edward G. Robinson**

200 Paul Lucas

201 Ann Harding

**202 Marlene Dietrich**

**203 Marlene Dietrich**

**204 Ben Lyon**

**205 Louise Brooks**

**206 Madeleine Carroll**

**207 John Beal**

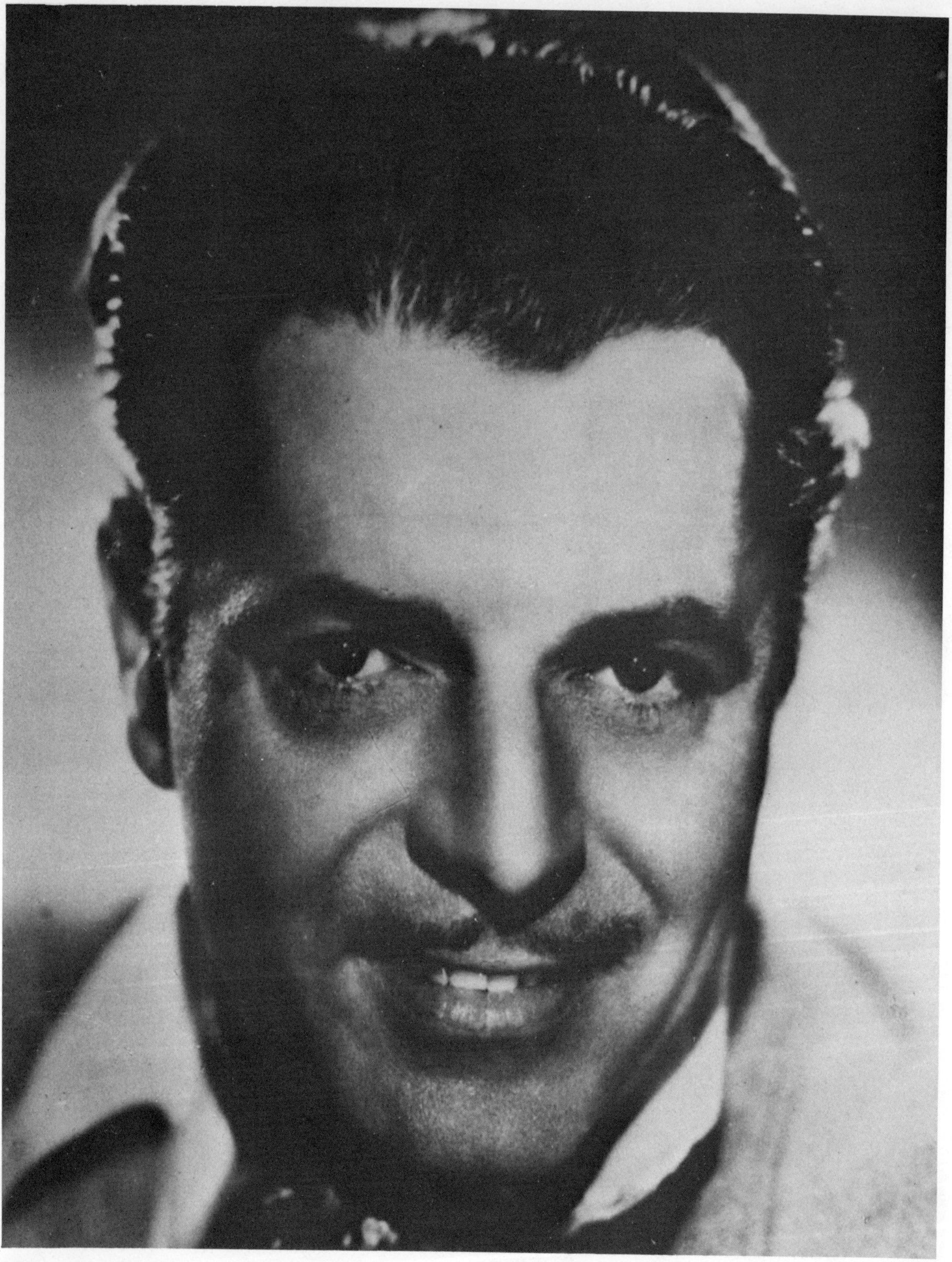

**208 Warner Baxter**

**209 Paulette Goddard**

**210 Claude Rains**

**211 Tallulah Bankhead**

**212 Jean Arthur**

**213 John Wayne**

**214 Ann Sheridan**

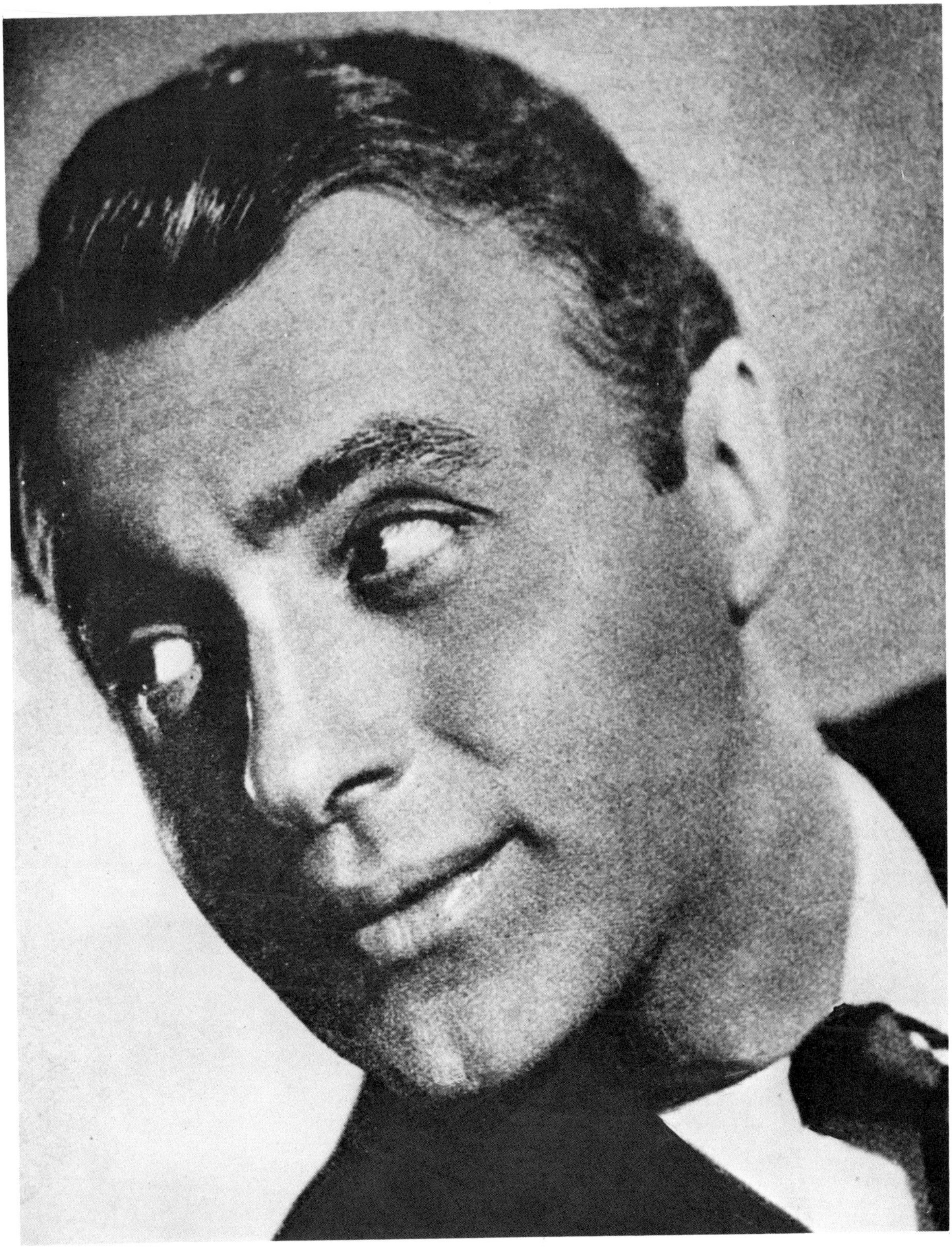

**215 Charles Boyer**

**216 Lucille Watson**

**217 Herbert Marshall**

218 Annabella

**219 Laurence Olivier**

220 Victor McLaglen

221 Barbara Stanwyck

**222 Clark Gable**

**223 Claudette Colbert**

**224 Clark Gable**

**225 Bette Davis**

**226 Loretta Young**

**227 Robert Montgomery**

228 Preston Foster

**229 Arthur Lake**

**230 Maurice Chevalier**

**231 Mae West**

**232 Edna May Oliver**

233 **John Carradine**

**234 Elizabeth Patterson**

**235 Paul Henreid**

236 Thelma Todd

**237 Groucho Marx**

**238 Chico Marx**

**239 Harpo Marx**

**240 Stan Laurel**

241 Oliver Hardy

**242 Al Jolson**

# INDEX AND PROFILES TO PART TWO

A

**ADOREE, Renee**—plate 90. Born in 1898, in Lille, France. Her father was the owner of a travelling circus and she became a circus rider and acrobatic dancer in early childhood. As a young girl she became a dancer in the Folies Bergères in Paris. Later, she danced and sang in a London cabaret and then went to America where she worked as a vaudeville entertainer. She made her screen *début* in THE STRONGEST, a screen play based on the life of Georges Clemenceau. Her most memorable starring role was in THE BIG PARADE with John Gilbert. Other starring roles came in MONTE CRISTO, THE PAGAN, REDEMPTION, LA BOHEME, and A CERTAIN YOUNG MAN with Ramon Novarro. She was the wife of film star Tom Moore. Height 5 ft. 2 in. Dark brown hair and blue eyes. She died in 1933 of tuberculosis.

**AGNEW, Robert**—plate 87. Born in Cincinnati, Ohio, on August 12, 1899. After a stage career of several years as a handsome and talented young juvenile, he entered films in 1919. Played supporting and co-starring roles, usually as the youthful hero. His film credits include SLIGHTLY USED, DANCING DAYS, BLUEBEARD'S EIGHTH WIFE, WILD OATS LANE, and THE HEART OF BROADWAY, among many others. Height 5 ft. 6 in. Dark brown hair and eyes.

**AHERNE, Brian**—plate 174. Born May 2, 1902, in Worcestershire, England. Graduated from London University in 1918. Went on the stage immediately after graduation and enjoyed a big success in the London production of WHITE CARGO. He made his film *début* in 1924 and played leading parts in a number of British films before going to America where he starred in many Hollywood films, among them SYLVIA SCARLETT, BELOVED ENEMY, THE GREAT GARRICK, and MAXMILLIAN OF MEXICO. Height 6 ft. 2½ in. Fair hair and blue eyes. Was married to American film star Joan Fontaine.

**ALEXANDER, Ross**—plate 55. Born in New York City on April 21, 1900. When he was sixteen he obtained a part in the Broadway production of ENTER MADAME starring Blanche Yurka. This auspicious beginning was followed by a succession of good roles in such plays as THE STORK IS DEAD, THE PARTY'S OVER, HONEYMOON, and LET US BE GAY—all top Broadway hits. Claimed by Hollywood, he played supporting parts in films until he was cast by Warner Brothers for the lead in FLIRTATION WALK. His greatest screen fame came with Warners where he starred in A MIDSUMMER NIGHT'S DREAM, SHIPMATES FOREVER, CAPTAIN BLOOD with Errol Flynn, WE'RE IN THE MONEY, and READY, WILLING AND ABLE. The greater part of his career was in the sound era. Height 6 ft. 1 in. Tall, dark, and handsome. Died at the peak of his career in 1937.

**ALVARADO, Don**—plate 94. Born in Albuquerque, New Mexico, on November 4, 1904. His parents were Spanish and his father a rancher. He went to Hollywood while still in his teens with the hope of "getting into the movies," but despite the fact that he was an unusually handsome and personable young man, it was more than a year before he obtained even an extras' part. His big break came in 1927 when he was cast with Constance Talmadge in BREAKFAST AT SUNRISE. D. W. Griffith then chose him for his male lead in DRUMS OF LOVE. Many successes followed including starring roles in RAMONA, THE LOVES OF CARMEN, THE BRIDGE OF SAN LUIS REY, and RIO RITA. Height 5 ft. 11 in. Black hair and brown eyes. Real name was Jose Paige. He died in 1967.

**ANNABELLA**—plate 218. Born on July 14, 1910, in Paris, France. Her chance to enter films came when her father entertained a film producer who, struck by her beauty and charming personality, gave her a part in a French film. It was not until she was starred in LE MILLION two years later that she was acclaimed. Famous in French films, she went to London to star in WINGS OF THE MORNING, UNDER THE RED ROBE, and DINNER AT THE RITZ. Already an international star when she arrived in Hollywood, she continued her film career with great success in America. She married film star Tyrone Power. Height 5 ft. 4 in. Light gold hair and brown eyes.

**ARLEN, Richard**—plate 62. Born on May 1, 1899, in Charlottesville, Virginia. Real name was Richard van Mattimore. He made his screen *début* in 1920 and struggled along in minor parts until 1926 when he was chosen for the leading role in WINGS. With his success in this picture, which co-starred Clara Bow and Buddy Rogers, his studio cast him in the title role of THE VIRGINIAN. Then THE LIGHT OF THE WESTERN STARS, THE FOUR FEATHERS, and BLOOD SHIP cinched his position as a star. Among his many other films was his departure to light comedy in FEEL MY PULSE with Bebe Daniels. Height 5 ft. 11 in. Brown hair and blue eyes. Married to film star Jobyna Ralston.

**ARLISS, George**—plate 11. Born in London, England, on April 10, 1868. He made his stage *début* at the age of eighteen at the Elephant and Castle Theatre in London. Later, became a leading member of Mrs. Patrick Campbell's London company. With this company he went to New York where he remained to become one of the most popular actors on Broadway. He played the lead in William Archer's THE GREEN GODDESS which ran for two years in New York. He then took the play to the St. James's Theatre in London for another year. Then, to Hollywood where he starred in the film version. Other of his films made in Hollywood include THE MAN WHO PLAYED GOD, DISRAELI, OLD ENGLISH, ALEXANDER HAMILTON, and EAST MEETS WEST. Height 5 ft. 9 in. Grey hair and brown eyes. Died in 1946.

**ARMSTRONG, Robert**—plate 185. Born in Saginaw, Michigan, on November 20, 1896. Graduated from law school at the University of Washington, but abandoned a law career for the stage. After gaining experience in stock, he attained success on the New York stage and was starred in the great Broadway success IS ZAT SO, which he later played in London. Hollywood followed and his successful career continued in films including BIG NEWS, THE RACKETEER, THE MAIN EVENT, and NOBODY'S BABY. Height 5 ft. 10 in. Dark brown hair and brown eyes. He died in 1973.

**ARNOLD, Edward**—plate 184. Born in New York City on February 18, 1890. His real name was Guenther Scheider. After a good deal of stage experience, he made his screen *début* in Chicago in 1918, when Chicago was an important movie-making center. Some years later in Hollywood, four studios vied for his services. Among his screen successes were BLOSSOMS ON BROADWAY, THE TOAST OF NEW YORK, EASY LIVING, and THE WHITE SISTER with Helen Hayes. He will always be remembered in the title role of DIAMOND JIM BRADY. Height 5 ft. 11 in. Dark brown hair and eyes. He died in 1956.

**ARTHUR, Jean**—plate 212. Born in New York City on October 17, 1906. Her real name was Gladys Greene. She began as a model and was discovered by a Fox talent scout, brought to Hollywood and given a contract with the Fox company. Her film *début* was in 1923. After working for a time in two-reel comedies, she was cast as the female lead in THE TEMPLE OF VENUS. She then made SINS OF THE FATHER with Emil Jannings and WARMING UP with Richard Dix. Among her film credits are included MR. DEEDS GOES TO TOWN, HISTORY IS MADE AT NIGHT, HALF-WAY TO HEAVEN, and THE EX-MRS. BRADFORD. Height 5 ft. 3 in. tall with blonde hair and blue eyes.

**ASTOR, Mary**—plate 21. Born on May 3, 1905, in Quincy, Illinois. Her real name was Lucille Langhanke. She made her screen *début* at the age of fifteen in a film called THE BEGGAR MAID. She was then given supporting roles until Douglas Fairbanks, Sr. chose her for his leading lady in DON Q. After that film and one with Milton Sills called THE SEA TIGER, her film career rocketed. Among her film credits are included THE

HURRICANE, DON JUAN, THE PRISONER OF ZENDA, LADY FROM NOWHERE, and DODSWORTH. Height 5 ft. 5 in. Auburn hair and brown eyes. Was married to Kenneth Hawks, the film director who was killed in an air crash in 1930.

**AUTRY, Gene**—plate 37. Born in Tioga, Texas, on September 29, 1907. Worked on his father's ranch in Oklahoma as a young man where he learned his trade as a professional cowboy. Tried his hand at silent Western films as a young man, but found composing music and playing his guitar on radio to be more rewarding. His screen career as such did not start until after the advent of sound where he had the opportunity to play and sing in the many Westerns he made. His first starring role was in THE BIG SHOW. Other films include THE SINGING VAGABOND, and RED RIVER VALLEY. He has composed more than two hundred songs. Height 5 ft. 11 in. Brown hair and blue eyes.

**AYRES, Agnes**—plate 95. Born on April 4, 1898, in Carbondale, Illinois. Began her screen career at Essanay as an extra, and rose to fame with Jesse Lasky and Paramount. THE AFFAIRS OF ANATOLE with Wallace Reid and SON OF THE SHEIK with Rudolph Valentino, were perhaps her two best films. Among her other films are included THE DONOVAN AFFAIR, HEART RAIDER, and FORBIDDEN FRUIT. Height 5 ft. 5 in. Golden brown hair and blue eyes. She died in 1968.

**AYRES, Lew**—plate 189. Born on December 28, 1906, in Minneapolis, Minnesota. He was educated at the University of Arizona where he studied medicine. His interest in music resulted in his becoming a competent pianist and singer. He was also adept on the banjo and guitar. He became a member of the university jazz band and later a professional musician with various orchestras. He made his screen *début* as the lover of Greta Garbo in THE KISS—a miraculous feat for an unknown. He rose to stardom in ALL QUIET ON THE WESTERN FRONT. Other of his films include EAST IS WEST, THE LAST TRAIN FROM MADRID, MURDER WITH PICTURES, THE NAVY SPIRIT, THE CRIME NOBODY SAW, and the DOCTOR KILDAIRE series with Lionel Barrymore. Height 5 ft. 10 in. Dark brown hair and brown eyes.

## B

**BANKHEAD, Tallulah**—plate 211. The fabulous "Tallu" was a belle of the South, born in Huntsville, Alabama, on January 31, 1902. She was the daughter of United States Senator W. B. Bankhead. She began with a stage career that did not fully blossom until she crossed the Atlantic to London where she captivated English theater-goers and then starred in a British film called HIS HOUSE IN ORDER. She replaced Gladys Cooper in the cast and the film was a great success. Back in the States, she then made film history with LIFEBOAT, THUNDER BELOW, TARNISHED LADY, and THE DEVIL AND THE DEEP. She was famous for addressing everyone as "dahling." She died in 1968. Height 5 ft. 2 in. with blonde hair and blue eyes.

**BARRYMORE, Ethel**—plate 24. The "first lady" of the American stage, she was born in Philadelphia, Pennsylvania, on August 15, 1879. From a long line of famous stage personalities, she made her *début* at the age of five at the old Empire Theatre in New York. From that moment there was never a doubt that another Barrymore had come into her own. She made several films in 1916 and 1917, but always returned to the stage until sound gave her scope for the great actress that she was. In all, she made twelve silent films and a long series of successful sound films. Among her screen credits are RASPUTIN AND THE EMPRESS, made with her famous brothers Lionel and John, YOUNG AT HEART, THE STORY OF THREE LOVES, THE PARADINE CASE, THE FINAL JUDGEMENT, THE KISS OF HATE, and NONE BUT THE LONELY HEART for which she won the Academy Award (Oscar). The last of the Barrymores, she outlived both her brothers and died quietly in Beverly Hills in 1959. Height 5 ft. 7 in. Light brown hair and brown eyes.

**BARRYMORE, John**—plate 27. Born in New York City on February 15, 1882, son of the famous stage stars Maurice Barrymore and Georgia Drew. Real name was Blythe. Began his stage career in 1903. Was famous for his role as Hamlet which he enacted both on the stage and on the screen. Among his other great stage successes were RAFFLES, PETER IBBETSON, and RICHARD III. Though known as a great dramatic actor, he made his film *début* in a comedy called ARE YOU A MASON in 1913. He later, of course, starred in many great films among them BEAU BRUMMEL, DON JUAN,

BELOVED ROGUE, ROMEO AND JULIET, and DR. JEKYLL AND MR. HYDE. He also made THE LOTUS EATERS with Colleen Moore and THE SEA BEAST with Dolores Costello, whom he later married. Was the younger brother of Ethel and Lionel Barrymore. Height 5 ft. 9 in. Brown hair and blue eyes. He died in 1942.

**BARRYMORE, Lionel**—plate 26. Born on April 28, 1878, in Philadelphia, Pennsylvania. Brother of Ethel and John Barrymore. Lionel spent his entire life on the stage or screen. A great Broadway star, he was acclaimed for THE COPPERHEAD, PETER IBBETSON, MACBETH, THE JEST, and many other great stage plays. His first screen work was done in early Biograph films. In 1909, D. W. Griffith induced him make a film called FRIENDS. The same year he made FIGHTING BLOOD with Blanche Sweet and then did THE NEW YORK HAT with Mary Pickford. He was in the EXPLOITS OF ELAINE with Pearl White, and then made the screen version of his famous stage success THE COPPERHEAD. Among his other films were THE BARRIER, SADIE THOMPSON with Gloria Swanson, MADAME X with Pauline Frederick, and in later years, the DOCTOR GILLESPIE series. Height 6 ft. Dark brown hair and blue eyes. Died in 1954.

**BAXTER, Warner**—plate 208. Born on March 29, 1892, in Columbus, Ohio. His first stage work began in Tulsa, Oklahoma, where he joined a stock company as the juvenile lead. He later became leading man for the company. In 1914, he headed for Hollywood where he literally almost starved trying to crash the movie industry. Oliver Morosco signed him to his Los Angeles stock company and when he produced LOMBARDI LIMITED in New York, he cast Baxter in the lead. It was his triumph in this play that finally got him into films. He made THE BELOVED TRAITOR with Mae Marsh in 1918, followed by ALIMONY with Grace Darmond, and then CRAIG'S WIFE with Irene Rich. His greatest hit was with Fox in the film IN OLD ARIZONA for which he won the Academy Award (Oscar). His other films include RAMONA, SLAVE SHIP, WHITE HUNTER, BROADWAY BILL, and THE PRISONER OF SHARK ISLAND. He died in 1951. Height 5 ft. 11 in. Dark brown hair and eyes.

**BEAL, John**—plate 207. Born in Joplin, Missouri, on August 13, 1905. His real name was James Bleidung. As a young actor on Broadway he was fortunate to be cast in MADAME X with Pauline Frederick and, later, with Helen Hayes in ANOTHER LANGUAGE. When the latter was made into a film he played the leading male role. He went back to the stage for a time, but returned to the screen in THE MAN WHO FOUND HIMSELF. He remained in films and perhaps his most remembered performance was in the title role of THE LITTLE MINISTER. Other film credits include BORDER CAFE, DOUBLE WEDDING, and MADAME X when it was screened with Pauline Frederick. Height 5 ft. 10½ in. Dark brown hair and eyes.

**BEERY, Noah**—plate 106. Born on January 17, 1884, on a farm near Kansas City, Missouri. He is the older brother of Wallace Beery. After a long and very successful stage career he came to films as a "heavy." He had a fine speaking and singing voice, which he used to great advantage with the coming of sound. Among his films were BEAU GESTE, THE ISLE OF LOST SHIPS, FOUR FEATHERS, UNDER A TEXAS MOON, THE ROUGH RIDERS, and PARADISE. Heights 6 ft. 1 in. Dark brown hair and eyes. He died in 1946.

**BEERY, Wallace**—plate 76, 77. Born on April 1, 1889, on a farm near Kansas City, Missouri. Before entering films was first a trainer of performing elephants in a circus and then an actor. His fine singing voice gained success for him in musical comedy on the New York stage. He made his film *début* with Essanay in 1914. He emerged as a fine dramatic actor in Marshall Neilan's THE UNPARDONABLE SIN. He went on to become the screen's most lovable character actor, after an early stint as a "villain." Among his films were THE LOST WORLD, THE SEA HAWK, DINNER AT EIGHT, TUG BOAT ANNIE, and PANCHO VILLA. Height 6 ft. Brown hair and eyes. Died in 1949.

**BENNETT, Constance**—plate 93. Born in New York City on October 22, 1904. Daughter of the famous stage and screen star Richard Bennett and sister of actress Joan Bennett. She had no particular theatrical ambitions but Samuel Goldwyn persuaded her to take a screen test. By 1925 she had played several major roles. She was best known for her brittle, sophisticated roles. Among her films were THE GOOSE HANGS HIGH, LADIES IN LOVE, CYTHEREA with Norman Kerry and Lewis S. Stone, SALLY, IRENE, AND MARY, THE COMMON LAW, THREE FACES EAST, and

TOPPER. Height 5 ft. 4 in. Ash blonde hair and blue eyes. She died in 1965.

**BENNETT, Joan**—plate 179. Born in Palisades, New Jersey, on February 11, 1909, the daughter of stage and screen star Richard Bennett and younger sister of Constance Bennett. As a child, she worked in silent films with her father. Later, she was cast by Samuel Goldwyn in the leading role opposite Ronald Colman in BULLDOG DRUMMOND. Film credits include THREE LIVE GHOSTS, THE MISSISSIPPI GAMBLER, DISRAELI with George Arliss, and THE WOMAN IN THE WINDOW with Edward G. Robinson. Height 5 ft. 3 in. Golden hair and blue eyes. She often appeared in films with black hair.

**BICKFORD, Charles**—plate 81. Born on January 1, 1892, in Cambridge, Massachusetts. After a "hitch" in the U. S. Navy, he obtained work in burlesque on Broadway and was on the legitimate stage for sixteen years before entering films in 1927. His first film was DYNAMITE. He was highly successful in ANNA CHRISTIE with Garbo and in such other films as PRIDE OF THE MARINES, THE PLAINSMAN, THE SEA BAT, HELL'S HEROES, and A STAR IS BORN. Height 6 ft. 1 in. Red hair and blue eyes. Died in 1967.

**BOARDMAN, Eleanor**—plate 53. Born in Philadelphia, Pennsylvania, on August 1, 1899. Had several years stage experience when she made her film *début* in 1922. Her first important film was THREE WISE FOOLS with William Haines and Claude Gillingwater. She gained stature with George Walsh and Harrison Ford in VANITY FAIR and then co-starred with Conrad Nagel in THE ONLY THING. Other film credits include MEMORY LANE, TELL IT TO THE MARINES, REDEMPTION, THE AUCTION BLOCK, and MAMBA. Height 5 ft. 6 in. Light brown hair and green eyes. Married to King Vidor, the producer.

**BOLES, John**—plate 182. Born in Greenville, Texas, on October 28, 1900. Studied to become a doctor, but gave up a medical career for the stage. Possessing a fine singing voice, he soon attained success in musical comedy. Gloria Swanson saw him on the New York stage and chose him to play in a film with her. He later appeared in the film success STELLA DALLAS. CRAIG'S WIFE, A MESSAGE TO GARCIA, and THE LITTLEST REBEL followed. With the coming of sound, he attained greater acclaim in RIO RITA, THE DESERT SONG, and SONG OF THE WEST. His film with Gloria Swanson was LOVES OF SUNYA. Height 6 ft. Brown hair and grey eyes. Died in 1969.

**BONDI, Buela**—plate 85. Born in Chicago, Illinois, on May 3, 1896. Came to the screen via Broadway and to Broadway via stock. Five years' experience playing more than two hundred varied roles, groomed her for screen success. She made her screen *début* in STREET SCENE, following which she varied her time between stage and screen. She finally settled for Hollywood and later appeared in such successes as CHRISTOPHER BEAN, MAKE WAY FOR TOMORROW, and THE BUCCANEER. Height 5 ft. 4 in. Brown hair and eyes.

**BOW, Clara**—plate 63. Born on August 5, 1906, in Brooklyn, New York. Was introduced to the screen after winning a beauty contest while still in school. Her first film, BEYOND THE RAINBOW, was made in 1922. This was followed by DOWN TO THE SEA IN SHIPS. Bursting at the seams with vivacious personality and charm as well as beauty, Clara Bow became known as the "IT" girl. She was the most popular young star of her time. Included in her many films were KID BOOTS with Eddie Cantor, BLACK OXEN, IT, DANGEROUS CURVES, THE SATURDAY NIGHT KID, and the never-to-be-forgotten WINGS with Buddy Rogers and Richard Arlen. Height 5 ft. 3 in. Red hair and brown eyes. She died in 1965.

**BOWERS, John**—plate 154. Born on December 7, 1891, in Indianapolis, Indiana. He made his film *début* in 1916 and played supporting roles until Samuel Goldwyn chose him to co-star with Pauline Frederick in ROADS OF DESTINY. Followed THE SILENT CALL with the famous dog star STRONGHEART which, strangely enough, won him millions of fans and the leading role with Colleen Moore in SO BIG. In 1926, he married film star Margaret de la Motte and they were co-starred in a film called PALS IN PARADISE. His other film credits include THE DANGER GIRL, LADDIE, CODE OF THE WILDERNESS, SKIN DEEP, and THE ROCKING MOON. Height 6 ft. Black curly hair and brown eyes.

**BOYER, Charles**—plate 215. Born in Figeac, France, on August 8, 1898. After two years at the French Conservatoire, was engaged at the Theater Antoine. He became a star on the French stage and made silent films in France and in Germany. His big international success came when he went to work in Hollywood. He starred in THE GARDEN OF ALLAH, HISTORY IS MADE AT NIGHT, MAYERLING, TOVARICH, and many other films. Height 5 ft. 11 in. Black hair and brown eyes. Married to Pat Patterson, the film star.

**BRENT, Evelyn**—plate 143. Born in Tampa, Florida, on October 20, 1899. Her real name was Betty Riggs. She began her theatrical career on the London stage and then went into English films. Was a star in English films in the silent days. Returning to the United States an accomplished film star she was cast in HELD TO ANSWER for Metro, co-starring with House Peters. She made FORBIDDEN CARGO in 1925, followed by such successes as BEAU SABREUR, THE WOMAN TRAP, THE QUEEN OF DIAMONDS, UNDERWORLD with George Bancroft and Clive Brook, THE SHOW DOWN, and INTERFERENCE. Height 5 ft. 4 in. Dark brown hair and eyes.

**BRENT, George**—plate 166. Born in Dublin, Ireland, March 15, 1902. His real name was George Nolan. He was an Abbey Theatre player in Dublin before emigrating to America. He spent two years in stock before appearing on Broadway. A good businessman as well as a talented actor, in a period of ten years he owned six stock companies and had acted in more than three hundred productions. Hollywood finally captured him and his first film, THE BIG TRAIL, was a success. Among his film credits are GOD'S COUNTRY AND THE WOMAN, GOLD IS WHERE YOU FIND IT, MOUNTAIN JUSTICE, and THE GO-GETTER. Height 5 ft. 11 in. Dark brown hair and brown eyes.

**BRIAN, Mary**—plate 4. Born in Corsicana, Texas, on February 17, 1908. Her real name was Mary Dantzler. Her first film was Herbert Brenon's production of PETER PAN in 1925. She made BROWN OF HARVARD with William Haines, and THE LIGHT OF THE WESTERN STARS with Richard Arlen. Other film credits included BEAU GESTE, THE VIRGINIAN, and CAPTAIN APPLEJACK. Height 5 ft. 2 in. Brown hair and blue eyes.

**BRONSON, Betty**—plate 18. Born in Trenton, New Jersey, on November 17, 1907. Before entering on a screen career she studied dancing under Fokine. In 1923, she was chosen by James Barrie to play the title role in the screen version of PETER PAN. There were over a hundred applicants for the part. Barrie's choice seemed to be the correct one as Miss Bronson won great acclaim in the film. Subsequent films included A KISS FOR CINDERELLA, THE LITTLE FRENCH GIRL, THE SINGING FOOL and SONNY BOY with Al Jolson. Height 5 ft. 4 in. Medium brown hair and blue eyes. She died in 1971.

**BROOK, Clive**—plate 105. Born on June 1, 1891, in London, England. Prior to 1914, he was a journalist of note. In the First World War, he rose to the rank of Major with many honors and was sent home to England after sustaining severe shell shock at the battle of Messines in 1918. After regaining his health, he went on the stage and played a leading part opposite actress Fay Compton in FAIR AND WARMER. Entering films soon thereafter he had starring roles in the English silent film productions of THE PENALTY and THIS FREEDOM. Lured to Hollywood by Thomas Ince, he made, among many others, FOUR FEATHERS, THREE FACES EAST, THE LAUGHING LADY, THE MIRAGE, UNDERWORLD, and HULA. He also played Holmes in THE RETURN OF SHERLOCK HOLMES. Height 5 ft. 11 in. Medium brown hair and blue eyes. He died in 1974.

**BROOKS, Louise**—plate 205. Born in Topeka, Kansas, in 1907, she came to the screen by way of the Ziegfeld Follies. Like many of the other Ziegfeld girls, she was "scouted" by Hollywood. She was beautiful, talented both as an actress and as a dancer, and it was only natural that she be starred in THE AMERICAN VENUS. She was featured in THE CANARY MURDER CASE, and starred in PANDORA'S BOX, ROLLED STOCKINGS, LOVE 'EM AND LEAVE 'EM, and THE STREET OF FORGOTTEN MEN, among many other films. She was married to actor-director Eddie Sutherland. Height 5 ft. 4 in. Brown hair and eyes.

**BROWN, Johnny Mack**—plate 137. Born in Dothan, Alabama, on September 1, 1904. Was a famous football player at the University of Alabama where he was educated. He went direct from the football field to films, virtually "snatched" by studio scouts. His first film was THE BUGLE CALL. In 1927, he made two college films with Marion Davies—THE VARSITY GIRL and

THE FAIR CO-ED. Two of the films in his career were made with Greta Garbo—THE DIVINE WOMAN and THE SINGLE STANDARD. Other film credits include FABULOUS, HURRICANE, and THE VALIENT. He was tall, dark, and handsome—6 ft. 1 in. Dark brown hair and eyes. Died in 1974.

**BRUCE, Virginia**—plate 194. Born on September 29, 1908, in Minneapolis, Minnesota. Her real name was Virginia Briggs. She was a Ziegfeld Follies girl before entering films. WHY BRING THAT UP? was her first film. She was a great beauty of her day and appeared as such in THE GREAT ZIEGFELD. She was a hit in THE BAD MAN OF BRIMSTONE, BORN TO DANCE, and WIFE, DOCTOR AND NURSES. These films helped to further her career. Other film credits include METROPOLITAN, WOMAN OF GLAMOUR, WHEN LOVE IS YOUNG, BETWEEN TWO WOMEN, and THE GARDEN MURDER CASE. Height 5 ft. 4 in. Golden blonde hair and blue eyes.

**BUCHANAN, Jack**—plate 157. Born in Glasgow, Scotland, on April 2, 1892. Started on the Glasgow stage with little or no success. Then, in London he obtained a spot in the chorus at the Empire Music Hall. He understudied Vernon Watson and when an opportunity came to play his part did so with such success that he was chosen for the principal touring company. He became a leading revue comedian in London and later in New York. He worked in silent films and, later when sound came, two of his greatest successes in America were MONTE CARLO, directed by Ernst Lubitsch, and THE BARKLEYS OF BROADWAY with Fred Astaire and Ginger Rogers. Height 6 ft. Brown hair and eyes.

## C

**CALHERN, Louis**—plate 149. Born in New York City on November 2, 1895, he made his stage *début* in Shakespeare's MUCH ADO ABOUT NOTHING. Later, blossomed forth as a leading man and achieved a Broadway reputation. He made his film *début* in the silent film era, but attained his greatest success with the advent of sound. He did smooth, sophisticated character parts with great perfection. He often played "villain" roles. His first film, made in 1921, was called THE BLOT and co-starred Claire Windsor. Among his film credits were THE LAST DAYS OF POMPEII, THE FACES, THE GORGEOUS HUSSY, and THE ARIZONIAN. Height 6 ft. 2½ in. Dark brown hair and eyes.

**CAREY, Harry**—plate 31. Born in New York City on January 6, 1880. His father was a judge of the Supreme Court and he himself was educated as a lawyer and started out in that profession. He gave up law for the stage and had considerable experience in the theater when he entered films in 1913 with the Biograph company. His films were mostly Westerns, although his greatest role was in TRADER HORN which was made in Africa. He co-starred with Irene Rich in DESPERATE TRAILS and among many other films made SATAN TOWN, THE BORDER PATROL, THE MAN FROM RED GULCH, THE LIGHTNING RIDER, and THE TEXAS TRAIL. Height 6 ft. Brown hair and blue eyes. He died in 1947.

**CARRADINE, John**—plate 233. Born in New York City, on February 5, 1906. After a successful stage career he reached Hollywood shortly before the advent of sound pictures. He went unnoticed in silent films, but by 1929 he was busy establishing himself and four years later came into great demand for his character portrayals. His films include THE GARDEN OF ALLAH, THE HURRICANE, CAPTAINS COURAGEOUS, ALI BABA GOES TO TOWN, ONE MILE FROM HEAVEN, and THE PRISONER OF SHARK ISLAND. Height 6 ft. 1 in. and very slender. Dark brown hair and eyes.

**CARROLL, Madeleine**—plate 206. Born in West Bromwich, Staffordshire, England, on February 26, 1906. Her father, John Carroll, married a French woman and Madeleine was bi-lingual in English and French. She was educated at Birmingham University and, after a short time as a teacher, became interested in the theatre and made her stage *début* in THE LASH. She made several silent films in England before beginning her Hollywood career. Among her films were THE SCHOOL FOR SCANDAL, MADAME GUILLOTINE, WHAT MONEY CAN BUY, THE GENERAL DIED AT DAWN, THE PRISONER OF ZENDA, and LLOYD'S OF LONDON. Height 5 ft. 5 in., with ash blonde hair and blue eyes.

**CARROLL, Nancy**—plate 155. Born in New York City on November 19, 1906. Her parents were from Ireland

and her real name was La Hiff. She is one of twelve children. Her stage experience before entering films in 1925, was in musicals. She had top billing in THE PASSING SHOW at the Winter Garden Theatre on Broadway when the films claimed her. She hit the jack-pot with the filming of THE WOLF OF WALL STREET and a long series of successful films followed among them THE SHOPWORN ANGEL, ILLUSION, CLOSE HARMONY, and LAUGHTER. Height 5 ft. 4 in. Red hair and blue eyes. She died in 1965.

**CHATTERTON, Ruth**—plate 96. Born in New York City, on December 24, 1893. She began her stage career at fourteen with a stock company in Washington, D. C. She rose to leading parts with such luminaries as Pauline Lord, Lenore Ulric, and Lowell Sherman on Broadway. At eighteen she was being starred. While presenting THE DEVIL'S PLUM TREE in a Los Angeles theatre, she was seen by Emil Jannings. He persuaded her to co-star with him in SINS OF THE FATHERS, which was her first film. Under contract to Paramount, she made SARAH AND SON, FRISCO JENNY, CHARMING SINNERS, and THE LAUGHING LADY. Her two greatest films were MADAME X for M-G-M and DODSWORTH, a Samuel Goldyyn production. Height 5 ft. 3 in. Light brown hair and blue eyes. Married to film star Ralph Forbes. She died in 1961.

**CHEVALIER, Maurice**—plate 230. One of the world's greatest entertainers, Maurice was born in Menilmontant, a quarter of Paris where everyone was poor and Maurice was no exception. His birthdate is September 12, 1889. He started on the Paris stage as an imitator of popular stars. He danced and sang and had a comedy routine. At eighteen, he became the dancing partner of the famous Mistinguette and appeared at the Folies Bergere and the Casino de Paris. He served in the French Army in the First World War, was severely wounded, and received the French Military Cross. After the war he returned to the Paris stage and also worked in several silent films in France. He was brought to Hollywood by Jesse Lasky where his first film, THE INNOCENTS OF PARIS, brought him fame on the American screen. Among his great musical films were THE LOVE PARADE, THE BIG POND, LOUISE, THE BELOVED VAGABOND, BREAK THE NEWS, GIGI, and CAN CAN. Height 5 ft. 10 in. Brown hair and blue eyes. He died in 1972.

**COLBERT, Claudette**—plate 223. Born in Paris, France, on September 13, 1905. Real name Claudette Chauchoin. Emigrated to America with her family in 1913 and was educated there. After gaining acting experience on the New York stage, she entered films in FOR THE LOVE OF MIKE, her first picture. Her greatest film was Cecil B. DeMille's MANSLAUGHTER. She was delightful in TOVARICH and enchanting in THE BIG POND with Maurice Chevalier. Her other films include THE YOUNG MAN OF MANHATTAN, UNDER TWO FLAGS, THE VORTEX, MAID OF SALEM, THE BARKER, LADY LIES, and BLUEBEARD'S EIGHTH WIFE. Height 5 ft. 5 in. Black hair and brown eyes.

**COLMAN, Ronald**—plate 128. Born on February 9, 1891, in Richmond Surrey, England. He served in the British Army in the First World War and began a stage career in London before coming to New York in 1920. While he was working in a Broadway production with Ruth Chatterton, Henry King, the film director, engaged him to play the leading role opposite Lillian Gish in the film version of THE WHITE SISTER. He was an instant hit and was immediately starred in ROMOLO. From then onward his film titles read like a fairytale: KISMET, BEAU GESTE, ARROWSMITH, RAFFLES, CLIVE OF INDIA, THE LIGHT THAT FAILED, RANDOM HARVEST, THE PRISONER OF ZENDA, LOST HORIZON, and many, many others. He won the Academy Award for ARROWSMITH. Height 5 ft. 11 in. Dark brown hair and eyes. Was married to Benita Hume. He died in 1958.

**CONKLIN, Chester**—plate 111. Born in Oskaloosa, Iowa, on January 11, 1888. Commenced professional career as a circus clown and then became a stage comedian. Made his film *début* with Keystone in 1914 and became one of that company's leading comedians. In addition to his comedies in the early days of films, he later played important character parts and was the comedy relief in feature pictures. Among his film credits are included STAIRS OF SAND, WE'RE IN THE NAVY NOW, THE DUCHESS OF BUFFALO, THE VIRGINIAN, and McFADDEN'S FLATS. Height 5 ft. 5 in. Brown hair and blue eyes. He died in 1971.

**COOGAN, Jackie**—plate 89. Born in Los Angeles, California, on October 26, 1914. His father, John Coogan, was a stage comedian and his mother appeared as a singer and dancer in vaudeville. Charlie Chaplin engaged him for the title role in THE KID when he was just five years old. He was world famous for this film. For several years thereafter he continued in films as a child actor. Among his credits were PECK'S BAD BOY, OLIVER TWIST, LITTLE ROBINSON CRUSOE, CIRCUS DAYS, and BUTTONS. Brown hair and blue eyes.

**COOK, Clyde**—plate 121. Born at Port McQuarrie, Australia, on December 16, 1891. Educated in Sydney and made his stage *début* in pantomime. He later won success as a dancer in London, Paris, and New York. He made his first film in 1919 with the Hal Roach studio in Hollywood. His work was principally in comedies but in later years he scored in comedy relief character parts in feature films. Among his film credits were JAZZ HEAVEN, WINGS OF ADVENTURE, A SAILOR'S SWEETHEART, and THE TAMING OF THE SHREW. Height 5 ft. 7 in. Brown hair and blue eyes. A great comic!

**COOPER, Gary**—plates 191, 192. Born in Helena, Montana, on May 7, 1901. Real name Frank Q. Cooper. Worked on his father's ranch and later as a newspaper cartoonist. In 1924, he embarked upon his screen career when he obtained a bit part in a two-reeler starring Eileen Sedgewick. THE WINNING OF BARBARA WORTH with Vilma Banky was one of his first successes. Although he played a wide variety of parts in his career, he rose to become one of the great Western stars of cinema history, winning an Oscar for HIGH NOON. Among his films were THE GENERAL DIED AT DAWN, A FAREWELL TO ARMS, LIVES OF A BENGAL LANCER, BEAU GESTE, THE PLAINSMAN, THE VIRGINIAN, SERGEANT YORK, THE TEXAN, and FOR WHOM THE BELL TOLLS. Height 6 ft. 2½ in. Reddish brown hair and blue eyes. He died in 1961.

**COOPER, Jackie**—plate 88. Born in Los Angeles, California, on September 16, 1923. His father was Johnny Cooper, the vaudeville actor, and his mother Mabel Leonard, a well-known professional actress. Jackie appeared in silent films at the age of three, working with Lloyd Hamilton in his comedy series. More recent films include PECK'S BAD BOY, DINKY, TOUCH GUY, DEVIL TAKES THE COUNT, and O'SHAUGHNESSY'S BOY. Fair hair and blue eyes.

**CORTEZ, Ricardo**—plate 92. Born in New York City on July 7, 1899. His real name was Jacob Kranz, but he changed it legally to Ricardo Cortez when he began his screen career in 1917. He had previously been a boxer. His first big role came with Jesse Lasky in a film called SIXTY CENTS AN HOUR. He played suave leading man roles with great success. In 1924 his role in FEET OF CLAY resulted in his elevation to stardom. Among his films were TALK OF THE DEVIL, THE SPANIARD, THE CASE OF THE BLACK CAT, THE SWAIN, THE EAGLE OF THE SEA, THE SORROWS OF SATAN, and THE PRIVATE LIFE OF HELEN OF TROY. Height 6 ft. 1 in. Black hair and brown eyes. Married to screen star Alma Rubens.

**COWARD, Noël**—plate 52. Born on December 16, 1899, in London, England. Although primarily a playwright, composer, and stage star, he did considerable film work almost up to the time of his death in 1974. One of his last films was BUNNY LAKE IS MISSING with Lawrence Olivier. In the early days of the film industry, he went to Hollywood to work in HEARTS OF THE WORLD, the great D. W. Griffith epic in 1918. Among his other films were TONIGHT IS OURS, THE VORTEX, and DESIGN FOR LIVING with Gary Cooper. In THE VORTEX, one of his finest films, he co-starred with Claudette Colbert and Frederic March. Although he did not personally appear in the film version of his operetta BITTER SWEET, with the great voices of Nelson Eddy and Jeanette MacDonald, this films made the name of Noël Coward immortal in screen history. Height 5 ft. 10 in. Brown hair and eyes.

**CRAWFORD, Joan**—plate 167. Born in San Antonio, Texas, on March 23, 1904. Real name Lucille Le Sueur. Started her professional career as a dancer. Her first film was PRETTY LADIES in which she had only a bit part. In 1925, she made SALLY IRENE, AND MARY with Constance Bennett and Sally O'Neill, and a film called OLD CLOTHES with Jackie Coogan. TRAMP, TRAMP, TRAMP, with Harry Langdon came in 1926, and then there was THE TAXI DANCER, THE UNKNOWN with Lon Chaney and Norman Kerry, DANCING DAUGHTERS, and OUR MODERN MAIDENS with Douglas Fairbanks, Jr., whom she later married. Already a star in silent films, she made the transition into sound to become one of the greatest stars in film history. After divorcing Fairbanks, she married film star Franchot Tone. Height 5 ft. 4 in. Auburn hair and hazel eyes.

D

**DAMITA, Lily**—plate 14. Born on July 20, 1906, in Paris, France. At eighteen, she was a leading member of the Folies Bergère and a year later succeeded Mistinguette as star of the Casino de Paris. She starred in French, British, German, and American films. Her greatest successes were in Hollywood where she made THE COCK-EYED WORLD with Victor McLaglen, THE RESCUE with Ronald Colman, and THE BRIDGE OF SAN LUIS REY with Don Alvarado. She was married to film star Errol Flynn and is the mother of Sean Flynn, who has also attained stardom. Height 5 ft. 2 in. Fair hair and brown eyes.

**DARWELL, Jane**—plate 125. Born in Palmyra, Missouri on October 15, 1892. Her earliest ambition was for the stage and, after a course in dramatics, she obtained a small part in a play. With some stage experience behind her, she was cast for an important role with Monroe Salisbury and Bessie Barriscale in the film THE ROSE OF THE RANCHO in 1914. In the same year with Jesse Lasky she made THE ONLY SON. It was her destiny to become one of America's finest character actresses. Among her films were SLAVE SHIP, DANGEROUSLY YOURS, FIFTY ROADS TO TOWN, LOVE IS NEWS, and ISN'T LIFE WONDERFUL. Height 5 ft. 6 in. Brown hair and blue eyes. She died in 1967.

**DAVIES, Marion**—plate 186. Born on January 3, 1897, in Brooklyn, New York. Real name Marion Douras. Daughter of a New York judge. Her great beauty caught the attention of the producer of the stage success CHU CHIN CHOW, who put her in the show's leading role. She was later with the Ziegfeld Follies. She modelled for the American artists Harrison Fisher, Montgomery Flagg, and Howard Chandler Christy and her portrait appeared on nearly every magazine cover in the country. She made her screen *début* in RUNAWAY ROMANY in 1917. She played the tomboy in LITTLE OLD NEW YORK. Other of her films included WHEN KNIGHTHOOD WAS IN FLOWER, THE RED MILL, QUALITY STREET, THE BEAUTIFUL REBEL, and PEG OF MY HEART. Height 5 ft. 5 in. Golden blonde hair and blue eyes. She died in 1961.

**DAVIS, Bette**—plate 225. Born in Boston, Massachusetts, on April 5, 1908. Real name Ruth Elizabeth Davis. After dramatic training at the John Murray Anderson school, she spent two years on the stage before making her screen *début* in BAD SISTER. Miss Davis was really a product of the sound era, but she actually worked in three silent films. She was to become one of the screen's greatest stars. The list of her films is truly formidable: THE MAN WHO PLAYED GOD with George Arliss, THE PETRIFIED FOREST, OF HUMAN BONDAGE, DARK VICTORY, THE LETTER, THE MAN WHO CAME TO DINNER, NOW VOYAGER, THE CORN IS GREEN, ALL ABOUT EVE, THE VIRGIN QUEEN, and WHAT EVER HAPPENED TO BABY JANE? with Joan Crawford, to name a few. Bette Davis always played Bette Davis, but her public liked it that way. She was married to film star Gary Merrill, who co-starred with her in several of her films. Height 5 ft. 3½ in. Blonde hair and blue eyes.

**DAVIS, Mildred**—plate 28. She was born on May 8, 1902, in Pasadena, California. She worked in comedies upon first entering films in 1919. She was chosen by Harold Lloyd as his leading lady and remained in that role for the balance of her career. She retired from films after her marriage to Lloyd. Among the films she made were SAILOR BEWARE, AMONG THOSE PRESENT, and SPEEDY. Height 5 ft. 4 in. Golden hair and blue eyes. There was a daughter, Gloria, and a son, Harold Lloyd, Jr., who is now working in films.

**del RIO, Dolores**—plate 101. Born on August 3, 1905, in Durango, Mexico. Educated at a convent and studied dancing in Spain. In 1925, while on a trip to Mexico, American producer Edwin Carewe was so deeply impressed by her singing and dancing that he persuaded her to come to Hollywood for a film career. Her first film was JOANNA and fourteen months later she was a star. Perhaps her greatest film was WHAT PRICE GLORY? with Victor McLaglen and Edmund Lowe. Among her other films were THE LOVES OF CARMEN with Don Alvarado, EVANGELINE, LANCER

SPY, IN CALIENTE, THE WIDOW FROM MONTE CARLO, and RESURRECTION. She was sometimes spoken of as the most beautiful woman on the screen. Height 5 ft. 5 in. Black hair and eyes. Her real name was Lolita Asunsolo and she was a cousin of film star Ramon Novarro.

**DENNY, Reginald**—plate 6. Born in Richmond, Surrey, England, on November 21, 1894. Son of famous English stage comedian W. H. Denny. He made his stage *début* at the age of five and was the original boy prince in THE ROYAL FAMILY when it was produced at the Theatre Royal in London in 1899. He came to Broadway with Mrs. Patrick Campbell, but left her company to accept an offer from Hollywood. He had been an amateur boxing champion in his college days in England and Universal first starred him as the boxer in THE LEATHER PUSHERS. Among his other films were KIKI with Mary Pickford, SKINNER'S DRESS SUIT, MADAM SATAN, THE CHEERFUL FRAUD, THE ABYSMAL BRUTE, and WHAT HAPPENED TO JONES. Height 6 ft. Medium brown hair and blue eyes. He served in the British Royal Air Force during the First World War. He died in 1967.

**DEXTER, Elliott**—plate 98. Born in Houston, Texas, on March 29, 1878. One of the veterans of American films. He co-starred with Mary Pickford in STELLA MARRIS, and with Marie Doro in THE HEART OF MARY FLYNN, THE LASH, and CASTLES FOR TWO. He worked with Marguerite Clark, Gloria Swanson, Leatrice Joy, Betty Compson, and Wanda Hawley. He co-starred with Alice Brady in WOMAN AND WIFE and with Ethel Clayton in MAGGIE PEPPER. He was a close personal friend of Cecil B. DeMille and was under contract to Famous Players and Paramount for many years. Among his other films were WE CAN'T HAVE EVERYTHING and THE AFFAIRS OF ANATOLE. Height 5 ft. 11 in. Dark hair and eyes. Married to film star Marie Doro.

**DIETRICH, Marlene**—plates 202, 203. Born in Berlin, Germany, on December 27, 1902, the daughter of a German Army officer. She studied the violin at an early age and became very proficient, but turned to the stage and then to films. She made a number of silent films in Germany, but it was not until after her work in THE BLUE ANGEL that she went to America under contract to Paramount. Her first American film was MOROCCO with Gary Cooper and Adolphe Menjou. She was an instant success and went on to be one of the most fabulous of international stars. Among her other early films were THE GARDEN OF ALLAH, DESIRE, KNIGHT WITHOUT ARMOUR, and ANGEL. Height 5 ft. 5 in. Red-gold hair and blue eyes.

**DIX, Richard**—plate 132. Born on July 18, 1895, in St. Paul, Minnesota. His real name was Ernest Brimmer. After being trained to be a surgeon, he decided that he preferred the stage as a career and became a leading man with the Morosco Stock Company. Cecil B. DeMille saw him in a play and was so impressed with his work that he gave him an important role in his epic film THE TEN COMMANDMENTS. Samuel Goldwyn then starred him in THE CHRISTIAN and he was on his way. He made ICE BOUND and THE VANISHING AMERICAN with Lois Wilson, MANHATTAN, SAY IT AGAIN, and THE REDSKIN. Then came MORAN OF THE MARINES, SHANGHAI BOUND, and CIMARRON. Height 6 ft. Brown hair and eyes. He died in 1949.

**DOVE, Billie**—plate 48. Born in New York City on May 14, 1903. Real name Lillian Bohny. She came to films from the Ziegfeld Follies. She made her film *début* in POLLY OF THE FOLLIES and then co-starred with Eddie Cantor in KID BOOTS. Douglas Fairbanks, Sr. chose her for a supporting role in THE BLACK PIRATE, and she made THE LOVE MART opposite Gilbert Roland. Other of her films were BEYOND THE RAINBOW, THE AMERICAN BEAUTY, THE STOLEN BRIDE, THE PAINTED ANGEL, HER PRIVATE LIFE, THE LADY WHO DARED, and WANDERER OF THE WASTELAND with Jack Holt. Height 5 ft. 5 in. Dark brown hair and eyes.

**DUNN, James** —plate 147. Born in New York City on November 2, 1903, He began his film career in Hollywood without any stage or acting experience. After working in silent films as an extra and in small parts, he joined a stock company where he gained considerable dramatic experience on the stage. He then returned to films where his work in A TREE GROWS IN BROOKLYN made him a star. Among his film credits are VENUS MAKES TROUBLE, MYSTERIOUS CROSSING, WE HAVE OUR MOMENTS, THE TWO-FISTED GENTLEMAN, and HEARTS IN

BONDAGE. Height 6 ft. Brown hair and blue eyes. He died in 1967.

**DVORAK, Ann**—plate 10. Born in New York City on August 2, 1910. Her real name was Ann McKim and her mother, Anna Lehr was an actress on both stage and screen. As a child, she worked in a number of silent films, sometimes with her mother. She was trained as a dancer and danced and did bit parts before the advent of sound. Her first important role came with Paul Muni in SCARFACE. Her other films include WE WHO ARE ABOUT TO DIE, DR. SOCRATES, SHE'S NO LADY, MIDNIGHT COURT, THANKS A MILLION, and RACING LADY. Height 5 ft. 4½ in. Brown hair and green eyes.

## E

**EILERS, Sally**—plate 146. Born in New York City on December 11, 1908. Started her film career as an extra in silent films. Was chosen as the Wampus "Baby Star" of 1928. She made many successful films in which she played supporting or starring roles. Among them were PURSUIT, STRIKE ME PINK, WITHOUT ORDERS, TALK OF THE DEVIL, ALIAS MARY DOW, SHE MADE HER BED, REMEMBER LAST NIGHT, and WE HAVE OUR MOMENTS. Height 5 ft. 3½ in. Red hair and brown eyes.

**EVANS, Madge**—plate 50. Born in New York City on July 1, 1909. Made her screen *début* as a child actress in 1919. Left films for school but returned in 1925 to appear opposite Richard Barthelmess in WINNING THROUGH. She remained on the Hollywood scene and included in the many films in which she appeared are THE LOVE DEFENDER, GATES OF GLADNESS, THE BLUEBIRD, THE LITTLE ACCIDENT, WINNING THROUGH, THE BANKS OF THE WABASH, MOONLIGHT MURDER, PENNIES FROM HEAVEN, and THE THIRTEENTH CHAIR. Height 5 ft. 4 in. Blonde hair and blue eyes.

## F

**FAIR, Elinor**—plate 59. Born in Richmond, Virginia, on May 15, 1902. Trained for a stage career as a young girl, studying dancing, voice culture, and music in France, Germany, and Italy. She began her acting career on the New York stage in musical comedy. Her film *début* was made with the famous Fox star William Farnham in THE END OF THE TRAIL. Other films included THE VOLGA BOATMAN with Theodore Kosloff, BACHELOR BRIDES, JIM THE CONQUEROR, and MY FRIEND FROM INDIA with William Boyd, whom she later married. Height 5 ft. 4½ in. Black hair and dark brown eyes.

**FAIRBANKS, Jr., Douglas**—plate 82. Born in New York City on December 9, 1909. The son of film star Douglas Fairbanks, Sr. Began film career in 1923. His first big role was in STEPHEN STEPS OUT. Worked in films in England as well as in America. One of his most successful films was THE PRISONER OF ZENDA. Other film credits include AMATEUR GENTLEMAN, MAN OF THE MOMENT, THE CORSICAN BROTHERS, and ACCUSED. He was at one time married to Joan Crawford. Height 6 ft. Brown hair and blue eyes.

**FARREL, Charles**—plate 78. Born on August 8, 1905, in East Walpole, Massachusetts. Educated for a business career at Boston University, but went on the stage instead. Made his screen *début* in 1924, and for two years played minor parts. His big break came when he was given a leading role opposite Janet Gaynor in SEVENTH HEAVEN. With the success of that film and his own personal triumph in it, he was on his way to stardom. His film credits include LUCKY STAR, THE ROUGH RIDERS, SUNNY SIDE UP, THE PRINCESS AND THE PLUMBER, and THE STREET ANGEL. Height 6 ft. 2 in. Brown hair and eyes.

**FAZENDA, Louise**—plate 30. Born on June 17, 1895, at Lafayette, Indiana. After a precarious existence on the stage where she got absolutely nowhere, she entered films with Mack Sennett in 1913. Her first film was with Bobby Vernon and was called MIKE AND JAKE AT THE BEACH. For several years she played slapstick farce for Sennett. DOWN ON THE FARM and THE SUMMER GIRLS were two of her best. In 1923, she began making feature films and was cast in MAIN STREET with Monte Blue, and Florence Vidor. She was "priceless" in the thriller THE BAT, which was followed by her big role in THE CRADLE SNATCHERS. She also cavorted with W. C. Fields and Chester Conklin in TILLIE'S PUNCTURED ROMANCE. Other Fazenda films include DANCING FEET, ON WITH THE SHOW, THE LADY AND THE ROSE, and NOAH'S ARK. Height 5 ft. 5 in. with fair hair and blue eyes. Married producer-director Hal Wallis. Died in 1962.

**FENTON, Leslie**—plate 49. Born in Liverpool, England, on March 12, 1903. Emigrated to America with his family and made his home in Columbus, Ohio, where he was educated. Interested in an acting career, he went to New York where he obtained a small part in the stage production of MY SON. After considerable stage experience, he entered films in THE GOOSE HANGS HIGH. He was in the big spectacular WHAT PRICE GLORY, followed by leading roles in THE LAST PERFORMANCE, EAST LYNNE, THUNDER MOUNTAIN, and CHINA PASSAGE. Height 6 ft. Dark brown hair and eyes.

**FERGUSON, Elsie**—plate 79. Born in New York City on August 19, 1883. She made her stage *début* in the chorus of THE BELLE OF NEW YORK in 1900. Miss Ferguson became a great star both on Broadway and the London stage before entering films. She made ROSE OF THE WORLD with Wyndham Standing in 1918. AVALANCHE was one of her big successes. She made BURNING DAYLIGHT and FOOTLIGHTS in Hollywood and then divided her time between stage and screen. She scored with Wallace Reid in FOREVER, and then made the OUTCAST followed by SCARLET PAGES. Height 5 ft. 5 in. Chestnut hair and brown eyes. She died in 1961.

**FINCH, Jack**—plate 5. Born in Milwaukee, Wisconsin, on October 15, 1903. Educated as a journalist and worked first in publicity at the Famous Players-Lasky studio in Hollywood where he met and struck up a great friendship with Wallace Reid. Was cast in several of Reid's films including ACROSS THE CONTINENT and EXCUSE MY DUST. Later worked in THE HUNCHBACK OF NOTRE DAME with Lon Chaney at Universal, in ROBIN HOOD with Douglas Fairbanks, Sr., and in THE IRON HORSE with George O'Brien. Was a close friend of Louella Parsons, the motion picture critic for Hearst publications. He was related to Flora Finch, the film comedienne. Height 6 ft. 1½ in. Reddish-brown hair and blue-grey eyes.

**FINLAYSON, Jimmy**—plate 120. Born on August 27, 1887, in Falkirk, Scotland. Real name William Claude Dukanfield. Emigrated to America as a young man and after considerable stage experience on Broadway entered films via Mack Sennett comedies. He was one of the original Keystone Kops. He later did comedy relief roles with equal success. Among his later films were HANDLE WITH CARE, PICK A STAR, WAY OUT WEST, THE BOHEMIAN GIRL, and BONNIE SCOTLAND. Height 5 ft. 8 in. Brown hair and eyes. Died in 1953.

**FORBES, Ralph**—plate 97. Born on September 30, 1902, in London, England, of Scottish parents. He made his screen *début* in England in a silent film called BROWN SUGAR with Clive Brook. After working on the London stage, he came to Broadway in HAVOC. He supported Ruth Chatterton in several of her stage productions, and then married her. He made his screen *début* as one of the brothers in BEAU GESTE. Other of his films include THE GREEN GODDESS with George Arliss, RECKLESS YOUTH, THE LAST OF MRS. CHEYNEY, and MR. WU with Lon Chaney. Height 6 ft. Fair hair and blue eyes. Died in 1951.

**FORD, Wallace**—plate 142. Born in Bolton, Lancashire, England, on February 12, 1899. Raised in an orphan's home under the name of Samuel Jones. Was adopted by a Canadian family in Manitoba, but ran away at the age of eleven because of ill treatment. After many harrowing experiences, he finally secured a job in a theatre as an usher. He later became an actor and worked in stock and then Broadway. He came to films as a seasoned actor and made many successful films among them STARDUST, JERICHO, and THE INFORMER with Victor McLaglen. Height 6 ft. Brown hair and blue eyes. Died in 1966.

**FOSTER, Preston**—plate 228. Born in Ocean City, New Jersey, on October 24, 1902. He worked as a newspaper reporter before going on the stage. Following several years of dramatic stage work, he made his film *début* toward the end of the silent era. With the advent of sound, he rose rapidly to starring roles. Among his films were THE PLOUGH AND THE STARS, SEA DEVILS, THE OUTCASTS OF POKER FLAT, ANNIE OAKLEY, THE LAST DAYS OF POMPEII, HOUSE OF FATE, WE WHO ARE ABOUT TO DIE, and WE'RE ONLY HUMAN. Height 6 ft. Dark brown hair and blue eyes. Died in 1970.

**FRANCIS, Alex B.**—plate 17. Born in London, England, in 1868. Entered a monastery to become a monk, then changed his mind and went on the stage. After successes on the London stage and on Broadway, Jesse Lasky signed him for Famous Players in 1916. He became one of America's most beloved character actors. Among his many films were THE TENDER HOUR, THE RETURN OF PETER GRIM, THE CASE OF SERGEANT GRISCHA, THE YANKEE SENOR, THE BISHOP MURDER CASE, and THE MISSISSIPPI GAMBLER. Height 5 ft. 11 in. Grey hair and blue eyes.

G

**GABLE, Clark**—plates 222, 224. Born in Cadiz, Ohio, on February 1, 1901. He began as a prop boy and scene shifter. Then an extra and a bit player in Westerns. Before the advent of sound he was virtually unknown. His first film that brought notice was THE PAINTED DESERT, and it was not until he made MUTINY ON THE BOUNTY that he was considered a star. But he *was* a star and indeed rose to the heights of stardom to become known in Hollywood as "The King." His role of Rhett Butler in GONE WITH THE WIND will never be forgotten. Among his many other films were PARNELL, SARATOGA, SAN FRANCISCO, CAIN AND MABEL, and MISFITS. Height 6 ft. 1½ in. Dark brown hair and grey eyes. Was married to Carole Lombard. He died in 1960.

**GARBO, Greta**—plates 71, 73. Born in Stockholm, Sweden, on September 18, 1906. Real name Greta Louvien Gustafsson. Once worked in a shop in Stockholm. Later entered the Royal Academy of Dramatic Art in Stockholm and was "discovered" by film director Mauritz Stiller, who cast her in his film THE ATONEMENT OF GÖSTA BERLING. She appeared in several other Continental films including one with UFA in Germany. Metro signed her in 1925 and she came to Hollywood. Her first American picture was THE TORRENT and her second THE TEMPTRESS. She became one of the screen's immortals with her portrayals in such films as GRAND HOTEL, QUEEN CHRISTINA, ANNA KARENINA, CAMILLE, MARIE WALEWSKA, MATA HARI, and ANNA CHRISTIE. Height 5 ft. 6 in. Light brown hair and blue eyes. She never married.

**GAYNOR, Janet**—plate 80. Born on October 6, 1907, in Philadelphia, Pennsylvania. Entered films in 1924 and attracted attention of the producers for her role in THE JOHNSTOWN FLOOD. Her great success came with her starring role in SEVENTH HEAVEN, and from then on her popularity was high and her position as a star assured. She rose to even greater heights in A STAR IS BORN. Other films included SUNRISE, THE STREET ANGEL, THE MAN WHO CAME BACK, and CHRISTINE, among many others. Height 5 ft. Golden red hair and brown eyes.

**GIBSON, Hoot**—plate 38. Cowboy star born in Tekamah, Nebraska, in January 1892. Real christian name Edward. Became a cowboy in his early youth and by the time he was twenty had won so many trophies for trick riding that he became recognized as one of the champion cowboys of America. Later joined a travelling circus. Embarked on his screen career in 1911. He made an almost endless series of Westerns among them THE FLAMING FRONTIER, PAINTED PONIES, PRAIRIE KING, TAMING THE WEST, SURE FIRE, ACTION, THE BEARCAT, and GALLOPING FURY. Height 5 ft. 10 in. Was married to film star Sally Eilers. He died in 1962.

**GILBERT, John**—plates 70, 72. Born on July 10, 1895, in Logan, Utah, of British parents. He was educated at a military school in San Rafael, California. Was on the stage as a child and had brief stage experience as a young man, but in 1915, when he was twenty, he began his screen career. He eventually starred in some of the greatest hits of his day—with Mae Murray in THE MERRY WIDOW, with Lillian Gish in LA BOHEME, with Greta Garbo in QUEEN CHRISTINA and WOMAN OF AFFAIRS, and with Estelle Taylor in MONTE CRISTO. His greatest film was THE BIG PARADE with Renee Adoree. Other film credits included CAMEO KIRBY, HE WHO GETS SLAPPED, THE SNOB, and FLESH AND THE DEVIL. Height 5 ft. 10 in. Black hair and brown eyes. Was married first to Leatrice Joy and then Ina Claire, both stars. Died in 1936.

**GILLINGWATER, Claude**—plate 151. Born in Pike County, Missouri, on August 2, 1870. One of the best-known players of "old men" roles in American pictures. He had a great deal of stage experience before entering films in 1920. His first film was LITTLE LORD FAUNTLEROY which starred Mary Pickford. He went on in films for picture after picture with delightful portrayals. There was SO LONG LETTY, POOR LITTLE RICH GIRL, WE MODERNS, THE TALE OF TWO CITIES, THE MAN WHO PAWNED HIS SOUL, THE PRISONER OF SHARK ISLAND, and many others. Height 6 ft. 2½ in. Grey hair and brown eyes.

**GODDARD, Paulette**—plate 209. Born in Great Neck, Long Island, in New York state on June 3, 1909. She left school at the age of fifteen to try for the stage and just a year later was appearing on Broadway in the Ziegfeld Follies. Hal Roach signed her for the films and she first appeared in Hal Roach comedies. She had made several other feature films including THE KID FROM SPAIN and PACK UP YOUR TROUBLES before Chaplin signed her to play opposite him in MODERN TIMES. With the advent of sound films, she went on to stardom. Her role in THE WOMEN was one of the best of her career. She was married to Chaplin at one time. Height 5 ft. 4 in. Dark brown hair and blue eyes.

**GRIFFITH, Corrine**—plate 7. Born on November 24, 1899, in Texarkana, Texas. Before commencing her screen career she was a professional dancer. Her fragile type of beauty had great appeal and following her triumph in DECLASSE she became established as a top star. Among her pictures were INFATUATION, THE LADY IN ERMINE, DIVINE LADY, SATURDAY'S CHILDREN, and THE GARDEN OF EDEN. She was the wife of Walter Morosco, the producer-director. Height 5 ft. 4 in. Golden brown hair and blue eyes.

**GRIFFITH, Raymond**—plate 169. Born in 1890 in Boston, Massachusetts, of theatrical parents. As a child he played LITTLE LORD FAUNTLEROY on the stage and was later with Barnum and Bailey's circus. He became known in musical comedy on the stage and then as a dramatic actor until he lost his voice. He then became an accomplished pantomimist and dancer. Entering screen work as a gag writer, he later began acting in films and in 1922 Marshall Neilan chose him for a leading role in FOOLS FIRST. He was next under contract to Paramount where his career blossomed. Among his films were included WEDDING BELLS, RAIN OR SHINE, TIME TO LOVE, FORTY WINKS, and ALL QUIET ON THE WESTERN FRONT. Height 5 ft. 6 in. Black hair and hazel eyes. Died in 1959.

## H

**HAINES, William**—plate 58. Born on January 1, 1900, in Staunton, Virginia. Was a "bit" player with the Goldwyn company until he was cast in a prominent role in THREE WISE FOOLS. Recognition came with this film and he was given the title role in BROWN OF HARVARD. Followed THE GAIETY GIRL, TELL IT TO THE MARINES, MIDNIGHT EXPRESS, and ALIAS JIMMY VALENTINE. His first important film was with Norman Kerry in BROTHERS UNDER THE SKIN. One of his little known but one of his best films was CIRCE with Mae Murray. Height 6 ft. Black hair and brown eyes.

**HALL, James**—plate 177. Born on October 22, 1900, in Dallas, Texas. Real name James Hamilton. Joined a travelling show at an early age and rose to be a dancer in the Ziegfeld Follies. After several years on the legitimate stage, he entered films in 1926, making his *début* as the hero in THE CAMPUS FLIRT with Bebe Daniels. His greatest role was in HELLS' ANGELS with Ben Lyon and Jean Harlow. Other of his films include HOTEL IMPERIAL, THE SATURDAY NIGHT KID, THE CANARY MURDER CASE, and FOUR SONS. Height 5 ft. 11 in. with brown hair and blue eyes. Died in 1940.

**HAMILTON, Lloyd**—plate 109. Born in Oakland, California, on December 22, 1891. Originated the character of "Bud" in the HAM AND BUD film series. He was famous for the cap he wore and seldom removed. His comedy was individualistic and uniquely appealing. Can be classed as one of the top comedians of the silent film era. Among his many films other than the HAM AND BUD comedy series were UP A TREE, WON BY A NECK, MARRIAGE ROWS, and HOTSY TOTSY. Height 6 ft. Brown hair and blue eyes.

**HAMMERSTEIN, Elaine**—plate 61. Born on June 16, 1897, in New York City, the daughter of Arthur Hammerstein, famous American theatrical producer. She was the niece of Oscar Hammerstein. After some stage experience on Broadway, including the lead in HIGH JINKS, she made her screen *début* in THE ARGYLE

CASE. She was then cast in a leading role in RUPERT OF HENTZAU with Bryant Washburn and Bert Lytell. Other film credits include ONE WEEK OF LOVE, THE FOOLISH VIRGIN, THE WAY OF A MAID, THE UNWRITTEN LAW, and LADIES OF LEISURE. Height 5 ft. 5 in. Dark brown hair and eyes.

**HARDING, Ann**—plate 201. Born in San Antonio, Texas, on August 7, 1904. Her real name was Dorothy Gatley. Her first film experience was as a script reader for Famous Players Lasky. Seeking a stage career, she went East and became a member of the Provincetown Players. She originated the leading role in THE TRIAL OF MARY DUGAN on the New York stage. She came to films in the leading role in PARIS BOUND, and then made CONDEMNED with Ronald Colman. Other film credits include LOVE FROM A STRANGER, THE GIRL OF THE GOLDEN WEST, HOLIDAY, THE WITNESS CHAIR, and THE LADY CONSENTS. Height 5 ft. 5 in. She was famous for her flaxen hair and blue eyes and was the "lady fair" of the first colour films.

**HARDY, Oliver**—plate 241. Born on January 18, 1892, in Atlanta, Georgia. Began his career in stock with his own singing act. He had considerable stage experience when he joined Vitagraph in 1918. He moved to Fox and then to Hal Roach. Working in Hal Roach comedies, he met Stan Laurel. As a comedy team they achieved great success and assured a place for themselves in film history. His screen credits include BABES IN TOYLAND, NIGHT OWLS, PACK UP YOUR TROUBLES, BLOCKHEADS, THE DANCING MASTERS, THE BULLFIGHTERS, GREAT GUNS, A CHUMP AT OXFORD, to name a few. Hardy was the "fat" man of the team. Height 6 ft. 1 in. Black hair and brown eyes. Died in 1957.

**HARLAN, Kenneth**—plate 178. Born in New York City on July 26, 1895. Son of the famous actress Rita Harlan and nephew of character actor Otis Harlan. Before he was eighteen, he had the experience of playing both brother and husband to his own mother on the stage. He also played her sweetheart, he made his film *début* working with both the famous Talmadge sisters, Constance and Norma. Among his many films were PARADISE ISLAND, ON THE STROKE OF THREE, THE GOLDEN STRAIN, and THE MAN WITHOUT A HEART. Was married to Marie Prevost, the film star. Height 6 ft. Dark brown hair and grey eyes. Died in 1967.

**HARLOW, Jean**—plates 190, 193. Born in Kansas City, Missouri, on March 3, 1911. Sheer chance brought Jean Harlow into pictures. While passing one of the Hollywood studios with a friend, she was seen by one of the studio officials who was so impressed that he stopped her on the street and arranged an interview with the studio's casting director. She was soon working in Hal Roach comedies. This was in 1925 when she was just fifteen. Before sound came she made MORAN OF THE MARINES with Richard Dix, and was in CITY LIGHTS with Charlie Chaplin. While working at the Christie Studio she met Lyon and James Hall who were about to start work on HELL'S ANGELS for Howard Hughes. They introduced her to Hughes who cast her for the lead in HELL'S ANGELS. She later starred with all the "greats"—Clark Gable, Cary Grant, William Powell, Spencer Tracy, Lionel Barrymore, Wallace Beery, and Robert Taylor. Her film credits include RED DUST, PLATINUM BLONDE, RIFF RAFF, CHINA SEAS, and DINNER AT EIGHT. Height 5 ft. 3½ in. Platinum blonde hair and grey-blue eyes. Died in 1937 at age twenty-six.

**HARRON, John**—plate 19. Born on March 31, 1900, in New York City. A younger brother of Robert Harron, the great D. W. Griffith star. He made his screen *début* in 1921 in THROUGH THE BACK DOOR with Mary Pickford. Like his brother, John Harron became an outstanding young actor in dramatic roles. Among his films were DULCY with Constance Talmadge, STREET GIRL, HELL BENT FOR HEAVEN, THE BOY FRIEND, and THE LITTLE IRISH GIRL. Height 5 ft. 11 in. Dark brown hair and eyes.

**HART, William S.**—plates 32, 33. The early screen's great Western star was born in Newburgh, New York, on December 6, 1872. He was a veteran of the screen and perhaps the greatest of all the cowboy stars. Before making his screen *début* he was a Shakespearian actor on Broadway. His first film was a two-reeler called TWO GUN HICKS made in 1914. The public was avid for his films and he made many. Among them were THE RETURN OF DRAW EGAN, RIDDLE GAWNE, SHARK MONROE, WOLVES OF THE TRAIL, BLUE BLAZES RAWDEN, THE TOLL GATE, WILD BILL HICKOCK, TUMBLEWEEDS, and HELL'S HINGES. Height 6 ft. Dark brown hair greying and blue eyes. Married to screen star Winifred Westover. Died on his ranch in Saugus, California in 1946.

**HATTON, Raymond**—plate 152. Born in Red Oak, Iowa, on July 7, 1892. Was a famous American stage comedian and star of musical comedy. He made his film *début* with the Kalem company in 1915. His comedy relief roles won him popularity the peak of which came during his years with Famous Players Lasky. Among his films were SINNERS TAKE ALL, BAD MAN FROM BRIMSTONE, YELLOWSTONE, WOMEN IN TROUBLE, JOAN THE WOMAN, and OLIVER TWIST. Height 5 ft. 7 in. Brown hair and blue eyes.

**HAWLEY, Wanda**—plate 133. Born on July 30, 1899, in Philadelphia, Pennsylvania, of British parents. She was trained for opera and did considerable concert work in the U.S.A. and Canada. She made her film *début* in 1919 as "Beauty" in EVERY WOMAN. Charles Ray requested her for his leading lady in GREASED LIGHTNING. She then embarked upon her career with Paramount where she starred with such great luminaries as Wallace Reid, Bryant Washburn, Elliott Dexter, Monte Blue, Bert Lytell, and Theodore Roberts. Her film credits include THE AFFAIRS OF ANATOLE, THE SIX BEST CELLARS, DOUBLE SPEED, THE TREE OF KNOWLEDGE, SECRET SERVICE, THE TRUTHFUL LIAR, COMBAT, and THE PHANTOM OF THE FOREST. Height 5 ft. 3 in. Golden blonde hair and blue eyes.

**HAYES, Helen**—plate 196. Born on October 10, 1895, in Washington, D. C. With Ethel Barrymore, Helen Hayes was classed as the greatest of dramatic stage stars. At the time she made her first film she was the toast of Broadway and she repeated on the screen some of her great stage successes. Among her films were THE SIN OF MADELON CLAUDET, ANOTHER LANGUAGE, THE WHITE SISTER in which she co-starred with Ronald Colman, and FAREWELL TO ARMS with Gary Cooper. Height 5 ft. 3 in. Honey blonde hair and blue eyes.

**HAYWARD, Louis**—plate 153. Born in Johannesburg, South Africa, on March 19, 1909. He was educated in France and then came to England to study for the stage. After gaining experience on the London and New York stages, he made his film *début*. ANTHONY ADVERSE brought him top recognition, although he had done some silent and a number of sound films prior to this film. Among his film credits are A SELF-MADE MAN, ABSOLUTE QUIET, THE SUICIDE CLUB, THE LUCKIEST GIRL IN THE WORLD, and THE WOMAN BETWEEN. Height 5 ft. 8 in. Dark brown hair and eyes.

**HENREID, Paul**—plate 235. The son of Baron von Henreid, he was born in Trieste, Italy, on January 10, 1905. His parents were Austrian. After silent film work in Europe, he came to Hollywood where his career became international and his services much in demand. Among his many films were BETWEEN TWO WORLDS, VICTOR THE GREAT, NOW VOYAGER, and CASABLANCA with Ingrid Bergman and Humphrey Bogart. Height 5 ft. 11 in. Light brown hair and blue eyes.

**HOLMES, Phillips**—plate 91. Born on July 22, 1909, in Grand Rapids, Michigan. Son of the famous stage star Taylor Holmes. Educated at Harvard and Cambridge universities. After gaining recognition on the stage, he entered films under contract to Paramount. Film credits include HOUSE OF A THOUSAND CANDLES, THE WILD PARTY, THE DOMINANT SEX, STAIRS OF SAND, CHATTERBOX, and GENERAL SPANKY. Height 6 ft. Fair hair and blue eyes. Died in 1942.

**HOLT, Jack**—plate 13. Born on May 31, 1888, in Winchester, Virginia. After a short stage career, he came to films in 1915 to play opposite Mary Pickford in THE LITTLE AMERICAN. This was followed by THE CLAW with Clara Kimball Young, and THE WOMAN THOU GAVEST ME with Katherine MacDonald. He also made THE SQUAW MAN with Miss MacDonald. He then made two films with Agnes Ayres —HELD BY THE ENEMY and BOUGHT AND PAID FOR. One of his best films was with Pola Negri in THE CHEAT. He did EMPTY HANDS with Norma Shearer, and other of his films include THE LITTLEST REBEL, VENGEANCE, FLIGHT, FORLORN RIVER and THE ENCHANTED HILL. Later in his long career he became known for his Westerns. Height 6 ft. Dark brown hair and eyes. Was the father of film star Tim Holt. Died in 1951.

**HOLT, Tim**—plate 43. Born on February 5, 1918, in Beverly Hills, California, the son of Jack Holt, the screen star. His father used him in many silent films as a child and he went on to an important film career of his own with the coming of sound. Among his films were HISTORY IS MADE AT NIGHT with Jean Arthur, STELLA DALLAS, THE MAGNIFICENT AMBERSONS, GOLD IS WHERE YOU FIND IT, and, perhaps the greatest film of his career, TREASURE OF THE SIERRA MADRE with Humphrey Bogart and Walter Huston. Height 5 ft. 10 in. Light brown wavy hair and blue eyes.

**HORN, Camilla**—plate 158. Born in Frankfurt, Germany, on April 25, 1907. Star of the Berlin music halls before entering German silent films with the UFA company. Her breath-taking blonde beauty won her the part of Marguerite in FAUST, which she played to the Mephistopheles of Emil Jannings. This was followed by successes in A STREET IN ALGIERS and NEMESIS, after which she was lured to Hollywood to play opposite John Barrymore in THE TEMPEST. She made a second film with Barrymore called THE ETERNAL LOVE. Her other films in America included THE ROYAL BOX, BRIEF DAWN, and THE GOLDEN STRAIN. Height 5 ft. 5 in. Slight and very beautiful with golden blonde hair and blue eyes.

**HOWARD, Leslie**—plate 195. Born in London, England, on April 24, 1893. His real name was Leslie Stainer. He was a bank clerk before serving in the First World War with the British forces. After the war he established himself on the London stage and then on Broadway. In Hollywood, he made a film with Mary Pickford and also did a film version of ROMEO AND JULIET. His career in Hollywood peaked with the coming of sound when he made OF HUMAN BONDAGE, THE PETRIFIED FOREST, THE SCARLET PIMPERNEL, STAND IN, INTERMEZZO with Ingrid Bergman, and GONE WITH THE WIND. Height 6 ft. Blond hair and brown eyes. Died in 1943.

**HOXIE, Jack**—plate 36. This famous cowboy star was born on his father's ranch in Oklahoma in 1890. The family later moved to Idaho where they kept a ranch of 16,000 horses and 20,000 cattle. Hoxie spent his boyhood in cowpunching and riding. While working in a rodeo, he was seen by a studio scout and signed for Westerns. He first worked in a serial called LIGHTNING PRICE. His fame as a Western star was sustained in such of his films as THE RED RIDER, THE LAST FRONTIER, FLYING HOOFS, FORBIDDEN TRAIL, and THE WESTERN WALLOP. His horse Scout was almost as well-known as Hoxie. Height 6 ft. Brown hair and blue eyes.

**HUGHES, Lloyd**—plate 15. Born in Bisbee, Arizona, on October 21, 1899. Educated in Los Angeles and went immediately into films as an extra. He made his first film, THE IMPOSSIBLE MAN, in 1918. Many leading roles and finally stardom followed. Perhaps his greatest film was THE LOST WORLD. Other film credits include LADIES AT PLAY, VALENCIA, CLIPPED WINGS, SWEETHEARTS ON PARADE, and THE RUNAWAY BRIDE. Height 6 ft. Dark brown hair and grey eyes.

**HUME, Benita**—plate 129. She was born in London, England, in 1905. Studied at the Royal Academy of Dramatic Art and had West End stage experience before making her first film at the age of seventeen. She was known in British silent films before making her Hollywood *début*. As the wife of film star Ronald Colman, she and her husband both enjoyed great success in American films. Among her film credits are included THE SOUTH SEA BUBBLE, HIGH TREASON, RAINBOW ON THE RIVER, and THE LAST OF MRS. CHENEY. Height 5 ft. 5 in. Dark brown hair and eyes. She died in 1967.

**HUNTER, Ian**—plate 171. Born in Kenilworth, near Capetown, South Africa, on June 13, 1900. Served in the British army and then began a stage career. After five years on both the London and Broadway stages, he made his screen *début* in 1924. His film credits include THE ADVENTURES OF ROBIN HOOD, CONFESSION, CALL IT A DAY, THE DEVIL TAKES THE COUNT, STOLEN HOLIDAY, ANOTHER DAWN, and THAT CERTAIN WOMAN. He played suave, sophisticated roles to perfection. Height 6 ft. Brown hair and grey eyes.

**HUSTON, Walter**—plate 131. Born in Toronto, Canada, on April 6, 1884. Trained to be an engineer, but abandoned this for the stage in 1901. After battling Broadway for four years, he returned to his profession of engineering. In 1909, he decided to have another try at the stage and this time he became a Broadway star.

D. W. Griffith brought him to the screen for his film ABRAHAM LINCOLN after which Walter again returned to the stage. With sound, he was persuaded to come back to the screen in GENTLEMEN OF THE PRESS. This film was a great personal success for him. He made THE BAD MAN with Holbrook Blinn, THE VIRGINIAN, RHODES OF AFRICA, DODSWORTH, and TREASURE OF THE SIERRA MADRE, among many others. Height 6 ft. Dark brown hair and blue eyes. He is the father of film director John Huston. Died in 1950.

## J

**JOLSON, Al**—plate 242. His real name was Asa Yoelson and he was born in Petrograd, Russia, in 1866, the son of a Jewish cantor. The family emigrated to America while Al was still an infant and settled in Washington, D. C. He was trained to become a cantor like his father but ran away from home and joined a travelling circus. Later, he worked in vaudeville in a singing act but was not a success until he became a "black face" minstrel. With this beginning, he was to become Broadway's most fabulous musical comedy star. He had the distinction of making the first feature-length sound film, THE JAZZ SINGER. His other films included SAY IT WITH SONG, MAMMY, SONNY BOY, WONDER BAR, THE SINGING FOOL, and CASINO DE PAREE. Height 5 ft. 8 in. Dark brown hair and eyes. Was married to stage and film star Ruby Keeler. He died in 1950.

**JONES, Buck**—plate 45. Born in Vincennes, Indiana, in 1889. His real christian name was Charles. He was a cowboy in Montana, served in the U. S. cavalry in the Philippines, and was a trick rider in a wild west show before starting his film career in 1914. He was a *protégé* of William Fox and the Fox studio made him one of the great Western stars of his day. His film credits include HEARTS AND SPURS, THE TIMBER WOLF, THE FLYING HORSEMAN, HILLS OF PERIL, and TROOPER O'NEIL, to name only a few. Height 5 ft. 11 in. Brown hair and grey eyes. Married and had one daughter. He died in 1942.

## K

**KARLOFF, Boris**—plates 160, 161. Born in London, England, on November 23, 1887. Real name was Charles Edward Pratt. Began his stage career with an English stock company. He later moved to Canada and then to Hollywood where he worked as an extra in silent films. He later worked with Lon Chaney and then Bela Lugosi, and became associated with horror films. Stardom came after his portrayal of the monster in FRANKENSTEIN. Among his films are included THE INVISIBLE RAY, THE WALKING DEAD, JUGGERNAUT, NIGHT KEY, and THE MAN WHO CHANGED HIS MIND. Height 6 ft. Dark brown hair and brown eyes. Died in 1969.

**KEATON, Buster**—plate 115. Born on October 4, 1895, in Pickwick, Kansas. Real name Joseph Francis Keaton. Was in vaudeville with his parents from early childhood. He was a successful comedian at twenty-one when he was set to star in a revue at the Winter Garden on Broadway, but instead went to Hollywood with Joseph M. Schenck to make two-reel comedies. His first film was THE BUTCHER BOY. He became one of the screen's greatest comedy stars and his films are still being shown today. Among his most memorable films are THE GENERAL, THE NAVIGATOR, FREE AND EASY, GO WEST, COLLEGE, and FORWARD MARCH. Was married to Natalie Talmadge and had two sons, Jimmy and Bob. Height 5 ft. 6 in. Black hair and brown eyes. Died in 1966.

**KELLY, Paul**—plate 162. Born in Brooklyn, New York, in 1901, he made his first appearance on the stage at the age of seven. When he was ten he was touring with a Shakespearean company. He was a Broadway star when he entered films. After working awhile in silent films he returned to the stage. One of his silent films was ANNE OF THE GREEN GABLES with Mary Miles Minter, made in 1919. His greatest screen successes came with sound. His film credits include NAVY BLUE AND GOLD, PAROLE RACKET, FRAME UP, BROADWAY THROUGH A KEYHOLE, and FIT TO FIGHT. Height 6 ft. Brown hair and eyes. Died in 1956.

**KENNEDY, Madge**—plate 66. Born in Chicago, Illinois, on April 19, 1898. Before entering films she enjoyed a fabulous stage career. She starred in such famous stage productions on Broadway as FAIR AND WARMER, TWIN BEDS, CORNERED, and POPPY. While in Los Angeles, where she had spent a great deal of her childhood, she was persuaded to sign a film contract. Among her films were BABY MINE, THE DANGER GAME with Tom Moore, STRICTLY CONFIDENTIAL, THE PURPLE HIGHWAY, BAD COMPANY, and LYING WIVES. Height 5 ft. 5 in. Brown hair and eyes.

**KENYON, Doris**—plate 57. Born in Syracuse, New York, on September 5, 1897. Was a star on the Broadway stage when she made her film *début* in 1919 in THE INN OF THE BLUE MOON. She made BORN RICH with Bert Lytell and Cullen Landis, and worked with Rudolph Valentino in MONSIEUR BEAUCAIRE. Other of her films included THE VALLEY OF THE GIANTS, BEAU BANDIT, STRICTLY BUSINESS, THE BLONDE SAINT, and INTERFERENCE. Height 5 ft. 6 in. Brown hair and grey eyes. She was married to film star Milton Sills.

**KOSLOFF, Theodore**—plate 47. Born in Russia in 1886, he became a master of a school of Russian ballet and trained many well-known dancers. He became prominent in Hollywood in 1919 when he moved his school from New York to the film capitol. He was pressed into acting by the studios and played important parts in many films. He was a favourite of Cecil B. DeMille, who gave him a prominent role in his KING OF KINGS. He also worked in DeMille's production of THE DOVER ROAD. Other of his films included THE VOLGA BOATMAN, and THE LITTLE ADVENTURESS. Height 5 ft. 9 in. Dark brown hair and brown eyes.

## L

**LAKE, Arthur**—plate 229. Born in a circus tent in Corbin, Kentucky, in 1905. His parents were circus performers and Arthur was trained to be a dancer. He played youthful roles in a great many films after coming to the screen in 1925. His first film was SKINNER'S DRESS SUIT with Reginald Denny. He is best remembered for the BLONDIE series originating from a popular newspaper comic strip. Among his film credits are included JACK AND THE BEAN STALK, WHEN LOVE IS YOUNG, HAROLD TEEN with Alice White, DANCE HALL, TANNED LEGS, and THE AIR CIRCUS. Height 6 ft. Brown hair and grey eyes.

**LANDI, Elissa**—plate 130. She was the Countess Elizabeth Marie Zanardi Landi Kuhnell, a descendant of an Empress of Austria. Born in Venice, Italy, on December 6, 1904, of an Italian father and an Austrian mother. She received a classical education and lessons in deportment, elocution, and dancing. She made her stage *début* in 1923 and became famous on the Continent and in London where she made her first film. With red-gold hair and green eyes, she was one of the beauties of her day. Among her Hollywood films were ECSTASY, THE THIRTEENTH CHAIR, MAD HOLIDAY, AFTER THE THIN MAN, UNDERGROUND, and THE PRICE OF THINGS. Height 5 ft. 3 in.

**LANGDON, Harry**—plate 114. Born in Council Bluffs, Iowa, on June 15, 1884. As a youth was an usher in a movie theater, then a property man in a small legitimate theatre. He next joined a touring company, followed by a medicine show and then a minstrel show. From this point he made his *début* as a vaudeville comedian. His film *début* came with Mack Sennett. Among the films that made him one of the screen's most popular comedians were TRAMP, TRAMP, TRAMP, THE STRONG MAN, LONG PANTS, and THREE'S A CROWD. His height was just 5 ft. Light brown hair and blue eyes.

**LAUREL, Stan**—plate 240. Born on June 16, 1895, in Ulverston, England. At seventeen he joined Fred Karno's London comedians as an understudy for Charlie Chaplin. Prior to joining Karno, he had received stage training in a circus, in musical comedy, drama, and vaudeville. When the Karno troupe toured the U.S.A. in 1910, Stan went along and remained in Hollywood where he made his film *début* with Universal. He was next with Hal Roach where he met Oliver Hardy. As a team they achieved phenomenal success as comedians. Film credits include THE ROGUE SONG, FLYING DEUCES, BABES IN TOYLAND, DANCING MASTERS, THE BULLFIGHTERS, and many others. Height 5 ft. 10 in. Auburn hair and blue eyes.

**LEBEDEFF, Ivan**—plate 20. Born in Lithuania on June 18, 1899. Was trained for the diplomatic service and served in the Tsar's army receiving the Cross of Saint George for gallant service. After the war he went to Paris and worked both on the stage and in silent films. Went to America from France and met D. W. Griffith who signed him to play the leading role in THE SORROWS OF SATAN. He was an immediate success and soon became a "matinee idol." Among his film credits are included SIN TOWN, FAIR WARNING, THEY HAD TO SEE PARIS, KING FREDERICK, and HISTORY IS MADE AT NIGHT. Height 6 ft. 1 in. Black hair and eyes.

**LEDERER, Francis**—plate 168. Born in Prague, Czechoslovakia, on November 6, 1905. Won a scholarship at the Prague Academy of Dramatic Art before he was eighteen. He proved himself as an accomplished actor on the stages of Berlin, Vienna, and Budapest, as well as Prague. After working in silent films on the Continent, he went to New York where he carved a niche for himself on Broadway before Hollywood claimed him. He made a great many films in America, the most important of which was MY AMERICAN WIFE. Other of his films included THE CAT AND THE FIDDLE, AUTUMN CROCUS, ONE RAINY AFTERNOON, and IT'S ALL YOURS. Height 6 ft. Dark brown hair and eyes.

**LEE, Lila**—plate 9. Born on July 25, 1905, in New York City. Made her stage *début* in early childhood in New York. Spent 10 years on the stage before entering films in 1918. Her first film was CRUISE OF THE MAKE BELIEVE. Reached the peak of stardom while under contract to Paramount in the Twenties. Film credits include TWO WISE MAIDS, FLIGHT, SOULS IN EXILE, SECOND WIFE, SUCH A LITTLE PIRATE, and MALE AND FEMALE. Height 5 ft. 3 in. Black hair and brown eyes. Married to James Kirkwood. Her real name was Augusta Appel.

**LOGAN, Jacqueline**—plate 126. Born on November 2, 1902, in Corsicana, Texas. She was a direct descendant of General Logan, a hero of the American Civil War. She was taught singing and dancing from early childhood and, following a short career as a newspaper society editor, went to New York seeking a stage career. Her titian hair, grey eyes, and great beauty caught the attention of Flo Ziegfeld who signed her for his famous Follies. Hollywood came next and her first film was THE PERFECT CRIME. Her career blossomed at Paramount. DeMille cast her in KING OF KINGS, she co-starred with Milton Sills in BURNING SANDS, and made THE BLOOD SHIP with Richard Arlen and Hobart Bosworth. Other film credits include EBB TIDE, SALOMY JANE, THE DAWN OF TOMORROW, GENERAL CRACK, and THE MIDDLE WATCH. Height 5 ft. 4 in.

**LOMBARD, Carole**—plate 141. Born in Fort Wayne, Indiana, on October 6, 1909. Real name Jane Peters. Studied for the stage but it was on the screen that she began her career. She started in the ranks with Mack Sennett, rose to bit parts, became a leading woman, and then blossomed into stardom. Her first starring role was for Fox in ME GANGSTER. She co-starred with Robert Armstrong in BIG NEWS and THE RACKETEER. Back in 1921, when she was just a child, she had made THE PERFECT CRIME with Monte Blue. She played opposite John Barrymore in TWENTIETH CENTURY and made MY MAN GODFREY with William Powell. Some of her other film credits included HANDS ACROSS THE TABLE, NOTHING SACRED, WE'RE NOT DRESSING, LOVE BEFORE BREAKFAST, NO MAN OF HER OWN, and TO BE OR NOT TO BE. One of her important films was BOLERO with George Raft. Height 5 ft. 2 in. Golden hair and blue eyes. Was married to Clark Gable when she died in a plane crash in 1942.

**LOWE, Edmund**—plate 135. Born on March 3, 1892, in San Jose, California. He was a star of the stage when he made his film *début* in 1921 in THE DEVIL with George Arliss. Followed THE PALACE OF THE KING with Pauline Starke, and THE WHITE FLOWER with Betty Compson. He made THE BAD ONE, THE KISS BARRIER, THE FOOL, EAST LYNN, and DRESSED TO KILL. But his three "big" films were THE COCK-EYED WORLD, IS ZAT SO, and WHAT PRICE GLORY, the latter with Victor McLaglen and Dolores del Rio. Height 5 ft. 11 in. Dark brown hair and blue eyes. Married to Lilyan Tashman, star of the Ziegfeld Follies and the screen. Died in 1971.

**LOY, Myrna**—plate 163. Born in Helena, Montana, on August 2, 1905. Trained at the Ruth St. Denis school as a professional dancer. She was discovered by the wife of Rudolph Valentino who had her husband prevail upon his studio to cast her for the lead in WHAT PRICE BEAUTY. She was then given the role of the siren in ACROSS THE PACIFIC. Followed KING OF THE KHYBER RIFLES with Victor McLaglen. She played a Chinese girl in THE CRIMSON CITY with the Japanese star Sojin, and in PARNELL co-starred with Clark Gable. Other of her films included WHY GIRLS GO BACK HOME, LADY OF THE ROSE, and THE GREAT DIVIDE. Height 5 ft. 6 in. Auburn hair and green eyes.

**LUGOSI, Bela**—plate 100. Born in Lugos, Hungary, on October 20, 1884. Made his stage *début* at the age of twenty as Romeo in a Hungarian production of ROMEO AND JULIET. Three years of Shakespearean repertoire followed. He came to New York in 1921, organised a Hungarian dramatic company and produced, directed, and starred in a play called THE RED POPPY which was acclaimed by the New York critics. His greatest stage success was in the role of Count Dracula in DRACULA. He made his film *début* in 1924, and played Count Dracula on the screen. Followed MURDERS IN THE RUE MORGUE, WHITE ZOMBI, CHANDU THE MAGICIAN, THE THIRTEENTH CHAIR, and the famous FRANKENSTEIN pictures. Height 6 ft. 1 in. Dark brown hair and blue eyes. Died in 1956.

**LUKAS, Paul**—plate 200. Born on a train that was entering Hungary on May 26, 1897. After working in amateur theatricals in college in Hungary, he made his screen *début* in silent films in 1917. After some success in screen work he returned to the stage in Berlin, Vienna, and Budapest. Then, Hollywood claimed him and he stepped immediately into leading roles. Among his films were DINNER AT THE RITZ, BRIEF ECSTASY, LADIES IN LOVE, and DODSWORTH. Height 6 ft. 1 in. Brown hair and eyes. He also made films in England.

**LYON, Ben**—plate 204. Born in Atlanta, Georgia, on February 6, 1901. His first love was the stage and his work in the stage play MARY THE THIRD secured him a small part in the film version of POTASH AND PERLMUTTER. Then the leading role with Barbara Stanwyck in SO BIG. Ben Lyon co-starred with Blanche Sweet in BLUEBEARD'S SEVEN WIVES, with Gloria Swanson in WAGES OF VIRTUE, with Pola Negri in LILY OF THE DUST, and with Barbara Lamarr in THE WHITE MOTH. That, indeed, is a formidable record, but his greatest of all was with Jean Harlow in HELL'S ANGELS. Height 5 ft. 11 in. Brown hair and blue eyes. He was married to film star Bebe Daniels.

**M**

**MacAVOY, May**—plate 83. Born on September 8, 1901, in New York City. She started life as a teacher but gave it up to carve out a career for herself in films. In 1920 Pathe cast her in THE HOUSE OF THE TOLLING BELL. After her role in CLARENCE with Wallace Reid, she was on her way. She made KICK IN with Bert Lytell, and THE ENCHANTED COTTAGE with Richard Barthelmess. Some of her other films include SENTIMENTAL TOMMY, LADY WINDERMERE'S FAN, TARNISH, and THE ROAD TO GLORY. Her greatest, however, was the leading role she played in BEN HUR with Ramon Novarro and Francis X. Bushman. Height 4 ft. 11 in. Dark brown hair and blue eyes.

**MacGREGOR, Malcolm**—plate 51. Born in Macon, Georgia, on October 27, 1900. As a newcomer to films with only a little stage experience as a background, he was given his big opportunity in THE PRISONER OF ZENDA, made in 1922 with Alice Terry, Barbara Lamarr, and Ramon Novarro. Followed BROKEN CHAINS with Colleen Moore and THE DANCER OF THE NILE with Carmel Myers. Other of his films include THE GAY DECEPTION, DON JUAN'S THREE NIGHTS, FLAMING WATERS, MATINEE LADIES, and INFATUATION. Height 5 ft. 11 in. Black hair and brown eyes.

**MACKAILL, Dorothy**—plate 68. Born on March 4, 1903, in Hull, England. Made her *début* on the London stage at the age of fifteen. Became the youngest member of the London Hippodrome chorus. At seventeen, she went to New York and obtained an interview with Flo Ziegfeld who engaged her for his chorus. Within two years she became a leading Ziegfeld star. Hollywood claimed her soon thereafter and she starred in many films there including THE LOVE RACKET, BRIGHT LIGHTS, MAN TROUBLE, HARD TO GET, and MIGHTY LIKE A ROSE. THE MAN WHO CAME BACK with George O'Brien, THE FIGHTING BLADE with Richard Barthelmess, and CHICKIE with John Bowers, were also among her films. Height 5 ft. 3 in. Hazel eyes and light brown hair.

**MacLANE, Barton**—plate 124. Born in Columbia, South Carolina, on February 26, 1895. Graduated from Wesleyan and went immediately on the stage. He had considerable stage experience before entering films. He had also written several plays. He was known for his "tough guy" and "cop" roles and was much in demand by the studios. He made a great many films among them YOU ONLY LIVE ONCE, THE PRINCE AND THE PAUPER, GOLD IS WHERE YOU FIND IT, BORN RECKLESS, and SMART BLONDE. Died in 1969. Height 6 ft. Brown hair and eyes.

**MARCH, Frederic**—plate 197. Born in Racine, Wisconsin, on August 31, 1898. His real name was Frederick Bickel. After starting as a bank clerk, he decided he wanted an acting career. He obtained a part with the Belasco Stock Company in New York. After gaining experience on the stage, he was given a part in a film with Ruth Chatterton called THE DUMMY. THE WILD PARTY with Clara Bow followed, then his role in MANSLAUGHTER with DeMille directing. Other of his films include ANTHONY ADVERSE, THE BUCCANEER, MARY OF SCOTLAND, THE ROAD TO GLORY, and A STAR IS BORN. Height 6 ft. Brown hair and eyes.

**MARSHALL, Herbert**—plate 217. Born in London, England, on May 23, 1890. Made his stage *début* in London in 1911. Also made his screen *début* in London in a silent film called MUMSIE with Pauline Frederick. This was followed by THE LETTER with Jean Eagles. In America, he became popular as a leading man known for his suave sophistication and appeared in a great many American films over a long period of years. Among his film credits were THE LADY CONSENTS, FORGOTTEN FACES, TILL WE MEET AGAIN, BREAKFAST FOR TWO, MAKE WAY FOR A LADY, and ANGEL. He saw military service in the First World War and lost a leg in action. Married to actress Edna Best. Height 6 ft. Brown hair and blue eyes. Died in 1966.

**MARX, Chico**—plate 238. The oldest of the Marx brothers, he was born in New York City on March 22, 1891. Took piano lessons at an early age and developed into an excellent boy pianist. He worked with his brothers, Groucho and Harpo, in a comedy act and the three, together with a fourth brother Zeppo, who later retired from show business, became a great Broadway hit. They worked in a number of short silent films, but their big opportunity came with sound when they made a highly successful comedy called COCOANUTS. So popular were the Marx brothers that their films are still seen in the theatre and on television. Chico was 5 ft. 6 in. tall with dark brown hair and eyes. Died in 1961.

**MARX, Groucho**—plate 237. Groucho was born in New York City on October 2, 1895. He commenced his stage career at the age of thirteen impersonating a girl with a falsetto voice. He worked with his brothers Chico, Harpo, and Zeppo, in vaudeville and later on the Broadway stage where they were a popular comedy team. Among the films Groucho and his brother made were ANIMAL CRACKERS, MONKEY BUSINESS, THE BIG STORE, HORSE FEATHERS, DUCK SOUP, A NIGHT AT THE OPERA, and A DAY AT THE RACES. Height 5 ft. 7½ in. Black hair and brown eyes. He always wore a false moustache in his films and carried a "prop" cigar. He died in 1977.

**MARX, Harpo**—plate 239. Harpo was so named because of his ability to play the harp. He could also play the flute, trombone, and piano. He was the brother that never spoke, working solely in pantomime. He wore a curly blonde wig on the screen. Harpo was the second brother in age, born between Chico and Groucho. His birth date is November 21, 1893. The three Marx Brothers made up a comedy team that was perhaps the greatest in screen history. They were all natural comedians. Harpo had brown hair and eyes. Height 5 ft. 7 in. Died in 1964.

**MAYNARD, Ken**—plate 41. Born in Mission, Texas, on July 21, 1895. Before he entered films was a real cowboy and rodeo champion. He held the world's championship for riding and roping. He also held a degree in engineering and served as a field engineer in the first World War. He began his screen career in 1922. To mention but a few of his many Western films—THE HAUNTED RANCH, SENOR DAREDEVIL, THE DEMON RIDER, IN OLD SANTA FE, LAWLESS RIDERS, HEROES OF THE RANGE, THE CATTLE THIEF, and SONORA. Height 5 ft. 11 in. Black hair, grey eyes.

**McLAGLEN, Victor**—plate 220. Born in London, England, on December 11, 1883. Spent his youth in South Africa, where his father was a bishop. He went to Canada and became a silver miner. A huge man, he turned to professional boxing and once fought the world champ Jack Johnson to a draw. Adventured in Australia, then Mesopotamia followed, and he was at one time Provost Marshall of Bagdad. During a hitch in service, he became heavyweight champion of the British Army. After the war, he worked in British films and in 1925 went to Hollywood where he rose to the peak of stardom in such films as WHAT PRICE GLORY, BEAU GESTE, THE RIVER PIRATE, KING OF THE KHYBER RIFLES, and his Academy

Award picture THE INFORMER. Height 6 ft. 4 in. Dark brown hair and grey eyes. Died in 1959.

**MERKEL, Una**—plate 144. Born in Covington, Kentucky, September 11, 1902, of German parents. While working with a touring stock company, she came to the notice of D. W. Griffith who engaged her as an understudy and double for Lillian Gish. He later gave her the role of Ann Rutledge in his production of ABRAHAM LINCOLN. She eventually switched to light comedy roles at which she was delightful and most adept. Among her films are included EYES OF THE WORLD, LOVE'S OLD SWEET SONG, THE OLD SOAK, THE BAT WHISPERS, BORN TO DANCE, TRUE CONFESSIONS, and SARATOGA. Height 5 ft. 6 in. Blonde hair and blue eyes.

**MILJAN, John**—plate 187. Born on November 9, 1898. His real name was Miljani and his parents came from Dalmatia. When he made his film *début* in 1923, he already had considerable stage experience and had served with the Marines in the first World War. His first film was LOVE LETTERS, which starred Shirley Mason. He became the screen's "smoothy" bad man. He worked with Lon Chaney in THE UNHOLY THREE, and played important roles in SUTTER'S GOLD, THE PLAINSMAN, OLD SAN FRANCISCO, NORTH OF NOME, SECRET INTERLUDE, and THE DESERT SONG, to mention only a few of his many films. Height 6 ft. Dark brown hair and eyes. Died in 1960.

**MILLER, Patsy Ruth**—plate 103. Born in St. Louis, Missouri, on June 22, 1905. When she was a visitor at a film studio in Hollywood at the age of seventeen, she accepted an invitation to appear in one of Buster Keaton's comedies. That was in 1922, and that same year Guy Bates Post cast her in his film OMAR THE TENTMAKER. Then, her big chance with Lon Chaney in THE HUNCHBACK OF NOTRE DAME. This film brought her stardom. She made THE WHITE BLACK SHEEP with Richard Barthelmess, ROSE OF THE WORLD, HERO OF THE NIGHT, SO LONG LETTY, THE YANKEE CONSUL, and SO THIS IS PARIS, among other films. Height 5 ft. 3 in. Dark brown hair and eyes.

**MILLER, Walter**—plate 40. Born in Johannesburg, South Africa, on December 25, 1892. A pioneer of silent films, he was a leading man in many of the first serials. In 1912, he had the leading male role with Lillian Gish in a Biograph film called THE MUSKETEERS OF PIG ALLEY. He made A GIRL AT BAY with Corrine Griffith and THE UNFAIR SEX with Nita Naldi. He then began playing "badmen" and did a series of Westerns among them THE UTAH KID, FIGHTING WEST, WYOMING, THE BIG STAMPEDE, and INDIAN TERRITORY. Other of his films included THE FIGHTING MARINE and THE GREEN ARCHER. Height 6 ft. Brown hair and grey eyes.

**MIX, Tom**—plates 34, 35. Born near El Paso, Texas, on his father's cattle ranch, on January 6, 1881. At seventeen, he fought in the Spanish American War. Also served with the Army in the Philippines, and in China during the Boxer Rebellion. Returning home after being badly wounded, he was made U. S. Marshall for the state of Oklahoma. He began his film career with the Fox studio in 1914, and he became a great Western star. With him in all his films was his famous black mare, Tony. His film credits include THE LONE STAR RANGER, SILVER VALLEY, SON OF THE GOLDEN WEST, THE CANYON OF LIGHT, THE WILDERNESS TRAIL with Colleen Moore, WESTERN BLOOD, and THE CIRCUS AGE. Height 5 ft. 11 in. Dark brown hair and eyes. Married Victoria Forde and had a daughter Thomasina. He died in 1940.

**MONTGOMERY, Robert**—plate 227. Born in Beacon, New York, on May 21, 1903. Worked as a labourer, a sailor, and as a property man in a theatre. He obtained a small part in a play and within eighteen months he was playing leading roles on Broadway. He came to the screen in a film called SO THIS IS COLLEGE, although he had done bit parts prior to this. With the advent of sound, his career blossomed rapidly. He made THE UNTAMED with Joan Crawford and THEIR OWN DESIRE with Norma Shearer. His role in NIGHT MUST FALL with Dame May Whitty brought him high praise. His other film credits include PICCADILLY JIM, THE SUICIDE CLUB, THE LAST OF MRS. CHEYNEY, EVER SINCE EVE, and LIVE LOVE AND LEARN. Height 6 ft. Dark brown hair and blue eyes. Married screen star Elizabeth Allen.

**MORAN, Lee**—plate 67. Born in Chicago, Illinois, in 1889. After considerable stage experience, mostly in musical comedy and vaudeville, films claimed him in 1914 and a year later he made WHAT COULD A

POOR GIRL DO with Billie Rhodes. He then teamed with Eddie Lyons, and together they made a series of comedies for the Christie studio. He had a leading role in THE ACTRESS with Norma Shearer. Other of his film credits include FIFTH AVENUE MODELS, SYNCOPATING SUE, MY LADY OF WHIMS, THE ROSE OF KILDARE, SPRING FEVER, and THE AVIATOR. Height 5 ft. 10 in. Brown hair and grey eyes.

**MORRIS, Chester**—plate 145. Born in New York City on February 16, 1902, of theatrical parents. Made his stage *début* at seventeen in THE COPPERHEAD which starred Lionel Barrymore. After appearing on the stage for two years with his parents, a sister and two brothers in a vaudeville sketch written by his father, he came to the screen in THE PERFECT ALIBI. In 1918, he made THE BELOVED TRAITOR with Mae Marsh. His other films include THE BIG HOUSE with Spencer Tracy, SHE COULDN'T SAY NO, THE WOMAN TRAP, THE BAT WHISPERS, I'VE BEEN AROUND, PRINCESS O'HARA. His greatest triumph was THE CASE OF SERGEANT GRISCHA in which he played the title role. Height 5 ft. 10 in. Black hair and grey eyes.

**MURRAY, Charlie**—plate 112. Born in Laurel, Indiana, in 1872, he began his professional career with a travelling circus at the age of fourteen. He became famous as a circus clown. He later played in musical comedy and vaudeville. With twenty years of stage experience behind him, he made his film *début* as a Mack Sennett comic. For many years he cavorted across the silver screen to delight film audiences. Among his films were A SMALL TOWN IDOL with Phyllis Haver, Ben Turpin, and Jimmy Finlayson, THE GORILLA, CLANCY ON WALL STREET, SWEET DADDIES, and THE COHENS AND THE KELLYS with George Sidney, Vera Gordon, and Kate Price. Height 6 ft. Red hair and grey eyes. Died in 1941.

**MYERS, Carmel**—plate 104. Born in San Francisco, California, on April 9, 1901. Her father was a Jewish rabbi and a scholar of some repute. She met D. W. Griffith when he sought her father's technical advise while filming INTOLERANCE. Griffith gave her a small part in the film. He then cast her with Dorothy Gish in STAGE STRUCK. After playing leading roles in films with Harold Lockwood, Bessie Love, Elmo Lincoln, and Harold Lloyd, she went to Broadway where she worked for a year in musical comedy. Returning to the screen, she made SLAVE OF DESIRE with George Walsh, THE DANCER OF THE NILE with Malcolm McGregor, SORRELL AND SON with H. B. Warner, TELL IT TO THE MARINES, LOLA, THE CARELESS AGE, and her greatest films—BEAU BRUMMEL with John Barrymore, and BEN HUR with Ramon Novarro and Francis X. Bushman. Height 5 ft. 3 in. Reddish brown hair and green eyes.

## N

**NAGEL, Conrad**—plate 159. Born in Keokuk, Iowa, on March 16, 1897. His parents were German and his father a professor of music at Highland Park College in Des Moines, from which school Conrad graduated with a B.A. degree. He began a stage career, but was lured to Hollywood for a role in LITTLE WOMEN in 1918. THE FIGHTING CHANCE with Anna Q. Nilsson followed and then WHAT EVERY WOMAN KNOWS with Lois Wilson. By this time this very handsome and very blond young man was much in demand. He made NICE PEOPLE with Wallace Reid and Bebe Daniels, BELLA DONNA with Pola Negri, FOOL'S PARADISE with Mildred Harris, THE SNOB with Norma Shearer, QUALITY STREET with Marion Davies, and Elinor Glynn's famous THREE WEEKS with Aileen Pringle. There were many other films including TESS OF THE D'URBERVILLES, SLIGHTLY USED, THE SACRED FLAME, and ONE ROMANTIC NIGHT. Height 6 ft. Yellow hair and blue eyes. He died in 1970.

**NIXON, Marion**—plate 176. She was born in Superior, Wisconsin, on October 20, 1904. She worked in a department store in Minneapolis before going on the vaudeville stage. Her first love had always been the movies and in Hollywood in 1922 she began her career in films as an extra. Two years later she was playing top leading roles. She made SPANGLES with Pat O'Malley, HOW TO HANDLE WOMEN with Glenn Tryon, and a long series of other films including THE RECKLESS WAY, ANNIE DOESN'T LIVE HERE, THE DRAGNET, and CAPTAIN CALAMITY. Height 5 ft. 2 in. Brown hair and eyes.

**NOVELLO, Ivor**—plate 25. Born in Cardiff, Wales, on January 15, 1894. He began his career as a composer and before he was nineteen had written "Keep the

Home Fires Burning." He made his film *début* in America with D. W. Griffith. He starred with Mae Marsh in Griffith's production of THE WHITE ROSE. He made several other films in America and France and many British pictures. He wrote mainly revues and musical comedies and some of the finest music ever written anywhere. Among his film credits are CARNIVAL, THE SOUTH SEA BUBBLE, THE CONSTANT NYMPH, THE LODGER, and THE BOHEMIAN GIRL with Ellen Terry and Gladys Cooper. Height 5 ft. 11 in. Black hair and brown eyes. Died in 1951.

## O

**OAKIE, Jack**—plate 102. Born in Sedalis, Missouri, on November 12, 1903. Was on the vaudeville stage as a comic before making his screen *début* in a film called FINDERS KEEPERS with Laura LaPlante. For many years he was popular with film goers, specialising in light comedy. Among his films were THE FLEET'S IN, HIT THE DECK, LET'S GO NATIVE, THE TOAST OF NEW YORK, THE MAN I LOVE, and ROAD HOUSE. In Charlie Chaplin's film THE GREAT DICTATOR he played the role of Mussolini. Height 5 ft. 11 in. Medium brown hair and blue eyes. Real name Lewis Offield.

**OLAND, Warner**—plate 172. Born in 1880 in Umea, Sweden. Came to America as a child and before entering films was well established in the legitimate theatre. He became a leading character actor on the screen and reached stardom in the CHARLIE CHAN detective series. His first film work was with Pearl White in her early serials. He played the title role in THE MYSTERIOUS DR. FU MANCHU, was in SIN, EAST IS WEST, TWINKLETOES, INFATUATION, THE MYSTERY CLUB, and DON Q. He also was in the first feature-length sound film with Al Jolson—THE JAZZ SINGER. Height 5 ft. 11 in. Dark brown hair and eyes. Died in 1938.

**OLIVER, Edna May**—plate 232. Born in New York City on January 12, 1890. Real name Edna May Nutter. She studied voice for the opera but abandoned it for the stage and joined a travelling stock company. Before entering films she was one of Broadway's favourite comediennes. After supporting roles in silent films, she came into prominence as a character actress with the advent of sound. Her screen credits include ROSALIE, MY DEAR MISS ALDRICH, ROMEO AND JULIET, PARNELL with Clark Gable, and OLIVER TWIST, to name but a few. She made a striking appearance, very tall for a woman at 5 ft. 10 in., she was also very slender. Light brown hair and blue eyes. She died in 1942.

**OLIVIER, Laurence**—plate 219. Sir Laurence Olivier, England's "first gentleman" of stage and screen, was born on May 22, 1907, in Dorking, Surrey, England. He was an accomplished Shakespearean actor before turning to modern drama. A success on both the stage and screen in England, he also made some silent films in Germany before coming to Hollywood via the New York stage. One of his never-to-be-forgotten films was REBECCA with Joan Fontaine. HENRY V was another triumph. He made several other Shakespearean films for the screen, many dramatic films, and even light comedy. He made one film with Marilyn Monroe, THE PRINCE AND THE SHOW GIRL. A recent film was SLEUTH with Michael Caine. Height 5 ft. 10 in. Dark brown hair and eyes. He was married to the late Vivian Leigh of GONE WITH THE WIND fame.

**O'NEIL, Sally**—plate 180. Her real name was Virginia Noonan and she was born in Bayonne, New Jersey, on October 23, 1907. A black-haired, blue-eyed Irish girl, she made her screen *début* in 1925 in SALLY, IRENE AND MARY with Constance Bennett and Joan Crawford. She had had stage training before coming to the screen and had no difficulty rising to screen popularity as a lovely and talented young actress. She played the juvenile in THE BATTLE OF THE SEXES with Belle Bennett aond Jean Hersholt. Other of her films include THE BRAT, MIKE, THE AUCTION BLACK, KATHLEEN MAVOURNEEN, MURDER BY THE CLOCK, BY APPOINTMENT ONLY, BEGGARS' HOLIDAY, and TOO TOUGH TO KILL. Height 5 ft. 1½ in. Her younger sister, Molly O'Day, was also a screen star.

## P

**PARKER, Jean**—plate 183. Her real name was Mae Green. She had reddish brown hair and hazel eyes and she was 5 ft. 3½ in. tall. She was born in Deer Lodge, Montana, on August 11, 1914. She worked in a number of silent films in child parts and then studied dancing, hoping for a musical comedy career. She was just seventeen when she returned to films in THE GHOST GOES WEST with Robert Donat. Other film credits include THE TEXAS RANGERS, FARMER IN THE DELL, LIFE BEGINS WITH LOVE, and THE BARRIER.

**PATTERSON, Elizabeth**—plate 234. Born in Savannah, Georgia, in 1882. Was a successful stage actress for many years before entering films. Played on both the American and British stages. She was three years with Ben Greet's English company in Shakespeare and several seasons with other English companies. She came to the screen as a character actress and became famous for her roles as the talkative, naïve mother type. Among her films were SMALL TOWN GIRL, THREE CHEERS FOR LOVE, OLD HUTCH, GO WEST YOUNG MAN, and THE RETURN OF SOPHIE LANG. Height 5 ft. 5 in. Dark brown hair and blue eyes. Died in 1966.

**PIDGEON, Walter**–plate 175. Born on September 23, 1898, in New Brunswick, Canada. After spending his early twenties in Europe where he studied voice, he returned to America and the New York stage. His fine singing voice and just as fine speaking voice helped materially in his rise to prominence on the stage. He made his screen *début* in 1925 in a film with Anna Q. Nilsson called MISS NOBODY. He did WOMAN WISE with June Collyer, then followed a long series of films including GATEWAY TO THE MOON, A MOST IMMORAL LADY, SWEET KITTY BELLAIR, SARATOGA, and THE FOUR MARYS. With the advent of sound, he sang in THE BRIDE OF THE REGIMENT and THE TOAST OF THE LEGION, both operettas. Height 6 ft. 3 in. Black hair and brown eyes.

**PITTS, Zasu**—plate 108. Born on January 2, 1898, in Parsons, Kansas. She began her screen career as an extra in 1917 and in that same year was cast in a film with Mary Pickford called THE LITTLE PRINCESS. After following with some comedy roles, at which she was very adept, she made BETTER TIMES with David Butler. Her big picture came in 1923 when she was cast with Gibson Gowland and Jean Hersholt in GREED. She continued her climb to stardom in SINS OF THE FATHERS with Emil Jannings. Later in her career she returned to light comedy and became noted for her dead-pan expression and fluttering hands. Among her films were EARLY TO BED, OLD SHOES, THE LOTTERY BRIDE, THE LITTLE ACCIDENT, EARLY TO WED, and SUNNYSIDE UP. Height 5 ft. 6 in. Brown hair and blue eyes. Married to film actor Tom Gallery. Died in 1963.

**POLLARD, Harry "Snub"**—plate 116. "Snub" as everyone knew him, was born in Melbourne, Australia, in 1888. He emigrated to America in his youth and settled in Chicago, Illinois. He worked there as an usher in a music hall, then became a box-office clerk, and finally turned to acting. In 1913, he met Broncho Billy Anderson, who signed him for Essanay. His comic roles as "Snub" Pollard delighted movie audiences and he was a comic on the screen for many years. He later devoted himself to directing. Among his films were OH DOCTOR, POKER FACES, I'LL SHOW YOU THE TOWN, and SHOW BOAT. Many of his films were made with Hal Roach. Height 5 ft. 7 in. Brown hair and eyes. Married to screen star Margarita Fischer. Died in 1962.

**POTEL, Victor**—plates 122, 123. One of the screen's veteran comedians. He worked with the Essanay company for many years, having joined them in 1910. He was born in Lafayette, Indiana, in 1887. After many years in comedies, he switched to Westerns in which he usually played the comedy relief. Exceedingly thin, 6 ft. 3 in. in height, and inclined to comic facial expressions, he was one of the screen's favourite comedians. Among his films are WHISPERING SMITH SPEAKS, SONG OF THE SADDLE, HARD ROCK HARRIGAN, THE VIRGINIAN, SNAKEVILLE, and THE OUTCASTS OF POKER FLAT.

**POWELL, William**—plate 140. Born in Pittsburgh, Pennsylvania, on July 29, 1892. After several years on the stage and travelling stock, he came to the screen in 1922 in a film called MORIARITY. In that same year he was cast in WHEN KNIGHTHOOD WAS IN FLOWER with Marion Davies. He made THE BRIGHT SHAWL with Dorothy Gish and Richard Barthelmess, DANGEROUS MONEY with Bebe Daniels, and UNDER THE RED ROBE with Mary McLaren. ROMOLA and THE FOUR FEATHERS followed. Other films include BEAU GESTE, THE EMPEROR'S CANDLESTICKS, THE LAST OF MRS. CHENEY, and his THIN MAN films with Myrna Loy. Height 6 ft. Black wavy hair and blue eyes.

## R

**RAINS, Claude**—plate 210. Born in London, England, on November 10, 1889. Made his stage *début* at the age of six. He was already an outstanding actor when he came to Hollywood and had made silent films in England. His first American film was THE INVISIBLE MAN. His film career in America was as distinguished as it had been in his native England. Among his many films were GOLD IS WHERE YOU FIND IT, THEY WON'T FORGET, ADVENTURES OF ROBIN HOOD, and, in very recent years, LAWRENCE OF ARABIA. Height 5 ft. 9 in. Black hair and brown eyes. He died in 1967.

**RALSTON, Esther**—plate 136. Born in Bar Harbour, Maine, on September 17, 1902. She rose to film fame through her portrayal of Mrs. Darling in PETER PAN, although she had previously played in THE MARRIAGE CIRCLE and other films. From a theatrical family, she began her early stage career in a family act. Before entering films, she appeared on both the London and Broadway stages. Among her film credits include OLD IRONSIDES with Charles Farrell and Wallace Beery, OLIVER TWIST, SHADOWS OF THE ORIENT, THE GIRL FROM MANDALAY, THE CASE OF LENA SMITH, THE AMERICAN VENUS, and THE BLIND GODDESS. Height 5 ft. 5½ in. Blonde hair and blue eyes.

**RAMBEAU, Marjorie**—plate 107. Born in San Francisco, California, on July 5, 1889. Was twelve years old when she began her stage career with a travelling stock company. She became famous as a dramatic actress on Broadway before coming to the screen. She has written several screenplays. She made THE GREATER WOMAN and MARY MORLAND in 1917, then returned to Broadway. Later, back in Hollywood, she made many films among them, UNDER PRESSURE, FIRST LADY, STRICTLY PERSONAL, MAN'S CASTLE, THE WARRIOR'S HUSBAND, HELL DIVERS, and GRAND CANARY. Height 5 ft. 6 in. Golden hair and blue eyes. She died in 1970.

**RATHBONE, Basil**—plate 156. Born in Johannesburg, South Africa, on June 13, 1892. Came to London for a stage career and worked with Sir Frank Benson, his cousin, in repertory. He went to America in 1921 and became a star on Broadway before entering films. One of his early films made at First National, was called THE GREAT DECEPTION with Aileen Pringle co-starring. He made THE MASKED BRIDE with Mae Murray and SUNYA with Gloria Swanson. Followed THE BISHOP MURDER CASE, LOVE FROM A STRANGER, THE GARDEN OF ALLAH, THE ADVENTURES OF ROBIN HOOD, and THIS MAD WORLD. He was famous for his role as SHERLOCK HOLMES. Height 6 ft. 1½ in. Black hair and hazel eyes. He also played in British films and was subsequently knighted. Died in 1967.

**RAWLINSON, Herbert**—plate 8. Born in Brighton, England, on September 16, 1885. Began his stage career in the West End of London, but his big success came on Broadway. He made his film *début* in 1912 with Hobart Bosworth and Eugenie Besserer in THE COUNT OF MONTE CRISTO for the Selig Studio. He also worked with Hobart Bosworth in THE SEA WOLF. With Universal, where his career peaked, he made FLIRTING WITH DEATH, THE BLACK BOX, THE VICTOR, and starred in that studio's spectacular DAMON AND PYTHIAS with Ann Little and an all-star cast. His other films included CHARGE IT with Clara Kimball Young, HOUR OF RECKONING, MEN OF THE NIGHT, THE BELLE OF BROADWAY, and FOOTLIGHTS AND SHADOWS. Height 6 ft. Brown hair and blue eyes. Died in 1953.

**REID, Wallace**—plates 1, 2, 3. Born in New York City on April 15, 1890, the son of Hal Reid, a well-known dramatic critic. He was educated at the New Jersey Military Academy and was first a journalist before going on the New York stage. He joined Vitagraph in 1911 and worked in THE DEERSLAYER with Florence Turner. He made THE TEST with Frank Lloyd for Nestor in 1914. His big break came with the part of the blacksmith in D. W. Griffith's BIRTH OF A NATION in 1915. From this modest beginning, Wallace Reid rose to become America's most popular male star. For eight straight years he topped the country's popularity poll. For many years he was Paramount's leading male star. Best remembered of his films are THE AFFAIRS OF ANATOLE with Gloria Swanson and an all-star cast, VALLEY OF THE GIANTS, THE DANCING FOOL, CLARENCE, EXCUSE MY DUST, and PETER IBBETSON. Height 6 ft. 1½ in. Light brown hair and blue eyes. Married to film star

Dorothy Davenport. Two children, a son William Wallace, and a daughter. Died January 18, 1923, at the peak of his career and just thirty-three years old.

**RICH, Irene**—plate 138. Born on October 13, 1890, in Buffalo, New York. Made her screen *début* in 1917 without previous acting experience. Her first good part came when she was cast in STELLA MARIS. She then made a film with Dustin Farnham and another good part followed with Lon Chaney in THE TRAP. Then a few Westerns with Harry Carey including DESERT TRAILS, BRAWN OF THE NORTH, and JUST CALL ME JIM with Will Rogers. With COMPROMISE, co-starring Clive Brook, and THE CLIMBERS, she began her society roles and young mother parts for which she became famous. Her films include LADY WINDERMERE'S FAN, CRAIG'S WIFE, DAUGHTERS OF DESIRE, MY OFFICIAL WIFE, and SO THIS IS LONDON. She was co-starred in several films with Will Rogers. Height 5 ft. 6 in. Dark brown hair and eyes.

**RITTER, Tex**—plate 39. Born in Murvaul, Texas, on January 12, 1907. Tex was primarily a music man and, although he had a bit of experience in silent Westerns, it was sound that brought him to prominence. With sound films his banjo and his voice brought the saga of the West to a great new audience. Tex, whose real name was Woodward Maurice Ritter, among many other films, made HEADING FOR THE RIO GRANDE, THE ROUND-UP, MOTHER LOVE, and GREEN GROW THE LILACS. In later years, he was best known by his recordings of folk and Western songs and he was immensely popular in that field up to the time of his death in 1973.

**ROBINSON, Edward G.**—plate 199. "Eddy" was born in Bucharest, Rumania, on December 12, 1893. His real name was Emanuel Goldberg. He came to America with his family at age ten and was educated in New York in public schools, at Columbia University, and the American Academy of Dramatic Art. He began his career in stock but was a celeberity on Broadway before entering films. He worked briefly in silent films, but his great recognition came with sound. After making LITTLE CAESAR he was a star. He was famous for his gangster roles, among them THE LAST GANGSTER, BULLETS OR BALLOTS, KID GALAHAD, and THUNDER IN THE CITY. Other film credits include A LADY IN LOVE, an early film made with Vilma Banky, EAST IS WEST, THE WHOLE TOWN'S TALKING with Jean Arthur. Height 5 ft. 8 in. Black hair and brown eyes. Died in 1973.

**ROBSON, May**—plate 150. She was one of the screen's greatest character actresses. Before entering films she spent twenty years under contract to Charles Frohman and was the delight of Broadway. Born in Melbourne, Australia, on April 19, 1865, she came to America as a young widow and worked first as a dress designer for theatrical people. She went on-stage as a substitute for an actress who had been taken ill and from that night the rest of her life was spent either on the stage or in films. She will never be forgotten for her screen portrayal of LADY FOR A DAY. Among her other films were RAINBOW ON THE RIVER, THE PERFECT SPECIMEN, THE CAPTAIN'S KID, WOMAN IN DISTRESS, and A STAR IS BORN. Height 5 ft. 6 in. Grey hair and blue eyes. She died in 1942.

**ROGERS, Roy**—plate 44. Born on November 5, 1912, in the great Western state of Wyoming. From early childhood he learned to ride and rope and worked as a cowhand in some of the silent Westerns as a young man. When sound came, Roy was ripe for cowboy stardom. With his famous horse Trigger, he became a legend in the films. His lovely wife, Dale Evans, was his leading lady in many of his pictures. Among his legion films were UNDER WESTERN STARS, SHINE ON HARVEST MOON, IN OLD CALIENTE, and THE ARIZONA KID. Height 5 ft. 10 in. Light brown hair that began to grey early in life, and blue eyes.

**ROGERS, Will**—plate 139. Born on November 4, 1879, in Colagah, Oklahoma. Educated at Kemper Military Academy and learned to ride and rope as a ranch hand in Oklahoma. He joined a Wild West show and toured the country with it. His rope-spinning act attained considerable notice and he appeared in New York at Madison Square Gardens. An instant and colossal hit, he was signed by Flo Ziegfeld for his Follies. While a star performer with Ziegfeld he introduced a line of patter with his rope act and his remarks swept the country. Although he made a series of films for Hal Roach in 1922, his greatest screen achievements came at Fox with the coming of sound. Among his films were LIGHTNIN', JUST CALL ME JIM, DOUBLING FOR ROMEO, A CONNECTICUT YANKEE,

STATE FAIR, and IN OLD KENTUCKY. Height 5 ft. 11 in. Brown hair and blue eyes. Died in 1935.

**RUSSELL, Rosalind**—plate 188. She began her stage career in tent shows and later toured the country in stock. She had attended a dramatic art school and had dreamed of being an actress from the time she was a little girl. Born in Waterbury, Connecticut, on June 4, 1906, she came up the hard way. But she finally reached Broadway and success. The films were where she really came into her own with her great roles in MORNING BECOMES ELECTRA, NIGHT MUST FALL with Dame May Whitty and Robert Montgomery, CRAIG'S WIFE, UNDER TWO FLAGS, THE SUICIDE CLUB, RECKLESS, and CHINA SEAS. Height 5 ft. 6½ in. Dark brown hair and eyes. She was also one of "them" in that great film THE WOMEN.

## S

**SEBASTIAN, Dorothy**—plate 164. Born on April 26, 1904, in Birmingham, Alabama. Worked in Broadway revues before making her film *début* in 1925 in SACKCLOTH AND SCARLET with Alice Terry. Followed WINDS OF CHANCE, THE SPITE MARRIAGE, THE UNHOLY NIGHT, FORGOTTEN WOMEN, THE RAINBOW WOMAN, THE DAY OF SOULS, and BLUEBEARD'S SEVEN WIVES with Ben Lyon. She was also in CIMARRON with Richard Dix. Height 5 ft. 3 in. Dark brown hair and hazel eyes.

**SHEARER, Norma**—plate 86. Born in Montreal, Canada, on August 10, 1904. She made her screen *début* with Fox at the age of sixteen. Her first important film was PLEASURE MAD. She made THE TOWER OF LIES with Lon Chaney, HE WHO GETS SLAPPED with John Gilbert, THE SNOB also with John Gilbert and Conrad Nagel, EMPTY HANDS with Jack Holt, and THE ACTRESS with Lee Moran. By this time she had married M-G-M's Irving Thalberg and was a celebrity and a star. Among her later films were THE BARRETS OF WIMPOLE STREET, LET US BE GAY, THE LAST OF MRS. CHENEY, THE DIVORCEE, ROMEO AND JULIET, STRANGE INTERLUDE, PRIVATE LIVES, INTERLUDE, and SMILING THROUGH. Height 5 ft. 3 in. Dark brown hair and blue eyes.

**SHERIDAN, Ann**—plate 214. Born in Dallas, Texas, on August 8, 1907. Her real name was Clara Lou Sheridan but she made her screen *début* under the name of Gloria Hellar with director King Vidor as her sponsor. She went to Hollywood as one of the thirty winners of the Paramount "Search for Beauty" contest. She had only small roles in films until she made EVERYBODY'S ACTING with Betty Bronson. Her career sparked with this film and she appeared in RED BLOOD OF COURAGE, BEHOLD MY WIFE, THE WAY OF ALL FLESH with Emil Jannings, ALCATRAZ, THE BLACK LEGION, ROCKY MOUNTAIN MYSTERY, and HOME ON THE RANGE. Height 5 ft. 5½ in. Red hair and blue eyes. She died in 1967.

**SILLS, Milton**—plate 56. Born in Chicago, Illinois, on January 10, 1882. Made his stage *début* in 1907 and became a successful star, famous for his role in THE MISER. His film career began in 1914 in Maurice Tourneur's production of THE PIT. One of his first successes was THE DEEP PURPLE with Clara Kimball Young. Another film with Clara Kimball Young and Jack Holt followed called THE CLAW. He made THE EYES OF YOUTH with Pauline Starke, BURNING SANDS with Jacqueline Logan, and ADAM'S RIB with Anna Q. Nilsson. A big one came with THE SPOILERS and then MADONNA OF THE STREETS with Alla Nazimova. Another big film for Sills was THE SEA HAWK. He made PARADISE with Betty Bronson, BURNING DAYLIGHT, THE ISLE OF LOST SHIPS, THE VALLEY OF THE GIANTS, and FLAMING YOUTH with Clara Bow, among many others. Height 6 ft. Brown hair and grey eyes. At the time of his death in 1930, he was married to Doris Kenyon, the stage and screen star.

**SIMON, Simone**—plate 148. Born in Marseilles, France, on April 23, 1912. She studied sculpture in Paris, but became deeply attracted to the stage. After a short time in the legitimate theatre, she entered films while still a little girl. Her portrayal of LAC AUX DAMES attracted the attention of an American talent scout and she eventually arrived in Hollywood. She captured American film audiences for her role in SEVENTH HEAVEN with Janet Gaynor and Charles Farrell. Then came another outstanding success, GIRLS' DORMITORY, and she was a star. Her other films included THE LITTLE FRENCH GIRL, LOVE AND

KISSES, LADIES IN LOVE, and FARAWAY. Height 5 ft. 3 in. Light brown hair and blue eyes.

**SMITH, C. Aubrey**—plate 84. Born on July 21, 1863, in London, England. He was educated at Charterhouse and Cambridge. He made his stage *début* in 1892, and became distinguished on the London stage before he went to Hollywood in 1916 to star in his first American film called THE WITCHING HOUR. He was much in demand for his always-convincing character roles. Among his films were THE PRISONER OF ZENDA, ROMEO AND JULIET, LLOYDS OF LONDON, THE GARDEN OF ALLAH, and FOUR FEATHERS. He was knighted before his death. Height 6 ft. 2 in. Grey hair and blue eyes. Died in 1948.

**STANWYCK, Barbara**—plate 221. Born on July 16, 1906. Real name Ruby Stevens. Began her theatrical career as a cabaret dancer and rose to stardom in the Ziegfeld Follies. She made her first screen appearance of note in a film called BROADWAY NIGHTS. Her career developed rapidly and with STELLA DALLAS she reached stardom. Among her many films were BANJO ON MY KNEE, THE LOCKED DOOR, DANCE MUSIC, THE PLOUGH AND THE STARS, BREAKFAST FOR TWO, HIS BROTHER'S WIFE, and DIAL M FOR MURDER. Height 5 ft. 5 in. Auburn hair and blue eyes. Married to Robert Taylor.

**STERLING, Ford**—plates 118, 119. Born on November 3, 1883, in La Crosse, Wisconsin. After a short career as a cartoonist on a Chicago paper, he became a circus clown. He left the circus in Hollywood to join Keystone comedies as a farcical, bearded Dutchman. He was one of the original Keystone Kops. A pioneer of the early films, he was one of its outstanding comedians. He later switched to comedy drama and had important roles in HE WHO GETS SLAPPED with Lon Chaney, THE FALL OF EVE, GENTLEMEN PREFER BLONDES, FOR THE LOVE OF MIKE, THE LADY WITH THE ROSE, and SALLY. Height 5 ft. 11 in. Black hair and brown eyes. Died in 1939.

**SWAIN, Mack**—plate 117. Born in Salt Lake City, Utah, on February 16, 1876. Made his stage *début* in 1891, and after twenty-two years of theatrical experience in vaudeville, minstrel shows, musical comedy, and comedy drama, he began his film career with Keystone comedies. He quickly became one of the rollicking, roistering Mack Sennett comics and his varied stage experience made him a master of slapstick. He made a number of films with Charlie Chaplin, including THE GOLD RUSH, and worked with Mabel Normand, Ford Sterling, Marie Dressler and all the great comedy stars of his day. His film credits include TILLIE'S PUNCTURED ROMANCE, WHISPERING WIRES, THE SHAMROCK AND THE ROSE, THE BELOVED ROGUE, and THE COHENS AND THE KELLYS. Height 6 ft. 2 in. Fair hair and grey eyes. He died in 1935.

**SWANSON, Gloria**—plate 99. She was born in Chicago, Illinois, on March 27, 1899. She should have been known as "Miss American Films" for if anybody ever deserved that title it is Gloria.She was very young when she joined the Essanay company and began her fabulous screen career. One of her first films was made with Ruth Stonehouse and was called ROMANCE OF AN AMERICAN DUCHESS. She went to Keystone next and became a Mack Sennett bathing girl. Her big break came when she signed with Famous Players Lasky and Paramount. She was their leading female star for many years Some of her many films include SOCIETY FOR SALE with William Desmond, DON'T CHANGE YOUR HUSBAND with Lew Cody and Elliott Dexter, co-starred with Wallace Reid and an all-star cast in DeMille's THE AFFAIRS OF ANATOLE, BEYOND THE ROCKS with Rudolph Valentino, MY AMERICAN WIFE with Antonio Moreno, WHY CHANGE YOUR WIFE with Thomas Meighan, THE IMPOSSIBLE MRS. BELLEW with Conrad Nagel, COAST OF FOLLY with Richard Arlen, LOVE OF SUNYA with John Boles, ZAZA with H. B. Warner, and SADIE THOMPSON with Lionel Barrymore. Her last film was SUNSET BOULEVARD with William Holden and Anna Q. Nilsson. Two of her husbands were Wallace Beery and the Marquis de la Falaise. Height 5 ft. 3 in. Reddish brown hair and blue eyes.

## T

**TASHMAN, Lilyan**—plate 134. Born on October 23, 1898, in Brooklyn, New York. She was a star of the Ziegfeld Follies before entering films. She scored from the very beginning. She was a sensation in THE TRIAL OF MARY DUGAN and was immediately offered and accepted a role with Richard Barthelmess in EXPERIENCE. She appeared in DECLASSE with Lloyd

Hughes and Corrine Griffith, and then made BULLDOG DRUMMOND with Ronald Colman. Her other films included ONE HEAVENLY NIGHT, PRESENT ARMS, and THE GOLD DIGGERS OF BROADWAY. Height 5 ft. 6 in. Light brown hair and blue eyes. Married film star Edmund Lowe. Died in 1934.

**TEARLE, Conway**—plate 60. Born in New York City on December 12, 1882, the son of English theatrical parents. Educated in England and went on the London stage in the company of Ellen Terry and Sir Charles Wyndham. Return to America and was cast with Ethel Barrymore in a Broadway production. Back in London again and for a considerable time played leading roles at the Drury Lane Theatre. He made his film *début* in 1910. In 1914, he was requested by Ethel Barrymore to play the leading role with her in THE NIGHTINGALE. He made THE COMMON LAW with Clara Kimball Young, STELLA MARIS with Mary Pickford, THE VIRTUOUS WIFE with Anita Stewart, THE ETERNAL FLAME with Norma Talmadge, and BELLA DONNA with Pola Negri. Other of his films include EVIDENCE, GOLD DIGGERS OF BROADWAY, ASHES OF VENGEANCE, and THE DANGEROUS MAID with Constance Talmadge. Height 5 ft. 11 in. Dark hair and eyes. Died in 1938.

**THOMPSON, Fred**—plate 42. Born in Los Angeles, California, in 1890. Educated at Princeton University. Was a famous athlete and won international championships. He became an ordained minister before entering films in 1914. He married Frances Marion, the screenwriter, who was responsible for many of his film plays. He became one of the great cowboy actors of his day. With him in all his films was his beautiful white horse Silver King. Films in which he starred include DON MIKE, HANDS ACROSS THE BORDER, THE TWO-GUN MAN, THE TOUGH GUY, and REGULAR SCOUT. Height 6 ft. Brown hair and grey-blue eyes.

**TODD, Thelma**—plate 236. She was born in Lawrence, Massachusetts, in 1904. She began her adult career as a teacher, but was "movie struck" and went to Hollywood where she obtained extra parts in silent films. She attended Paramount's acting school and her first big role was in THE POPULAR SIN. She did TRIAL MARRIAGE with Norman Kerry, HER PRIVATE LIFE, THE HOUSE OF HORRORS, BACHELOR GIRL, and FOOTPRINTS TO SATAN, among many others. Height 5 ft. 4 in. Brown hair and blue eyes. Died in 1935.

**TOLER, Sidney**—plate 173. Born in Warrensburg, Missouri, in 1890. He began as a playwright and then became an actor. THE BELLE OF RICHMOND, one of his plays was a Broadway hit. He had considerable acting experience when he entered films. His forte was dramatic character roles. Film credits include THE LONGEST NIGHT, THIS IS THE LIFE, THE DARING YOUNG MAN, THE THREE GODFATHERS, THE GORGEOUS HUSSY, CALL OF THE WILD, and CHAMPAGNE FOR BREAKFAST. His career peaked when he starred in the CHARLIE CHAN series as the Chinese detective. Height 6 ft. Brown hair and eyes. Died in 1967.

**TOOMEY, Regis**—plate 127. Born in Pittsburgh, Pennsylvania, on August 13, 1902. Started in the theatre as a property boy in his home town of Pittsburgh. This brought him eventually to acting and he carved out a career for himself on Broadway and on the London stage. His film career began with a supporting role in THE PERFECT ALIBI. He was a leading man for many years in both silent and sound films. Among his film credits are ILLUSION, THE WHEEL OF LIFE, BIG CITY, and ONE FRIGHTENED NIGHT. Height 5 ft. 9 in. Curly light brown hair and blue eyes.

**TORRENCE, David**—plate 74. Born in Edinburgh, Scotland, on September 23, 1880. Made his stage *début* in New York in BEAU BRUMMEL. He became a leading baritone in musical comedy and then, for eight years, acted in dramatic roles. He made his screen *début* in 1921 in the film INSIDE THE CUP, then supported Mary Pickford in TESS OF THE STORM COUNTRY. He made HEARTS IN EXILE with Dolores Costello, and THE DAWN OF TOMORROW with Jacqueline Logan and Alma Bennett, THE ISLE OF REDEMPTION, UNTAMED JUSTICE, and he played an important part in DISRAELI with George Arliss. Height 6 ft. 1 in. Black hair and hazel eyes. He is the younger brother of the famous film star Ernest Torrence.

**TORRENCE, Ernest**—plates 64, 65. Born in Edinburgh, Scotland, on June 26, 1878. He was trained in music and won a scholarship as a pianist. He went on the comic opera stage in London and then musical comedy. On Broadway he starred in many productions over a period of nine years. He made his film *début* in 1922 with Richard Barthelmess in TOL'ABLE DAVID. In the same year, he made BROKEN CHAINS with Colleen Moore, then THE TRAIL OF THE LONESOME PINE with Antonio Moreno and Mary Miles Minter. DeMille cast him for an important part in THE KING OF KINGS, and he scored a tremendous hit in the epic film THE COVERED WAGON. Other film credits include THE BRIDGE OF SAN LUIS REY, PONY EXPRESS, CAPTAIN BLOOD with J. Warren Kerrigan, SIDE SHOW OF LIFE with Anna Q. Nilsson, RUGGLES OF RED GAP, and STEAMBOAT BILL, JR. Height 6 ft. 2½ in. Black hair and hazel eyes. Among the finest of character actors.

**TURPIN, Ben**—plate 113. Born on September 17, 1874, in New Orleans, Louisiana. Began his film career with the Essanay company at the time it was first organised by Broncho Billy Anderson. He was Essanay's leading comedian for a number of years prior to his joining Mack Sennett. He was one of the original Keystone Kops. He worked with Charlie Chaplin in A NIGHT OUT and starred in the SNAKEVILLE series of shorts. Some of his later films include THE PRODIGAL BRIDEGROOM, COLLEGE HERO, UNCLE TOM'S CABIN with Marie Prevost and Charlie Conklin, A SMALL TOWN IDOL with Phyllis Haver, A BLONDE'S REVENGE, and SHOW OF SHOWS. Height 5 ft. 4 in. Fair, with "crossed" blue eyes.

**TRYON, Glenn**—plate 165. Born in Julietta, Idaho, on September 14, 1899. He made his stage *début* at the age of eight in "Rip Van Winkle." He was a veteran of the stage when he made his film *début* in 1924. He was delightful in light comedy roles and became a top star because of them. His first film was THE WHITE SHEEP, made at the Hal Roach studio. He then co-starred with Marion Nixon in a Universal film called HOW TO HANDLE WOMEN. SKINNER'S DRESS SUIT elevated him to screen prominence. The star and the film were so popular that a sequel was made called SKINNER STEPS OUT. Other of his films include BARNUM WAS RIGHT, HERO FOR A NIGHT, THE KING OF JAZZ, BROADWAY, DAMES AHOY, and THE KID'S CLEVER. Height 5 ft. 10 in. Dark brown hair and green eyes.

## V

**VALLI, Virginia**—plate 54. Born in Chicago, Illinois, on June 3, 1899. She was a Ziegfeld Follies girl before entering films. Having worked on the stage with Taylor Holmes, he chose her for his film EFFICIENCY EDGAR'S COURTSHIP. Rod LaRocque was also in the cast, and the film was made in 1917. She made A LADY OF QUALITY at Universal, was in THE ISLE OF LOST SHIPS, JUDGMENT OF THE HILLS, and SEIGE. Perhaps her greatest role was in THE STORM with House Peters. Her other films include THE ESCAPE, WHY THE WOMAN, BEHIND CLOSED DOORS, THE PLEASURE GARDEN, and MR. ANTONIO. She was expert in swimming, fencing, and as a horsewoman. She was also a dancer of no mean ability. Height 5 ft. 5 in. Dark brown hair and blue eyes. She died in 1968.

**VARCONI, Victor**—plate 69. Born in Kisvarda, Hungary, on March 31, 1896. Studied for the stage in Budapest and later appeared as Romeo at the National Theatre in the Hungarian capital. He made his screen *début* in Hollywood with Pola Negri in BELLA DONNA in 1917. He later played the Greek hero in THE LAST DAYS OF POMPEII. Under contract to Paramount, he made THE KING OF KINGS with DeMille directing. Other of his films include CHICAGO with Phyllis Haver, THE VOLGA BOATMAN, WHITE GOLD, THE DIVINE LADY, ETERNAL LOVE, THE GAY CABALLERO, ANGEL OF BROADWAY, and FOR WIVES ONLY. Height 5 ft. 10 in. Dark brown hair and eyes.

**VELEZ, Lupe**—plate 170. The famous "Mexican Spitfire" was born in San Louis Potosi, Mexico, on July 18, 1907. She was discovered by stage and screen star Richard Bennett in Mexico City where she was appearing in musical comedy. In Hollywood she obtained her first screen work with Hal Roach in Laurel and Hardy comedies. Her first important role was with Douglas Fairbanks, Sr. in THE GAUCHO. She made LADY OF THE PAVEMENTS, THE CUBAN LOVE SONG, EAST IS WEST, TIGER ROSE, WOLF SONG, THE BROKEN WING, RESURRECTION, and HOT PEPPER with Victor McLaglen and Edmund Lowe. Her latin mannerisms, and her volatile language characterized her vivacious personality. Height 5 ft. Black hair and brown eyes. She died in 1944.

**VERNON, Bobby**—plate 110. A great comedy star of the early silent era. He was born in Chicago, Illinois, on February 2, 1895, the son of Dorothy Vernon, the dramatic actress of stage and screen. Bobby was only 5 ft. 2 in. tall—an energy-packed, talented comic who enjoyed his best years with Christie Comedies. A handsome little man with flaxen hair and blue eyes, very youthful in appearance, he was Hollywood's standout "boy" comedian. Among his dozens of films made for Christie were WIFE SHY, SHORT SOCKS, NO LIMIT, THE ALL-DAY SUCKER, and SURE FIRE. Before joining Christie he was with Mack Sennett and was one of the original Keystone Kops. He also made films with Gloria Swanson, Phyllis Haver, Mabel Normand and Polly Moran while with Sennett.

**VIDOR, Florence**—plate 16. Born in Houston, Texas, on July 23, 1895. Her real name was Florence Arto. She came to Hollywood as a young girl and obtained work at various studios. Her dramatic ability was first brought to light in a bit part she played in A TALE OF TWO CITIES. In 1915 she married King Vidor, the film director. She was given her big chance in HAIL THE WOMAN and from that time onward all her films gave her starring roles. She made HONEYMOON HATE, THE PATRIOT, THE MAGNIFICENT FLIRT, CHINATOWN NIGHTS, THE VIRGINIAN with Kenneth Harlan, ALICE ADAMS, MAIN STREET with Monte Blue, CHRISTINE OF THE HUNGRY HEART with Ian Keith, and BARBARA FRITCHIE with Edmund Lowe. Height 5 ft. 4 in. Dark brown hair and eyes. In 1928, after divorcing King Vidor, she married Jascha Heifetz, the concert violinist.

**von STROHEIM, Erich**—plate 29. Born in Vienna, Austria, on September 22, 1885. His mother came from Prague and his father was a Jewish merchant from Gleiwitz (Stroheim himself always claimed a grander background: his mother a lady-in-waiting to Empress Elizabeth of Austria, his father a colonel in the Dragoons). After emigrating to America in 1909, where he acted in films from 1914 onwards, he was hired by D. W. Griffith as an actor and assistant on THE BIRTH OF A NATION. He also played the German officer in Griffith's HEARTS OF THE WORLD. He later turned to directing, where he achieved his greatest success. Among his films were FOOLISH WIVES, GREED, THE MERRY WIDOW, THE WEDDING MARCH, THE GREAT GABBO, and THREE FACES EAST. Height 5 ft. 8 in. Fair, close-cropped hair and blue eyes. Died in 1957.

## W

**WARWICK, Robert**—plate 23. Born on June 2, 1881, in Sacramento, California. Real name Robert Taylor Bien. Served in the First World War as an officer on the staff of General John J. Pershing. He studied music and voice in Paris with an operatic career in view, and became a leading light on Broadway before entering films. He made HUMAN DRIFTWOOD in 1916 and THE SILENT MASTER with Ann Little in that same year. Followed TOLD IN THE HILLS, SECRET SERVICE, and MIZZOURA with Monte Blue. He then made HUNTING TROUBLE with Walter Hiers, THE TREE OF KNOWLEDGE, JACK STRAW, THE QUEEN'S HUSBAND, and CAPTAIN DIEPPE. Later in his career he made THE LIFE OF EMILE ZOLA, THE BOLD CAVALIER, CAN THIS BE DIXIE?, THE PRINCE AND THE PAUPER, and THE AWFUL TRUTH. Height 6 ft. Dark brown hair and eyes.

**WATSON, Lucille**—plate 216. Born in Quebec, Canada, on May 27, 1879. She studied for the stage at the American Academy of Dramatic Arts and made her stage *début* in Ottawa in 1900. Before entering films she enjoyed a long and very successful career as a dramatic actress both on Broadway and the London stage. In films, she became one of the most popular character actresses. Among her films were WHAT EVERY WOMAN KNOWS, THREE SMART GIRLS, THE BISHOP'S MISADVENTURE, and THE GARDEN OF ALLAH. Height 5 ft. 6 in. Grey hair and eyes.

**WAYNE, John**—plate 213. Marion Mitchell Morrison who became the fabulous John Wayne of the movies, was born in Winterset, Iowa, on May 26, 1906. He played football for the University of Southern California and worked in a few silent films before Raoul Walsh gave him a part in his epic film THE BIG TRAIL. This began what is perhaps the longest and most fabulous film career any star has ever enjoyed. "Big John" is still making movies as this book goes to press. To name a few of his early films—CONFLICT, BORN TO THE WEST, THE SEA SPOILERS, and CALIFORNIA STRAIGHT AHEAD. Two of his later films which were especially outstanding were THE HIGH AND

THE MIGHTY and THE QUIET MAN. Height 6 ft. 2 in. Brown hair and blue eyes.

**WEST, Mae**—plate 231. Born in Brooklyn, New York, on August 17, 1891. She began her stage career when she was six years old. She later performed the first "hula" dance ever done in America. She wrote and acted in her own plays on Broadway and was not only the "toast" but the "talk" of Broadway for many years. She, rather reluctantly, did some work in silent films, but it was not until sound provided her with her famous spoken ad-libs and mannerisms that she deserted the stage for the screen. Her screen dialogue became the delight of the American public. Her first film was NIGHT AFTER NIGHT. She then made I'M NO ANGEL, BELLE OF THE NINETIES, KLONDIKE LOU, GO WEST YOUNG MAN, and EVERY DAY'S A HOLIDAY. Her films made with W. C. Fields are still classics. A short time ago, at the age of seventy-nine, she made MYRA BRECKINRIDGE with Raquel Welch, and was still the same sexy, fabulous Mae—looking not a day over forty. Height 5 ft. 4 in. Platinum blonde hair and blue eyes.

**WILLIAM, Warren**—plate 181. Born in Aitken, Minnesota, on December 2, 1896. Although not generally known, he played the male lead in some of the Pearl White serials in 1914. He was a very successful leading man on Broadway when he was persuaded by Jack Warner to come to Hollywood for the leading role opposite Dolores Costello in EXPENSIVE WOMEN. Early in his film career he co-starred with Bebe Daniels in THE HONOR OF THE FAMILY. He was in DeMille's CLEOPATRA, THE MOUTHPIECE, IMITATION OF LIFE, THE MAN IN THE IRON MASK, MADAME X, SATAN MET A LADY, STAGE STRUCK, MIDNIGHT MADONNA, and THE FIREFLY to mention only a few of his films. His real name was Warren William Krech. Height 6 ft. 1 in. Dark brown hair and blue eyes. Died in 1948.

**WILSON, Lois**—plate 12. Born in Pittsburgh, Pennsylvania, on June 28, 1896. Started her career as a schoolteacher but was "discovered" and entered films under the auspices of Lois Weber, the woman producer. Her first film was made in 1918 when she appeared with Frank Keenan in THE BELLS. Followed THE ROSE OF HONOR with Henry B. Walthall and IT PAYS TO ADVERTISE with Bryant Washburn and Walter Hiers. She made WHAT EVERY WOMAN KNOWS with Conrad Nagel and ICEBOUND with Richard Dix. Her two most important films were the epic THE COVERED WAGON with J. Warren Kerrigan, Tully Marshall and an all star cast, and MONSIEUR BEAUCAIRE with Rudolph Valentino. Other of her films included THE THUNDERING HERD, PONY EXPRESS, THE VANISHING AMERICAN with Richard Dix, NORTH OF 36, and THE GREAT GATSBY with Warner Baxter. Height 5 ft. 5 in. Medium brown hair and hazel eyes.

**WINDSOR, Claire**—plate 22. Born in 1901 in Cawker City, Kansas. Her parents were Scandinavians and her real name was Ola Kronk. Trained in voice and dancing, she began her screen career after winning a beauty contest in Seattle. Her first film TO PLEASE ONE WOMAN was made in 1921. In the same year she made THE BLOT with Louis Calhern. Then came BORN RICH with Bert Lytell and Cullen Landis, THE BUGLE CALL, SOULS FOR SABLES, CAPTAIN LASH, THE WHITE DESERT, THE LADY WHO LIED, SONS OF THE SAHARA, and SATAN AND THE WOMAN. Her most important role was in RUPERT OF HENTZAU with Bryant Washburn and Bert Lytell. Height 5 ft. 6½ in. Fair hair and hazel eyes. Married to film star Bert Lytell. They had one son.

**WONG, Anna May**—plate 46. Born in Los Angeles, California, on January 3, 1907. Made her screen *début* in 1922 and became known to the public by her role of the Chinese slave girl in THE THIEF OF BAGDAD with Douglas Fairbanks, Sr. She played in many of the big productions based upon stories of China and the Orient. Her screen credits include TOLL OF THE SEA with Kenneth Harlan, SHANGHAI EXPRESS with Marlene Dietrich, DAUGHTER OF THE DRAGON, THE CHINESE PARROTT with Warner Oland, ACROSS TO SINGAPORE, and OLD SAN FRANCISCO, among many others. Height 5 ft. 4½ in. Black hair and brown eyes. She died in February 1961.

**WRAY, Fay**—plate 198. Born in Wrayland, Alberta, Canada, on September 17, 1907. She began her film career as a girl comedienne and then played a wide variety of roles until she was chosen by Erich von Stroheim for his film THE WEDDING MARCH. She was then cast as Emil Jannings's leading lady in THE KING OF SOHO. She worked with Gary Cooper in some of his early Westerns, and had a co-starring role in WILD HORSE STAMPEDE. Her other films include THE ONE MAN GAME, THE FOUR FEATHERS, THE SEA GOD, WHEN KNIGHTS WERE BOLD, and, of course, she will never be forgotten as the heroine of KING KONG which still plays on both screen and television. Height 5 ft. 3 in. Light brown hair and blue eyes. Married scenario writer John Monk Saunders.

**WYNYARD, Diana**—plate 75. Born on January 16, 1906, in London, England. Her real name was Dorothy Cox. Two of her greatest films were RASPUTIN AND THE EMPRESS and CAVALCADE. After some stage and film work in England, she went to Hollywood in 1926 to make a film called THE LOVE GAME. A year later she made A MIDSUMMER NIGHT'S DREAM. It was perhaps CAVALCADE, which co-starred Clive Brook, that brought her the greatest acclaim. It was a story that moved her through a period from youth to old age and gave her scope to show her ability as a fine actress. Height 5 ft. 6½ in. Light brown hair and blue eyes. She was married to Carol Reed. She died in 1964.

## Y

**YOUNG, Loretta**—plate 226. Born in Salt Lake City, Utah, on January 6, 1911. Her family moved to Hollywood when she was a child and she became a child actress in films. She appeared in THE SHEIK with Rudolph Valentino, with Lon Chaney and Nils Asther in LAUGH CLOWN LAUGH, and with Otis Skinner in KISMET. By the time sound came along she was an accomplished young actress. She was elected by the film industry as the Wampus Baby Star in 1929. Among her screen credits are THE MAGNIFICENT FLIRT, THE ROAD TO PARADISE, THE UNGUARDED HOUR, SECRET INTERLUDE, SHANGHAI, THE CRUSADES, CAFE METROPOLE, SECOND HONEYMOON, LOVE UNDER FIRE, LADIES IN LOVE, and RAMONA. Her real name was Gretchen Belzer and she had a sister in films who went by the name of Sally Blane. She was married to screen star Grant Withers. Height 5 ft. 3 in. Light brown hair and blue eyes.